Family Fragments?

For Daniel and Jessica

Family Fragments?

Carol Smart & Bren Neale

Polity Press

The right of Carol Smart and Bren Neale to be identified as authors
of this work have been asserted in accordance with the Copyright,
Designs and Patents Act 1988.

First published 1999 by Polity Press
in association with Blackwell Publishers Ltd

Editorial office:
Polity Press
65 Bridge Street
Cambridge CB2 1UR, UK

Marketing and production:
Blackwell Publishers Ltd
108 Cowley Road
Oxford OX4 1JF, UK

Published in the USA by
Blackwell Publishers Inc.
Commerce Place
350 Main Street
Malden, MA 02148, USA

A catalogue record for this book is available from the British Library.

Library of Congress Cataloging-in-Publication Data

Smart, Carol.
    Family fragments? / Carol Smart & Bren Neale.
        p.   cm.
    Includes bibliographical references and index.
    ISBN 0-7456-1893-6. — ISBN 0-7456-1894-4 (pbk.)
    1. Divorced parents.   2. Divorce.   3. Family.   4. Family policy.
    I. Neale, Bren.   II. Title.
    HQ814.S63   1999
    306.89—dc21   98-33672
                                                                CIP

Typeset in 10½ on 12½ pt Palatino
by Ace Filmsetting Ltd, Frome, Somerset
Printed in Great Britain by MPG Books Ltd, Bodmin, Cornwall

This book is printed on acid-free paper.

Contents

Acknowledgements

We would like to acknowledge the support of the Economic and Social Research Council, who funded the research project (R000234582) which is the basis of this book.

We owe a particular debt of gratitude to Professor Selma Sevenhuijsen (Utrecht), who acted as adviser to the project and whose work on feminist ethics has been a constant source of inspiration to us. We are also grateful to Jeremy Roche (Open University), who collaborated with us throughout and was an immensely valuable source of knowledge on the workings of English family law. We would also like to acknowledge an intellectual debt to both Janet Finch (Keele) and Mavis Maclean (Oxford), who both, from different perspectives and in different ways, have unwittingly guided our work. Needless to say none of these colleagues is responsible for any of the inadequacies or intellectual limitations of this book.

Many other colleagues and friends helped us through the months of analysis and writing and our families had to endure the trials and tribulations of the research process with us. Often they were very neglected and we are both very grateful for their unstinting support. Other people helped in different ways. Pauline Windsor transcribed our interviews with immense speed and accuracy and we feel very lucky to have found her. Many local solicitors and voluntary organizations helped us to contact parents and without their help the project would never have got started.

Finally we would like to thank all the parents who participated in this research project. They gave their time freely, not once but twice, and many of them are allowing us back into their lives to interview their children in the next stage of this empirical work. All the names we have used for the case studies in this book are fictional to preserve the anonymity of the individuals involved.

1

Rethinking Family Life

Introduction

> Family research is only gradually waking up from its
> drowsy fixation on the nucleus of the family. (Beck and
> Beck-Gernsheim, 1995: 147)

> It takes quite a lot of empirically fortified wishful thinking
> to over-look the upheavals in social and family structures
> being brought about by millions of divorces. Family re-
> search which continues to think in terms of nuclear fami-
> lies and suggests by amassing data on them that they are
> not subject to change will someday find itself on the shelf
> beside the other curious products of a blind empiricism.
> (Beck and Beck-Gernsheim, 1995: 150)

These are of course highly contentious statements but they do,
perhaps, provide a useful starting-point for this book in that they
indicate the low status that family research tends to have in
mainstream sociological thought. What Beck and Beck-Gernsheim
seem to be suggesting in *The Normal Chaos of Love* is that family
research has been uninformed by theoretical insights and thus
has failed to note the momentous significance of changes to intimate relationships and the way in which these changes are part of
wider shifts in late modernity in Western societies. While we
would not fully support the way in which family research is
dismissed in these statements, Beck and Beck-Gernsheim do seem

to have identified a problem with what we might call the family research industry, namely its isolation from developments in sociological theory. But equally we could say that it has been an astonishing omission in mainstream sociological thought since the 1970s that so few theorists have seen family life as worthy of concern or conceptual attention.

It is important not to overstate this point but it is perhaps fair to say that family life lost its core significance to sociological think-ing after the decline of functionalist thought in the 1960s. David Morgan (1996) has remarked on the marginalization of family sociology and, while he argues that it may have simply been waiting in the wings of the more centre-stage concerns of class, labour studies, Marxism and post-Marxism and so on, he would probably agree that 'the family' did not excite much theoretical interest. It was left to radical psychoanalysts and feminists to find 'the family' significant and conceptually challenging. R. D. Laing (1971) challenged the mythic harmony of family life which in-fected the work of sociologists like Young and Willmott (1973) or Ronald Fletcher (1966). Following this tradition, Alice Miller (1987) still writes on the harmfulness of intensely powerful adult/child relationships in which children are routinely abused. These analy-ses of family life were quintessentially about power and its work-ings but because it was power in the context of the 'private sphere' it did not attract the interest of sociology in general because of the intensity of the sociological gaze on the 'public sphere'.

Feminist work did, of course, treat 'the family' seriously both for its political significance and for the conceptual challenges it offered. Feminists wrote and argued extensively on how to theo-rize 'the family' and how to understand the relationship between the private and the public and whether there was really a distinc-tion to be made between these spheres. Throughout the late 1970s and early 1980s conceptual and theoretically informed empirical work flourished and arguments raged as to whether or not 'the family' was the key site of gender oppression and, if so, how it reproduced gender inequalities. Yet, in spite of the immense energy of this work, mainstream sociology seemed unaffected at a theoretical level (Cheal, 1991). So although mainstream empiri-cal studies of family life could no longer ignore gender differ-ences, the primary concerns of sociological theory really did not shift at all. Conceptual work on 'the family' was mostly left to the feminists and their friends. Then feminist work itself in this area seemed to change. After the great debates about domestic labour and the (re)discoveries of forms of gendered power in the private sphere the early theoretical work gave rise to predominantly empirical work. While this empirical work was theoretically driven by the earlier debates there were no new theoretical developments to nourish or challenge these studies. Meanwhile feminist theorizing redirected attention towards other issues such as identity, sexuality, agency, the body and, of course, the thorny question of the very concept of Woman and its homogenizing tendency (Riley, 1988; Butler, 1990). While initially feminist theorizing had understood 'the family' to be the core site of women's oppression, trends in theorizing by the 1990s rejected the idea that there could be such a thing as a core site of oppression, dispensed with the idea that 'the family' could have the same significance for *all* women, and challenged the idea that one could speak of women as if they were a unitary category at all. Thus what had made 'the family' so significant to feminist theorizing was swept away on a tide of criticism from black feminists initially, and then from the growing post-structuralist tendency in feminist thought.

Thus, while important empirical work was still being progressed it began to seem far removed from the theoretical reconceptualizations and intellectual problems being tackled by key feminist thinkers. Questions being posed and tackled in this empirical work were and are significant but they have tended to be of a limited scope when compared with the 'big' questions being asked by more theoretically engaged sociologists. Thus questions might be about whether men really are doing more childcare now than ten years ago, or whether women are returning to the labour market sooner after childbirth, or whether cohabitation is less stable than marriage. While we would insist that these are the sort of questions that we need answers to (and indeed we ask such empiricist questions ourselves), they cease to have any great sociological significance if they are not part of an enquiry into the broader picture of how we should understand 'the family' in the context of late modernity/postmodernity (Finch, 1993).

Thus it is clear that although feminist work transformed general understanding of 'the family' and that this in turn was part of a wider analysis of the workings of patriarchal societies, this work ran alongside mainstream sociology in a kind of parallel universe. Then, at the point when the sheer volume of feminist theorizing and research might have overwhelmed mainstream indifference, feminists themselves moved on to other issues leaving the core theoretical debates on 'the family' frozen in an intellectual time warp created in the early 1980s. It is somewhat ironic now, therefore, to find that 'the family' has been taken up by mainstream sociological theorists in the mid-1990s and found to be conceptually significant and theoretically challenging. It is to this sociological rediscovery of 'the family' that we now turn.

'The family' becomes interesting again!

We want to suggest that there are three main reasons why 'the family' has become interesting to mainstream and theoretical sociology. The first reason relates to empirical findings of changes in family life and relationships. Higher rates of divorce, increasing cohabitation, the increase in so-called 'reconstituted families' and other related trends have social consequences which start to demand analysis and understanding. This can be seen as an empirically driven motivation towards reconsidering 'the family'.

The second reason is that 'the family' has become an issue of acute political debate. To some extent empirical studies of family change have fuelled this, albeit usually unintentionally. But empirical studies which map change without offering a wider analysis within which to understand shifts and transformations can be easily taken up and used as data in support of highly ideological or crudely partisan/political positions. This tendency has been further accelerated by the fact that those most vociferous in offering explanations for change have seen change as synonymous with decline and degeneration. Thus, the most populist explanations of change have tended to come from one direction, namely the alliance between the New Right and Ethical Socialists (Dennis and Erdos, 1993; Morgan, 1995; Phillips, 1997). We shall discuss some of their ideas later, but here the point we wish to make is that the analysis offered from this quarter has at least put 'the family' back into the centre of social life. While mainstream sociology has almost always seen 'the family' as an institution which *reacts* to other social changes in a passive fashion, the New Right and Ethical Socialist writers see 'the family' as giving rise to other social changes. Ironically it is these accounts which have acceded a considerable amount of agency to women and family members. Thus, it is argued, women cause crime by rejecting men as potential breadwinners and thus blocking young men's transition into responsible adulthood.

The point about the tenacity and popularity of accounts such as these is that they have no real opposition. Because most of the available empirical work has been used as the bedrock of precisely these explanations, it cannot alone also refute such analyses. Although empirical findings are always open to interpretation, alternative interpretations are available only if there are alternative conceptual frameworks within which to reformulate the dominant account. The sort of feminist theories of the 1980s which used to offer competing accounts of family life are no longer easily marshalled as alternative frameworks because they have been surpassed but not replaced. Thus there is revealed a conceptual paucity which has come about because of sociological indifference to analysing 'the family' and feminism's shift of conceptual focus. However, it is now keenly apparent that the dominant and highly politicized accounts of the New Right and Ethical Socialists should not stand unchallenged and this alone is giving rise to a renewed interest in 'the family' from different conceptual standpoints.

The third reason for a renewed interest in 'the family' is that mainstream sociological theorists have, through their conceptual work on a broad canvas, come to see 'the family' or intimate relationships as requiring analysis if changes taking place elsewhere in conditions of late modernity are to be understood. The sociologists we refer to are Giddens (1992) and Beck (1992) (also with Beck-Gernsheim in 1995). We shall proceed to discuss and evaluate their work below but the point we wish to make here is not that their analysis is necessarily fuller or more convincing than the work of sociologists who have long been in the field (viz. Morgan, 1991, 1996; Allen, 1985; Finch, 1989, 1993) but that these are theorists who, according to the tenets of mainstream theory, would normally be assumed to be interested in more important things than family life (or women's work). The machismo of mainstream sociology has undoubtedly created a hierarchy in which work on 'the family' has a rather lowly status and thus to see this status suddenly inverted is slightly shocking but also highly significant.

In highlighting the work of Giddens and Beck we do not wish to disparage the work of others who have long researched on 'the family' in a less flamboyant way. On the contrary we will later argue that this work is the foundation for the conceptual framings developed (and sometimes simply reiterated) in Beck and Giddens. But the significance of Beck's and Giddens' contributions is that they have (potentially) brought 'the family' back into the centre of sociological concerns as well as providing analyses of family life and intimacy which are not segregated from the sorts of explanation which are being provided for other changes in late modernity. More than this, both Beck and Giddens seem to provide members of families/relationships with agency and identify 'the family' as a site of change without assuming that 'the family' merely responds to more important changes elsewhere. In this sense they are not dissimilar to the Ethical Socialists, but unlike the latter they do not isolate 'the family' as a cause of social ills and their work is not geared to reversing social change to try to preserve a particular family form above all others. Put simply, Beck and Giddens have a sociological agenda, not a political or a policy agenda. Perhaps one of the most important conceptual contributions made by their focus on family life and intimacy is that their work at no time separates 'the family' from other social institutions or processes. It is ironically significant that they are not sociologists of the family because their attention to 'the family' somehow gives 'proof' that it is worthy of attention by others besides feminists and sociologists of the family.

The contributions of Giddens and Beck/Beck-Gernsheim

Giddens and The Transformation of Intimacy *(1992)*

Giddens' work on intimacy can be seen as a development from his work on the self and society in the late modern age.[1] This work was of a broad scope, seeking to answer questions about the nature of society in late modernity and, most especially, to understand the significance of human agency in the construction of the self and modern society. Giddens has, of course, been foremost in rediscovering the concept of the self for sociology and in incorporating human perceptions into an understanding of the process of change. Central to his thesis has been the idea of the reflexive self, which he sees as a defining element of late modernity, as well as part of the explanation of the nature of change in modern society. Thus practices of the self are seen as possible only because of social and cultural conditions available in the twentieth century, but at the same time once the reflexive self has an existence it acts, reinterprets and seeks to re-order social life.

This focus on the self, the production of narratives of the self (as a way of giving meaning to modern life) and the search for ontological security among massive (global) social change, brings Giddens directly to the spheres of intimacy and personal life while still understanding these fields in relation to wider concepts like globalization, post-industrialism, history or chaos. It is interesting that he rarely uses the term 'family' and, when he does, it is often in the context of discussing the work or framework of other authors rather than using the term as one that is meaningful to his own analysis. Perhaps this is because the very term 'family' can push one back into an older sociological paradigm of precisely the sort that Giddens' work seeks to transcend. Once we invoke the concept of 'the family', we are back in an old-style structuralism in which the family is one institution among others, although less important, and where it seems to denote the private sphere rather than the public sphere. Once we invoke 'the family', we invoke a lot of baggage that we then need to free ourselves from, most particularly the divide between private and public lives or selves. Giddens avoids having to perform these laborious disengagements by talking of intimacy, child-parent relationships, sexuality, the body and so on.[2] Thus one of the major achievements of his work is that it permits us always to see the individual as imbued with history, culture, language and the social, while the social is always the product of human agency.

It is through this approach that 'the family' (which is location, experience, kinship as well as ideological construct) returns to the mainstream sociological agenda. It is impossible to talk of the self and agency adequately if bits of the social are parcelled up and put aside. It is unimaginable that we could understand the production of the self without exploring intimate relationships just as it would be without addressing language or cultural inheritance, the organization of labour or the distribution of health and welfare. Thus in a stroke, so to speak, what was once defined as the private sphere has no boundaries to define it separately from the public sphere. Conceptual frameworks which kept 'the family' apart from the *real* concerns of sociologists simply evaporate and in retrospect seem incredibly trivial.

In *The Transformation of Intimacy* (1992) Giddens develops, in a popular form, ideas present in his earlier *Modernity and Self-identity* (1991). In particular he expounds upon his notions of the pure relationship and confluent love. By pure relationship he means:

> a social relationship [which] is entered into for its own sake, for what can be derived by each person from a sustained association with another; and which is continued only in so far as it is thought by both parties to deliver enough satisfactions for each individual to stay within it. (Giddens, 1992: 58)

And in explaining confluent love he states:

> Confluent love is active, contingent love, and therefore jars with the 'for-ever', 'one-and-only' qualities of the romantic love complex. (Giddens, 1992: 61)

These two concepts fit together to identify a new form of intimacy. In contradistinction to romantic love, which Giddens sees as being dominant since the nineteenth century when people began to marry for love rather than for economic or familial reasons, confluent love does not presume that falling in love is the threshold of a permanent relationship. The idea that one finds the right person and then stays committed to him or her through thick and thin is supplanted by the idea that if that person proves to be inadequate in some way, he or she can be replaced with a more suitable or compatible partner. Most importantly, the pure relationship is based upon a negotiated normative framework in which people decide upon how they want to live together and how they wish to collaborate and communicate. Unlike the old-style romantic relationship, which was sealed by a marriage that brought with it an imposed normative order, the pure relationship could be highly individualized to meet the needs of different couples or households. The pure relationship has an inevitable tendency towards instability because it is continuously subject to re-evaluation. Moreover, because the individuals who participate in this relationship are engaged in a 'project of the self' which involves personal growth, change and assessment, then it is more likely that needs and desires will change and become incompatible, or at least will be subject to re-negotiation.

Interestingly Graham Allen made a very similar point about modern marriage some seven years earlier than Giddens. He states:

> [M]arriage comes to be seen as more of a private, though legally recognised, arrangement between the two individuals most closely involved. Its rules are not fixed by convention, in any absolute fashion, but worked out by the couple, in theory without too much regard for the preferences of others. . . . [T]he purpose of marriage is not to sustain social order but to satisfy the idiosyncratic, and changing, personal needs of the couple. (1985: 102)

The difference between Giddens and Allen is perhaps only that Allen locates his analysis of marriage, family and divorce in terms of concepts like 'the individual' and 'social structure', leaving the relationship between the two to the reader's imaginings. Giddens, however, strives to overcome this dualism and produces a more dynamic, less functionalist account of similar tendencies. Thus Allen argues that these changes have come about because the economic needs of the wider kin group have changed with industrialization. He reproduces the classic sociological paradigm in which changes in 'the family' are seen to come about because of changes (usually economic) that have occurred elsewhere. The couple merely react to structural changes. Giddens' account is quite different. He argues that changes come about because in modern society individuals understand *themselves* (their reflexive selves) differently and because they are conscious agents of change (most particularly women) in the sphere of intimacy. The difference between these two approaches may not seem great but it symbolizes a complete transformation in sociological analyses of family life.

Giddens' work (like that of Beck and Beck-Gernsheim, which we discuss below) is profoundly influenced by an aura of feminist thinking without actually engaging with feminist work on intimacy or the personal. By this we mean that Giddens takes it as a basic tenet that women are active agents who have brought about change and who are seeking further changes. In his construction of the pure relationship and confluent love he considers women as equally significant as men – if not more so – in the sociological analysis of the transformation of intimacy. He also acknowledges that male power in 'the family' has not changed significantly. He states:

> For the sexual division of labour remains substantially intact; at home and at work, in most contexts of modern societies, men are largely unwilling to release their grip upon the reins of power. (1992: 131)

And he is fully aware that the structure of power in 'the family' is sustained by the social and economic order. Nevertheless he envisions change which is already occurring and which will become more pronounced. Interestingly he sees the vanguard of this change in lesbian and gay relationships, which he argues come closest to the pure relationship of his model. Lesbian and gay relationships are, he argues, more likely to be based on negotiations between individuals than simple adherence to social norms which govern marital relations (see Weeks et al., 1998; Dunne, 1997; Weston, 1991). This is obviously because lesbians and gays have been excluded from the institution of marriage, but also because there are no normative assumptions about gender inequalities and differences already embedded in the relationship. Thus Giddens points to the way in which gays and lesbians must construct relationships outside pre-existing guidelines and how they need to negotiate things afresh in a context of gender (if not personal) equality.

It is Giddens' argument that although heterosexual marriage is still hampered by patriarchal power relations, it is inevitably undermined by the rise of the pure relationship and confluent love elsewhere. The high rate of divorce is, for example, an indication of a shift away from the romantic love complex to confluent love for heterosexuals. But it is clear that he recognizes the actuality of the obstacles to change because the pure relationship does require equality and democracy and these remain elusive in the heterosexual matrix. He argues:

> If orthodox marriage is not yet widely seen as just one lifestyle among others, *as in fact it has become*, this is partly the result of institutional lag and partly the result of the complicated mixture of attraction and repulsion which the psychic development of each sex creates with regard to the other. (1992: 154. Our emphasis)

Thus there is unlikely to be a straightforward adoption of the pure relationship by heterosexuals in the immediate future. For a start, he suggests, they will enter into marriage for the sake of having and raising children. However, in his view children *per se* will not reduce the tendency towards the pure relationship. Instead marital relationships will take one of two likely forms which fall short of the pure relationship but which indicate a shift towards it. The first is the modern form of companionate marriage, in which the relationship is really akin to a friendship based on equality and mutual sympathy, but with little sexual involvement. The second is a form of co-residence, in which a home is shared but where there is little emotional investment in each other. Neither of these two forms resembles the earlier marital ideal of romantic love based on inequality, mutual dependence and role segregation.

The most compelling point about Giddens' argument is his vision that the current dominant form of intimacy (namely heterosexual marriage) cannot remain unchanged. Moreover his discussion of the potential rise of democracy in intimate life is also central to a renewed interest in 'the family' as a site where new debates about moralities and ethics can be played out. (The issue of moralities is discussed in chapter 6.) His ideas and his theoretical framework build on existing empirical work as well as linking 'the family' to a wider understanding of modern life. As will be revealed, many of his arguments are reflected in the findings of our own work, giving substance to his points about divorce and how people negotiate different life-styles once they are outside the normative ordering of the romantic love complex and legal marriage. There are, however, certain problems with the story that Giddens provides.

Inasmuch as his starting-point is the 'reflexive self' and 'the project of the self' in late modernity, he presumes, rather than addresses directly, that there remain differences of social class, ethnicity, religion and so on. In *Modernity and Self-identity* (1991), which provides the foundation for his work on intimacy, he talks of 'life-style choices', which suggests a certain glossing of class differences and inequalities. However, Giddens argues that he is aware of differential access to life-style choices and the extent to which post-traditional societies produce exclusions and marginalizations. While these apparently 'mesh' with his analysis, he argues that they are not his preoccupation because they are

already implied in the workings of life-style choice. The trouble is
that he does not dwell on how differential access to 'life-style
choices' might actually work. Sociologically speaking it is important to understand how this differential access works and how the
pure relationship is mediated by religion, ethnic difference, wealth,
employment status and so on. This is not to imply that only the
wealthy, white secular communities who are in full-time employment might access the pure relationship. It may be the poor, urban,
unemployed white sectors who, being less enmeshed in property
concerns and for whom marriage might entail financial impover-
ishment, incline more towards this model. But the point is that
Giddens does not reflect upon the significance of difference. This
unfortunately gives the impression that confluent love and the
pure relationship is available to all men and women who are able
to free themselves from the normative constraints of the romantic
love complex (and patriarchal power). The quotation from Giddens
above, for example, implies that the only thing stopping a whole-
sale move towards the pure relationship is 'institutional lag' and
the odd internal dynamics of heterosexuality. By institutional lag
he presumably means pension provision, childcare provision and
so on (although this is not clear), while the interpersonal gender
dynamics refer to psycho-sexual development, producing attach-
ments to outmoded and outgrown styles of gender relationships.
There is nothing here about class-based inequalities and how they
might stop this shift. Nor is there any recognition that racism
might in fact exert a push towards traditional marriage rather than
away from it for some communities. Put simply there are not
enough contradictions in the model that Giddens provides.

One other criticism we would like to make concerns Giddens'
treatment of children. Smart (1997) has argued elsewhere that the
pure relationship, where one can end a commitment once the
relationship has ceased to be satisfactory, ignores the impact of
having children. Some couples do stay together for the sake of
their children, but having children often makes it much harder
for individuals (usually mothers) to leave relationships and to be
financially independent. We need therefore to understand how a
triadic relationship might alter the essentially dyadic one of
Giddens' model. But Giddens does not ignore the existence of
children altogether, rather what little he has to say about them
sits ill with his own ideas about the reflexive self. Children, at
least young children, are depicted somewhat as objects or bur-

dens or a source of strain. Unlike the couple, they are not seen as having agency and thus are not seen as raising a voice at the point at which the adults decide to abandon their pure relationship. What is more, Giddens seems ignorant of the trend (for which there is as much evidence as there is for the trend towards the pure relationship) towards ongoing parenting after divorce. A sexual relationship may end, but parenting is harder to abdicate. It is not clear, therefore, that couples can simply end relationships and move on even if this is what they most want to do for themselves. Interestingly, Beck and Beck-Gernsheim offer a very different kind of analysis where children are concerned and so we will now turn to their work.

Beck and Beck-Gernsheim: The Normal Chaos of Love *(1995)*

Like Giddens' work, that of Beck and Beck-Gernsheim has its theoretical roots in an earlier work which maps out a new analysis of modernity. In this earlier work (*Risk Society*, 1992) Beck outlines the process of individualization that occurs under conditions of late modernity and the extent to which older sociological concepts of class no longer capture social inequalities which come about under new conditions of globalization and individualization. Inasmuch as his focus is upon the demise of traditional life (in a way not dissimilar to Giddens) he is drawn to focus on gender relations and in particular the new strains put upon women by the pull of tradition and the push of modernity. He states:

> In this way, the lives of women are pulled back and forth by this contradiction between liberation from and reconnection to the old ascribed roles. . . . They flee from housework to a career and back again, and attempt in different phases of their lives to hold together the diverging conditions of their life 'somehow' through contradictory decisions. . . . Divorce law and divorce reality, the lack of social protections, the closed doors of the labour market and the main burden of family work characterize some of the *contradictions* which the individualization process has brought into the female life context. (1992: 111–12)

Beck's work therefore foregrounds the idea of contradictions and the way in which individuals try to manage these. He does not

give the impression of smooth transitions from one state to another and in this sense he captures the complexities of modern
life.[3] Also like Giddens, Beck seeks to understand marriage and
'the family' in the context of all the other changes that are occurring under late modernity. He does not isolate 'the family' as if it
could be imagined as standing apart from other institutions,
maintaining a matrix of relationships which are somehow un-
touched by individualization, globalization, risks of unemployment or environmental damage and so on. His sociological
perspective challenges the idea that 'the family' can be preserved
unchanged or even returned to some prior idealized model. He
notes, for example, that to return to 'the family' of forty years ago
one would have to completely restructure the labour market, the
welfare state, remove women's legal rights, change women's
access to education and so on.

These ideas are taken up in the later jointly authored *Normal
Chaos of Love*. While there are strong similarities with Giddens'
work, this book focuses more on the way in which 'love' has
grown in significance in the modern era. The love of which they
speak is not a kind of cool negotiation with a touch of sexual
passion that Giddens implies in his pure relationship. Rather, the
love described by Beck and Beck-Gernsheim is needy, desperate
and magical in its powers to transform and heal (at least tempo-
rarily). And also, quite differently to Giddens' approach, they
include the love of children in this kind of new straining for
meaning through love which they see as central to modernity.
Consider the following:

> By now we have reached the next stage; traditional bonds
> play only a minor role and the love between men and
> women has likewise proved vulnerable and prone to fail-
> ure. What remains is the child. It promises a tie which is
> more elemental, profound and durable than any other in
> this society. The more other relationships become inter-
> changeable and revocable, the more a child can become
> the focus of new hopes – it is the ultimate guarantee of
> permanence, providing an anchor for one's life. (1995: 73)

From this we can see similarities with Giddens, but also a major
difference. For Beck and Beck-Gernsheim, once the adult relationship is over, the focus may become the child rather than yet
another adult relationship. They refer to the growth of autonomous motherhood where women, having failed to find a suitable

partner, decide to have a child outside a relationship. They also pay a lot of attention to what they see as a trend towards both mothers and fathers wanting to keep the children on divorce. The reasons that Beck and Beck-Gernsheim offer for this new tendency is the growth of individualism in late modernity. They cite the decline of social classes and forms of collective solidarity in cultures based upon the unrestricted flow of market forces combined with an ethos of self-improvement and self-absorption. Ironically, however, they point out that the more individualistic we become the more we yearn for closeness, security and identification with significant others. They see these as push/pull factors which, on the one hand, make relationships insecure and fragile, but on the other, keep us looking for just such a relationship. As an extension of this push/pull factor they also outline what is happening to women in modern societies. They suggest that they are suffering from forces that push them towards traditional domestic roles (in particular the impossibility of combining employment with the care of children) while also being pushed towards independence (the high rate of divorce, the desire for a life of one's own, and the need to earn money). Like Giddens, Beck and Beck-Gernsheim focus much of their analytical attention on the contradictions facing women and they give theoretical centrality to gender divisions as the very foundation of the bourgeois family and, in turn, industrial society. Thus they acknowledge that shifts in these gender divisions produce seismic changes elsewhere. But what is less clear in Beck and Beck-Gernsheim is how much agency women have. While Giddens sees women as developing intentionality and acting with social consequence, Beck and Beck-Gernsheim seem to depict women (and men) as subject to forces beyond their understanding which are generated by wider social changes. They give the impression of there being people who seek to satisfy yearnings without knowing why. While we might agree that individual actors may not have a sociological grasp of their place in the process of global change, Beck and Beck-Gernsheim tend to give the impression that individualism has produced not a reflexive self so much as an automaton.[4]

> The boom in love reflects current living conditions and the anonymous, prefabricated pattern forced on people by the market relegating their private needs right to the end of the list. (1995: 179)

It is hard not to be reminded of Herbert Marcuse's work, particularly his concepts of sublimation and repressive desublimation. Marcuse (1955) developed the former concept to explain how capitalism repressed our sexual libido in order that it might be sublimated into the work ethic and away from pleasure for the purposes of increased production. Later he replaced this idea with repressive desublimation. This concept was used to explain the rise of commercialized sex and pornography which harnessed sexual libido into a form of consumerism, rather than redirecting it into labour. The former explained alienated production, the latter alienated consumerism. Certainly Beck and Beck-Gernsheim seem to see love as the new opiate of the masses. They see love as taking over from religion (or patriotism or class solidarity and so on) to become the addiction that gives a kind of spurious meaning to alienated lives. They suggest that 'love is the best ideology to counteract the perils of individualization' (1995: 181).

This aspect of their analysis is the least satisfactory because, although it does not rely on a kind of conspiracy theory which was part of the Marcusian thesis (i.e. inevitably meeting the needs of capital), it does seem to rely on certain naturalistic assumptions about human beings. Thus it is not explained sociologically why, as we become more individualized, we should seek love; nor why we should seek security and so on. Rather love is treated as a kind of functional equivalent to religion and because we (apparently) once 'needed' religion, we now 'need' love in its absence. But Beck and Beck-Gernsheim see this modern form of love as rather dangerous:

> It is our conjecture . . . that love has become a blueprint for
> hopes and actions untrammelled by old ties and constraints
> previously enforced by the state, the law and the church,
> and developing its own inner logic, conflicts and paradoxes.
> . . . One fundamental cause of so much emotional upheaval
> is the inherent contradictoriness of a form of living erected
> on rapidly changing feelings and the hopes of both partners
> that they can 'become themselves'. (1995: 171)

In chapter 6 we challenge this conjecture, which seems to equate processes of individualization with the abandonment of ethics and rampant self-interest.[5] Our analysis is much closer to that of Giddens (and also Finch, 1989), who seeks to tease out new styles of moral thinking in intimate life, rather than presuming a growth of amorality or immorality.

Notwithstanding some of the problems in *The Normal Chaos of Love*, we wish to return to the authors' focus on children and their arguments about the changing nature of divorce. As suggested above (pp. 14–15), we find ideas about the changing significance of the child to be worth investigating further (this issue is examined through our empirical data in chapter 5). Beck and Beck-Gernsheim suggest that as married and/or sexual love becomes more fragile, love for the child appears to take on the promise of greater permanence and hence satisfaction. They argue that this generates new conflicts between men and women because it has meant that men begin to re-evaluate their relationships with their children at the point of divorce, which is the point at which they anticipate losing their children; they claim that men have started to envy women because of their closeness to children, going on to suggest (in a way very reminiscent of Christine Delphy, 1976) that the old bargain on divorce was that women got the children and men walked away with the economic benefits of uninterrupted employment. However, they also suggest that with more women in the labour market, men feel the bargain is now too one-sided.[6] They (i.e. the men) *imagine* that women have both the children and the benefits of employment. In his earlier work Beck argues:

> But to the degree that the economic inequality between men and women is decreased . . . *fathers become aware of their disadvantage*, partially naturally and partially legally. The woman has *possession* of the child as a product of her womb, which we all know does belong to her, biologically and legally. . . . The men who free themselves from the 'fate' of a career and turn to their children come home to an empty nest. (1992: 113) (Emphasis in the original)

In this way Beck and Beck-Gernsheim attempt to understand the growth in men's anger about recent[7] custody laws and their willingness to challenge mothers legally, as part of a wider process of individualization through which there develops a yearning for a permanent bond which only children can (apparently) provide. But it is also seen as a reaction to structural changes in employment and shifts in gendered relationships in marriage. This argument is compelling and the rise of fathers' rights organizations throughout the Western world lends weight to the thesis (see Neale and Smart, 1997a). However, it is a weakness in the thesis that the authors do not differentiate between the *perception* of a child as provider of permanent unconditional love and the actuality of parent-child relationships. Feminists have long striven to challenge the myth of motherhood in which it has been assumed that the birthing process gives rise to love and bonding and that mothers and children unambiguously love one another. A huge amount has been written problematizing this relationship and recognizing ambivalence, anger, suffocation and many negative emotions alongside some of the more positive ones (e.g. Rich, 1985; Ribbens, 1994; Everingham, 1994). Loving children requires as much 'work' (Finch and Groves, 1983) as loving adults and it can be just as unrewarding at times. If children are perceived as an easy source of love, stability and contentment then the fathers depicted by Beck and Beck-Gernsheim are probably destined to be disappointed. But more importantly from a sociological viewpoint, we need to understand why men might see children in this way and to explore whether it is their distance from day to day care which produces an idealized vision of this form of love.[8]

The focus on children in *The Normal Chaos of Love* produces a very different understanding of divorce to the one implied by Giddens. In the Giddens version when the pure relationship ends there is, effectively, a clean break and people go their own way to find another relationship. But Beck and Beck-Gernsheim present a very different analysis of post-divorce life. They state:

> Only someone equating marriage with sex, loving and living together can make the mistake that divorce means the end of marriage. If one concentrates on problems of material support, on the children and on a long common biography, divorce is quite obviously not even the legal end of marriage but transforms itself into a new phase of post-marital 'separation marriage'. (1995: 147)

It is difficult to reconcile these two very different versions unless we assume that the couples who are the focus of Giddens' analysis are financially independent of one another and childless. But at least the individuals who go to make up his couples are not presumed to be heterosexual and they are presumed to be reflexive about their relationship and its qualities. Beck and Beck-Gernsheim, however, seem to perceive only heterosexual love and bonding; their lovers are driven by forces beyond their control but at least they recognize the significance of children.

Both of these sociological accounts of family life under late modernity are interesting in that, while they contextualize fully 'the family' in modernity and see families as part of change rather than as a group which merely reacts to changes that are generated elsewhere, they depict intimate relations and/or love in very narrow terms. There are no mothers-in-law, no cousins, no grand-children, step-grandparents and so on. The field of intimacy seems very empty of players. It is almost as if Giddens and Beck have entered into the myopic vision of those who have recently fallen in love and who forget that other obligations and commitments continue. Even if we accept that relationships with wider kin are now negotiated rather than governed by strict rules and norma-tive expectations (Finch and Mason, 1993) it does not mean that they are insignificant. In our conclusion, therefore, we wish to look at another sociological account of modern family life which, while it sits comfortably with the broader scope of both Giddens' and Beck's work of bringing intimate relations into the main-stream of sociological thinking, does not focus simply on the 'couple' and enquires much more closely into everyday life and intimate practices.

Conclusion

David Morgan: Family Connections *(1996)*

Morgan is a theorist of 'the family' rather than a grand theorist of modernity and so, while his work is theoretically driven, he is more concerned about the interiority of familial relationships than either Giddens or Beck. But Morgan is equally committed to reconceptualizing 'the family' and to analysing 'the family' through contemporary sociological theory rather than staying within the older, more familiar structuralist paradigm which isolates 'the family' from other social relationships, experiences and meanings. This means that he renders significant aspects of everyday life that were invisible to earlier sociologists of the family. He does this gradually, starting with familiar territory of class and gender and the reproduction of both within 'the family'. He then discusses *care*, which has long been a significant focus of feminist work on intimacy and 'the family'. This focus on care and caring rather than on housework reflects an important shift in sociological (and feminist) thinking about 'the family'. Caring is qualitatively different from housework because it involves negotiations with others and responsiveness to others' needs; it is both a form of labour and of love. Work on care, he maintains, became highly significant precisely because it expanded our understanding of the complexity of intimate relationships and because it is a mixture of acts, intentions and sentiments.[9] As the concept of care became more and more refined, it became possible to see how carers were engaged in a reflexive project requiring skills and agency. In a way, feminist and sociological work on caring transformed women into sociological agents for the first time. No longer were they merely the 'put upon' and symbolic housewives of the domestic labour debate, nor were they simply a natural resource for other family members as implied in functionalist sociology; instead they entered, conceptually speaking, into a sociological citizenship for the first time. Work on caring, he suggests, has therefore effected a very important conceptual transition between the older-style structuralist approaches to 'the family' and more recent post- or neo-structuralist approaches.

Following his discussion of caring, Morgan moves into much newer terrain for family sociology, namely the body, time and space, food and home. Of course all of these were 'elements' within older styles of sociological thinking, but they were taken for granted and regarded as having no special conceptual significance. Using these concepts in the context of family life means that Morgan is challenging the split between sociological theorizing and family sociology referred to in our opening remarks. But equally important in Morgan's work is his discussion of terminology. While the sociological fascination with terminology can sometimes seem like obsessive pedantry, in this case Morgan is dealing with a fundamental problem – one which is essential to address here. The problem is which term is appropriate to refer to 'the family'. Clearly we cannot use the term 'the family' without the inverted commas any more. It is far too naive a concept. It implies that there is a naturalistic grouping which always, everywhere, is *the* family with its fixed gender roles. It distorts differences of class, race, region and so on. Because this traditional definition is based on a unit of reproduction, it presumes heterosexuality as the norm, and it presumes that only those linked by blood or marriage can be part of a family. Feminist work in the 1980s strove to abandon this term altogether except when one was self-consciously using it to refer to an ideological construct (Barrett and McIntosh, 1982). The preferred term in feminist work became 'household'. This concept emphasized the idea of co-residence without marital or kinship ties, it did not import the ideological content of the idealization of the natural family, and it tilted our perception of family life towards economic constructs like house-work, unpaid domestic labour, unwarranted power differentials and so on. But Morgan argues that people still use the term family. Indeed the term has become radicalized through the no-tion of 'families of choice' (Weston, 1991). Thus to banish the term altogether might well mean the loss of something significant. Families, for example, do not have to co-reside as households do and families imply an emotional commitment and even caring in a way that the concept of household does not. In any case, the way people live in families has changed. If a gay couple can call themselves a family, then the power of the concept always and inevitably to refer to a married man and wife with their children is fundamentally challenged. Thus the ideological power of the term is changed.

Notwithstanding these shifts, it is still impossible to talk inno-cently of *the* family. There is too much diversity in family life to use such a homogenizing concept. So Morgan opts for the term 'family practices'. He uses this in order to challenge the idea that 'the family' is a thing. Rather it is variable set of relationships which change and are modified and so the term 'practices' em-phasizes fluidity. More than this the term 'practices' allows us to conceptualize how family 'practices' overlap with other social practices (e.g. gendering practices, economic practices and so on). Moreover, while 'practices' are historically and culturally located, they allow us to imagine the social actor who engages in these practices and who may choose to modify them. We are therefore back on Giddens' territory and his emphasis on the self and agency. Morgan does not use these terms, but rather speaks of the auto/biographical turn in sociology which has started to recog-nize the importance of the individual to the construction of histo-ries and cultures. Obviously, if we use the term family practices, we cease to see 'the family' as an institution and this means, in turn, that we can sidestep the interminable debate about whether this institution is in decline or not. Instead of seeing the family as being under 'threat', or undermined, we can start to see a variety of shifts which may have different significances rather than see-

ing all change rolled up into some terrible attack on a homogeneous bloc called *the* family. In this way (and this is important for
the analysis in this book) we can stop imagining that all change is
either simply good or bad. We can also locate change differently,
ceasing to blame economic forces on the one hand, or rampant
individual self-interest on the other.

We therefore tend towards using the concept of 'family practices' in this book. Our focus is on fluidity and change, on gendered
practices, on adult-child relationships and on shifts within intimate relationships and between relationships. Following Morgan,
this means that our understanding of power relations is quite
distinct from earlier feminist work on the heterosexual family
and we do not proceed with an automatic assumption about how
power in the sphere of intimacy and family practices will always
work. But we will also be following the ideas initiated by important feminist work on kinship obligations and on caring.

The former is the focus of Janet Finch's work (1989, and Finch
and Mason, 1993), which sought empirically to investigate how
notions of moral obligation between kin might be changing in the
light of changing family structures and other social change. Her
ideas flow through this book and were, in large part, the genesis
of the research project on which this work is based. The major
significance of this work (discussed further in chapter 6) is its
redefinition of obligations and commitments as arising from em-
pathy and affinity rather than from a static concept of duty.
Focusing specifically on kinship rather than on couples and children as we do here, she argues that shared understandings about
'the proper thing to do' emerge over time and in specific contexts.
She argues that the key element about moral decisions is their
ambiguity, which is to say that there is always more than one
solution to a moral dilemma: people will disagree about the right
thing to do in particular circumstances. She goes on to point out
that even where people agree to a principle in the abstract, they
may well feel that it is inappropriate in a specific circumstance. In
talking of the way in which ideas about the proper thing to do
'emerge', Finch is not ignorant of power imbalances, particularly
of gender and class, nor is she unaware of the way in which
situations change such that there may be no fixed morality. She
refers to 'patterned changes' which may be events like marriage
or widowhood. Such patterned changes bring with them normative expectations and thus they are not experienced as a major

upheaval in terms of moral actions, but they too are negotiated. Following these ideas we start our enquiry into shifting family practices at the point of divorce or separation, precisely one of those key moments when a new 'moral order' needs to be individually crafted.

This book is therefore much concerned with morality, but in the sense that Finch uses it, not in the foundational sense that the Ethical Socialists might prefer (Smart and Neale, 1997a). But it is equally concerned with the concept of care. Again this idea flows through the book, although we develop the concept most systematically in chapter 9. We look at care both empirically (in the sense of exploring who does the work of caring) but also conceptually (in the sense that it is a quality of relationships and a state of reflexive awareness about the needs of others). When we started the empirical project which is the basis of this book we adhered to a rather limited notion of care with an emphasis on care as (unrecognized) work. However, our position shifted particularly under the influence of increasingly important feminist work on the meaning of care as an ethical practice (Sevenhuijsen, 1998; Tronto, 1993; Benhabib, 1992). As the discussion in chapter 9 reveals, we argue that a concept of care is vital to the conceptualization of policies (particularly family law policies) which seek to intervene in and influence moral relationships within and across families. It is our hope that we have woven together these crucial concepts of family practices, moral obligations and care in a narrative which will produce a new, more optimistic, way of understanding family fragments at the turn of the century.

2

Family Policy and the Research Agenda

Introduction

> [T]he aim of policies should be to facilitate flexibility in family life, rather than to shape it into a particular form. It is a proper role for the state to ensure that people have maximum opportunity to work out their own relationships as they wish, to suit the circumstances of their own lives. It is not the proper role of governments to presume that certain outcomes would be more desirable than others. (Finch, 1997:13)

This argument, presented by Janet Finch, is a logical outcome of the sort of theories discussed in chapter 1. The more we start to think in terms of 'family practices' and negotiated kinship, the more it becomes apparent that a fixed or rigid notion of the proper family on which to base policy developments is inappropriate. Policies as diverse as the planning of housing provision through to immigration laws would all vary considerably if the basic unit was taken to be mutable and in flux, rather than as fixed and unchanging. But in the context of the UK we have to recognize that there is not a unified 'family policy' as such. Indeed, as Fox Harding (1996) has argued, there is no explicit, intentional 'family policy' at all and we have to derive a sense of an overall policy from a variety of sources. In addition, she argues that while it is very common for policies to be initiated rhetorically in terms of preserving family life, in practice such policies may end up having little impact on families or even achieving the opposite of their stated aims.

Leaving aside the question of whether a unified family policy would be workable or desirable, the situation in the UK as far as policy on family life is concerned is necessarily complex and contradictory. Policies affecting families can be quite contradictory and tracing the effects of policies can be an impossible task simply because of the diversity of family practices upon which the policy impacts. Moreover, policies affecting family life are generated in diverse quarters and usually deal with only one aspect of intimate relationships. Thus family law may deal with divorce and its consequences, but the Child Support Agency deals with financial matters governing children, while social security legislation impacts upon cohabitation and marriage. Moreover, the likelihood is that each sphere has different priorities and principles, giving rise to differing outcomes which compete with each other. For this reason it is really quite impossible to state with any authority that in practice 'family policy' supports a particular form of family life.

However, as Fox Harding (1996) also remarks, there may be a much clearer vision of how family life should be organized within the political rhetoric (rather than practice/policy) which surrounds the family. The rhetorical idealization of the authoritarian family and the commensurate bemoaning of its loss, have a very long history in England. Each decade produces a fresh chorus on the subject of the decline of the family or family values, and each decade seeks to preserve exactly the family which previous Jeremiahs have condemned as an inferior version of the true authoritarian family. In the popular rhetoric of the family, the institution is in permanent decline and new depths are always being plumbed (Humphrey, 1996). Thus, any change to family life seems inevitably to be greeted with alarm and despondency. This change is, moreover, usually construed as arising from 'unbridled' individualism (Dench, 1996) or from a lack of moral restraint. Changes that are occurring because of social, historical or cultural shifts are constantly reduced, in popular discourse, to symptoms of individual moral decline. In other words, families are changing but the public debate separates these changes from other wider, social transformations and then seeks to admonish family members for their failure to stand still while the conditions that supported specific forms of family organization in the past are demolished.

It has now become commonplace for policies affecting family life to be introduced in terms of how they will *re*stabilize the family, or how they will *re*inforce parental responsibility. There is a dominant inferential framework into which policy is inscribed, and this is the idea of *getting back* to a specific family form. While market principles, competition and innovation are meant to dominate the labour market, education policy, health provision and so on, the family is meant to embrace old values of altruism, unpaid labour, implicit contracts and co-operation. Quite specifically changes to the law on divorce in England and Wales throughout the twentieth century have almost always been introduced as measures to stabilize marriage and the family. In the 1950s the Royal Commission on Marriage and Divorce (Morton, 1956) argued that if it could find the evidence that easier divorce destabilized marriage, it would recommend that all divorce should be banned (McGregor, 1957; Smart, 1984). The crucial Divorce Reform Act of 1969 was steered through parliament on the back of the argument that abolishing matrimonial fault and making the grounds for divorce less arduous would stabilize the institution of marriage. It was said that allowing people to divorce was the only way to allow them to remarry and thus have legitimate children by their new relationships. Then in the 1990s Lord Mackay introduced the Conservative Government's White Paper, *Looking to the Future*, which proposed various changes to the law on divorce, as a measure that 'supports the institution of marriage' (Lord Chancellor's Department, 1995: 73).

There is clearly an unresolved tension here. Governments have altered the law on divorce in substantial ways, most particularly since the end of the Second World War. Each time government has acted, it has promised to stabilize the family. Then, some years later, it has introduced a new measure to restabilize the family because it has discovered that the previous measures either failed or actually seemed to accelerate the destabilization of the family. So the recent history of family law reform is marked by a repetitive incantation of the ideal of the unchanging, stable family and its preservation, alongside the development of new legal policies on divorce and marital breakdown which increasingly normalize the process. This pattern has rarely been broken. The Conservative Government's Family Law Bill in the mid-1990s was a good example of this rhetorical invective which seems now to be an essential part of any measure dealing directly with family life. In its progress through parliament the Lord Chancellor insisted that it was a measure which would strengthen marriage. But this interpretation was challenged by Tory backbenchers for being yet another measure which promised more family stability while in reality offering 'easier' divorce. In consequence the Bill was revised to ensure that it would obtain passage through parliament and measures were strengthened to delay divorce proceedings and to further encourage the possibility of reconciliation. It was then, somewhat ironically, accepted as a measure which would indeed strengthen the idealized nuclear family. Thus the Family Law Act of 1996, like so much preceding family law legislation, continued the tradition of committing itself to maintaining a particular form of family life and preserving marriage as the basis of the family. Its chances of success seem remote, of course, given the extent to which the ideal to which it aspires is increasingly incompatible with how families are now 'lived' over the life course.

Changes in family living

In this debate on the Family Law Bill during 1996 it was clear that some saw previous divorce legislation as the cause of detrimental changes to the idealized nuclear family unit, while others seemed to imagine that restrictions imposed through the law on divorce could actually prevent further changes occurring to family life (Smart and Neale, 1997a). This betrayed a belief that what was required to sustain a particular family form were measures to reduce the existing escape routes from unhappy marriages combined with a remoralization of family members. In the debates in parliament almost every contribution rested on a statistical fact which was, in turn, interpreted as a trend or slippery slope. This comment by Paul Boateng is typical of the way in which such statistics were used:

> By the turn of the century 3.7 million children will have experienced at least one parental divorce. The impact on a child of its parents divorcing is considerable. The valuable research that has been carried out in this area highlights the need for effective multi-agency intervention to counter the negative impact of divorce on children. (Paul Boateng, Hansard, vol. 279, col. 591, 17 June 1996)

Morgan (1998) has pointed out that many popular and policy accounts of family life also start with lists of 'facts'. These lists always include statements on the rise in the divorce rate, the numbers of children who experience their parents' divorce, the numbers of lone mothers, the numbers of children born outside wedlock, and the numbers of mothers in the labour market. Additional 'facts', usually generated from *Social Trends* or other sources of statistical data (e.g. Haskey, 1996), might include rates of juvenile delinquency or the numbers of old people living alone. These statistically generated 'facts' are presented as constituting an overall package and hence a full picture of the nature and quality of modern family life. As Morgan suggests:

> In other words they are not a set of more or less random facts about the modern family. In some cases there might be causal linkages between some individual elements (divorce rates and re-constituted households and lone parents, for example) but more generally we are invited to view these items as signifiers of some underlying set of causes (or perhaps a single cause) or as a series of symptoms of some deeper social disorder. (Morgan, 1999: 14)

The lists of facts are further constructed as 'trends', which in turn inevitably invite an interpretation of how things are getting worse, or how they were once much better. Of course such an interpretation is aided by the tendency to use the 1950s as the benchmark for all subsequent developments. As a consequence family life in the 1950s becomes seen as the 'traditional' family because it is discursively constructed as the way the family was before change began. So, although family life in the 1950s was quite dissimilar to family living during the war or in the 1920s or the 1890s, contemporary accounts of changing family structures give the impression that 'once upon a time' the family did not change. Yet, as Nicholson (1997) has argued, the type of family which emerged in the 1950s was quite 'new' in many ways, in particular in its emphasis on excluding anyone from the household except spouses and children and in the transformation of the home into a site for consumption and leisure for husbands and children. The discussion of family life in the context of trends is therefore highly problematic if the benchmark era is treated as if it signifies a moment in history when the family took its 'natural' form – prior to the onset of decline.

Maclean and Eekelaar (1997) use trends in family life to a slightly different end. Rather than starting in the immediate post-war era they collect earlier data to point out that in some respects (such as average age at marriage for women or the rate of marriage) patterns are returning to those more typical of previous centuries. This means that the great rush to marry at a young age which affected the majority of young women born immediately after the Second World War was unusual. Delayed marriage and the avoidance of marriage altogether are therefore not in themselves new developments. This use of statistical data on trends provides the basis for a much more informed understanding of how the very idea of family, and the centrality of marriage to families, might fluctuate. Unfortunately, however, many of the recorded trends in family life often have a much shorter history than this. Statistics on cohabitation are a recent innovation, and modern trends cannot be compared with illicit cohabitations at a time when divorce was almost impossible, because such statistics could not have been collected. Unintentionally, therefore, many accounts of changes to family life can contribute to a sense of recent decline or 'instability', simply because records are so recent.

The choice of terminology to describe change is also important. Family life is now typically measured in terms of something called 'stability'. Stability is good and instability is bad. But the main, supposedly objective, measure of stability (namely divorce) is an exceptionally crude instrument which does not even measure co-residence, let alone the quality of relationships (Gibson, 1994). The existence of violence in households as a measure of 'stability' might yield a completely different picture of how stable married family life is. The description of instability is, in any case, selectively applied. For example, families where the death of a spouse triggers change are not referred to as unstable families, even though children may be distraught and the family becomes a lone-parent family. The term unstable therefore always carries a connotation of fault and inadequacy; it is normative rather than descriptive.

> Such constructed facts pervade a wide range of writings about and pronouncements on the family from public religious or political statements, . . . including more theoretical analyses of modern family life. The more theoretical accounts both reflect and constitute the changes under consideration. The choice of whether to write about 'change', 'decline' or 'de-institutionalisation' does not simply arise from the facts as presented but goes a long way towards constituting such facts and their subsequent interpretations. (Morgan, 1999: 14–15)

We would go further than Morgan here to suggest that not only does the listing of 'facts', and the terminology used to represent the collective effect of these 'facts', create an impervious tautology and an almost irrefutable 'common sense' about the dreadful state of family life, but that they increasingly form the supposedly scientific basis of policy developments. Our argument is not so much against the use of statistics as a tool for understanding social processes as it is against the unfortunate consequences of the assumption that statistics are objective and that they embrace all that needs to be known about family life in the formulation of policy. To a very considerable extent, this book is intended to address precisely the impressions of family life popularized by accounts based on overly simplistic readings of lists and statistics. It is also an attempt to offer a different vision of family life to those which assume that a moral decline has led to the so-called 'parenting deficit' (Etzioni, 1993).

Policy, research and the Children Act

We have argued that legislation on divorce has tried to assert the primacy of marriage to the family and that, through the concern generated by statistical trends, an irrefutable argument has become established which insists that marriage must always be prioritized to safeguard the family. In this context, the Children Act 1989 is something of an anomaly. This Act, or at least the private law provisions of the legislation which concern us here, did not have its origins in questions of marriage, nor did it idealize the married nuclear family.[1] Rather its locus was in the question of child welfare (Hoggett, 1989). In its progress into policy it did not therefore fall into the maws of the debate on the decline of marriage and the family; metaphorically speaking it was able to strike out in a different direction espousing children rather than promoting (fictitiously or otherwise) marriage and the authoritarian family. The Children Act was implicitly about the family and marriage, but because it framed the issues differently it was able to bring about a policy – almost surreptitiously – that separated parenthood from matrimony in policy terms and which focused on relationships rather than on the ideal of an institution. Most certainly it was informed by statistical trends, in particular the numbers of children experiencing their parents' divorce and the numbers of fathers who lost contact with their children, but these research data, combined with powerful psychological research (Richards, 1982), did not give priority to marriage but to parenthood. The Children Act is a clear attempt at social engineering but it is based on a vision of ideal post-divorce relationships, not, we contend, an attempt to reproduce or to celebrate a former family structure based on marriage. In many ways the Children Act – in principle if not in practice – comes close to the ideal posited by Janet Finch at the start of this chapter because its focus is on the quality of relationships (which can take a multitude of forms) rather than types or models of relationships which cohere into a fixed shape. But our argument is running ahead of itself and so it is necessary to explain the policy background to this legislation and the influence of research on the formulation of this policy, as well as outlining the key elements of the private law provisions of the Act, before progressing in subsequent chapters to an evaluation of it based on our empirical study of parents who were affected by its provisions.

Policy and the Children Act

As we have noted, the Children Act was the first clear statement of the way in which parenting, and in particular post-divorce parenting, was starting to be seen as more significant in family law terms than marriage. Although case law was beginning to reflect changing ideas about the relative importance of fatherhood and motherhood after divorce, it was this Act which codified these ideas and created a clear new ethos about post-divorce parenting (Neale and Smart, 1997a).

The origins of these changes lay in part in the debates on marriage and divorce in the mid-1980s which attempted to reconceptualize divorce as a form of injustice to men and to discredit the arguments which had prevailed until that time which suggested that it was women who were mostly (economically) disadvantaged at the point of divorce (Eekelaar and Maclean, 1986). There emerged a men's lobby which initially focused on the financial aspects of divorce and which argued successfully that – in an age of (apparent) gender equality – men should not be expected to pay for the maintenance of their wives on divorce. The

Matrimonial and Family Proceedings Act, introduced in 1984 as a result of this pressure, basically removed women's entitlement to maintenance for themselves and promoted the ideal of the 'clean break' between spouses on divorce. As a consequence of this legislation, husbands and wives were to be free of one another and to have no lingering financial entanglements which would sustain resentments and a sense of injustice (Gibson, 1994).

But the Matrimonial and Family Proceedings Act also provided for an increase in the levels of maintenance men would have to pay for their children because it was argued that child support would have to include an element for the carer of the children if she (or he) had to remain outside the labour market to raise the children. The problem that this caused for the men's lobby was that it meant that the overall amount of maintenance they would have to pay was not necessarily reduced, while the custom and practice of awarding custody of children to their wives remained undisturbed (Maidment, 1981). The focus of the men's lobby therefore shifted towards the perceived unfairness of maternal preference in matters of child custody (Bainham, 1989; McCant, 1987). The equality argument therefore shifted from a focus on the financial aspects of divorce to the question of care and responsibility for children.

It was in this context that the Law Commission (1986) formulated proposals to change the law relating to custody and parental relationships after divorce. As Brophy (1989) has pointed out, the concerns of the liberal lawyers in the Law Commission and the fathers' rights movement were distinct, but they came to coalesce because they both settled on the same solution to the different problems they perceived. The Law Commission was concerned with how children adapted to divorce and with reducing conflict on divorce, while the fathers' rights movement was concerned with a lack of rights for fathers in relation to children. Yet for both the solution became the idea of automatic joint legal custody of children on divorce.

> Although the initial concerns of the liberal lawyers and FNF [Families Need Fathers] were largely different, the former eventually came to focus on the position of non-custodial fathers. Both came to the same ultimate conclusion, namely joint legal custody of children on divorce, either as the preferred outcome or as a mandatory outcome. (Brophy, 1989: 224)

Later Brophy argues:

> It was at this point that joint custody became seen as the
> panacea to the whole range of problems it was presumed
> were experienced both by fathers and children. (1989: 224)

Fatherhood therefore became central to thinking around the post-divorce family and the situation of children, and the goal of retaining father involvement became the automatic subtext of the focus on children's welfare.

When the Children Act was finally drafted and then passed by parliament it did not in fact endorse the idea of automatic joint custody, but rather created the legal situation within which divorce no longer altered parents' legal relationship to their children. Thus the courts no longer made orders for custody at all because it was an automatic presumption that mothers and fathers simply retained all the parental responsibility they enjoyed during marriage beyond the legal divorce.[2] The courts could make orders for residence (where the child should live) and for contact (formerly access), but the Act made it clear that there was to be a preference for 'no orders' and that where possible parents should simply work out arrangements between themselves. The question that arises, however, concerns the process whereby parents actually work out these arrangements. The Law Commission's final report envisaged something of a continuation of pre-divorce arrangements in that it acknowledged that 'clearly in most cases one parent carries a much heavier burden of responsibility than does the other' (1988: 24). However, it wanted to encourage greater responsibility on the part of fathers by removing what were perceived to be the obstacles to post-divorce fathering created by the old legislation. But the apparently simple desire that parents should make their own arrangements for raising children after divorce, just as they would have done before divorce, pays little attention to the extent to which divorce removes most of the material – and also much of the emotional – foundation to the parenting project which is ongoing during a marriage. This was, in effect, a black hole inherent in the legislation which either no one had the foresight to think through or which was beyond the imaginings of the policy makers at the time. But the legislation basically pushed parents into an empty space with only one guideline – that nebulous concept of the welfare of the child – and expected them to refashion parenthood. This issue is of course central to this book.

The Law Commission at the end of the 1980s did therefore seem particularly concerned about fatherhood, but this concern was not formulated on the principles of equality which so excited the men's lobby but on the principle of the welfare of the child. The point was, however, that by the end of that decade the welfare of the child had become very closely associated with enhancing the position of fathers and this had, in turn, come about through an important shift in focus of scientific research. In the following section we shall explore the significance of research findings to the development of policy.

Research, child welfare and the Children Act

The erosion, towards the end of the nineteenth century, of father-right as the prime consideration in custody issues was initially due to the gradual ascendancy of the counter-discourse of maternal love. This discourse combined an assertion of the importance of the kind of love and care that 'only' a mother could provide, with a new notion of child welfare. This notion emphasized the importance of a child's need for emotional care and warmth over the need for discipline and moral instruction (Brophy, 1982). This argument grew in influence and by the turn of the twentieth century it was further validated through the establishment of the new 'child welfare science' (Piper, 1993). There emerged at this time what we might call a modern welfare principle which was based on science rather than sentiment. This approach was introduced formally into legal practice in the Guardianship of Infants Act of 1925, which made it clear that any disputes between mothers and fathers were to be made subsidiary to the welfare of the child. At this point welfare was established as the paramount consideration of the courts, albeit that this still occurred within the context of a fault-based divorce law which could find an adulterous wife to be an undesirable mother by virtue of her matrimonial offence.

Over this period father-right (Mason, 1994) was therefore gradually replaced with the tender years doctrine, which became a virtual orthodoxy in the 1950s and 1960s. At this stage the scientific discourse of welfare had been construed in popular rhetoric as insisting that the presence of the mother was essential to the well-being of her children (Winnicott, 1971; Bowlby, 1965). An orthodoxy was thereby established which saw child welfare as best served by preserving the mother/child bond above other relationships. In terms of research on early child development, the role of the father seemed to have dwindled to insignificance and the courts did not really concern themselves with the quality of the father/child relationship.

Following the Divorce Reform Act of 1969, issues of child custody became gradually separated from issues of the moral rights and wrongs of marriage. The courts were less able to make decisions concerning custody simply in relation to the legal finding of matrimonial guilt. Thus questions of justice between spouses ceased to be a relevant factor in deciding post-divorce arrangements for children and the erosion of a justice criterion left welfare alone as the dominant principle governing the regulation of post-divorce parenthood. This meant that there was no longer a bar to adulterous wives being seen as perfectly good mothers. In the face of a rapidly rising divorce rate, the tender years doctrine continued to guide decisions and the courts typically concurred with the recommendations of psychologists that children fared best remaining with their mothers and with minimal disruption to their emotional ties (Goldstein et al., 1979). This coincided with a general assumption among both professionals and parents that the pre-existing, gendered pattern of childcare within marriage would continue beyond it (Richards, 1982).

The courts were also keen to minimize conflict over children. Although they were not always successful in this aim, the idea that it was bad for children to have their parents fighting over them was given substance by research findings which confirmed that parental conflict following a separation is associated with poor outcomes for children (Maccoby et al., 1990, 1992; Cockett and Tripp, 1994). There was therefore little motivation to alter the legal practice of awarding custody to the mother and access to the father, which obviated the need for most legal battles over children.

Even the phenomenon of waning paternal interest after divorce did not really attract a great deal of interest in the 1970s. Indeed it was assumed that it was best for children if mothers remarried and replaced the missing father figure. Divorced fathers, on the other hand, were expected to remarry and start new families. Research indicated a marked falling-off in contact between children and the non-resident parent over time, with as many as 47 per cent of fathers failing to maintain any form of contact beyond two years, and in 61 per cent of cases paying no maintenance for their children (Eekelaar and Clive, 1977; Gingerbread and FNF, 1982; Mitchell, 1985). While there was some concern about fathers who would not pay maintenance, it was assumed that a clean break between parents was desirable and that the stability created by remarriage and a cessation of contact was an adequate solution to divorce (Goode, 1965; Théry, 1989).

But this situation soon changed as research began to come to rather different conclusions about the effect of divorce on children. Two American studies of mother custody families conducted in the late 1970s indicated that children fared best if they had continuing close contact with both parents after the separation (Hetherington et al., 1978, 1982; Wallerstein and Kelly, 1980[3]). These studies inaugurated a growing belief among psychologists that children suffered harm by losing contact with the non-custodial parent (Richards, 1982, 1993; Walker, 1993; Cockett and Tripp, 1994). Within this radically new welfare discourse, non-custodial fathers were constructed as vital to their children's well-being and as symbolizing stability, order and economic security for a child. Father absence became linked with outcomes such as poor performance in school, poor job prospects, promiscuity in girls and delinquency in boys.

It was in the midst of this paradigmatic shift in psychological thinking, which Maclean and Eekelaar (1997) have referred to as 'the emergence of a new orthodoxy', that the Law Commission was formulating reforms to the laws on custody after divorce in England and Wales. In this new framework 'disengaging' fathers became more than an economic problem and it became important to create ways of consolidating paternal commitment after the demise of the marital relationship. It seems that the architects of the Children Act were considerably influenced by this shift in thinking and strove to create a legal structure in which continuing contact with the non-residential parent could thrive. Given that the primary concern of family law was to preserve the welfare of children it is hardly surprising that the new family law reflected the dominant scientific thinking which was rewriting old ideas on what was best for children on divorce.[4] The question for the Law Commissioners was therefore how to meet the concerns of the new psychology, how to respond to the growing demands of fathers' rights groups, and yet how to recognize the significance of mothers as primary carers of children. Brophy (1989) predicted that the compromise would favour the new welfare principles and fathers' rights over the interests of mothers. As shown in subsequent chapters, the situation seems much more complex than this prediction suggests. However, before exploring that question it is necessary to look briefly at the principles of the legislation and to outline the nature of our empirical research into the consequences of the Act.

The core objectives of the Children Act 1989

It is possible to identify four core objectives of the private law provisions of the Act. These are:

1   to decrease hostility between the parties

2   to pursue a policy of non-intervention by the courts

3   to encourage joint parenting after divorce

4   to promote the welfare of the child.

These are not listed in order of priority because the Act makes it clear that the paramount and/or first principle is simply the welfare of the child. However, we shall deal with them in this order because the effect of each principle is cumulative and they build towards the final stated goal of improving child welfare.

Decreasing hostility

The Law Commission (1988) took the view that hostility between parents could create conditions detrimental to the future welfare of the child. Based on the premise that the most important decisions that parents have to take relate to the children, the Law Commissioners felt that it was important to remove any other factors that could induce antagonism between parents. As it was felt that one of the main reasons that fathers often became hostile was the custom of awarding 'sole custody' to mothers, it was recommended that the concept of custody be abolished, thus removing a main source of conflict. The Act dispensed with the practice of awarding custody on divorce by separating parental rights and duties from spousal rights and duties. Thus while divorce would end the latter, it would no longer affect the former. On divorce parental rights and duties would remain the same as during marriage.

A policy of non-intervention

The key element of this policy was the stated preference in the Act that, wherever possible, no court order should be made in relation to the children. This policy stressed the idea that parents themselves should resolve their differences in relation to the children and that it was not appropriate in the normal course of events for an outside authority to do this. The preference for no orders was also linked to the idea that parents should not try to resolve their conflicts over children in court. To some extent it was hoped that courts would become redundant. This aspiration coincided with the growing emphasis on mediation and with a growing dislike of the adversarial methods formerly adopted by some solicitors.

Encouraging co-parenting

Hoggett (1994), who was the main architect of the Act, argued that the new law was an experiment in joint parenting. By this she meant that it would remove all obstacles to the continuation of a proper parental relationship on the part of both parents after divorce, as well as positively encouraging such developments. As discussed above, the whole ethos of the legislation stressed the importance of keeping fathers involved with their children and it rapidly overturned the idea that the primary carer should have special consideration after divorce. This in turn gave support to the idea of abolishing the old terms of 'custody' and 'access' which, it was felt, were too deeply mired in the idea of winning and losing children. Moreover, the term access was seen as giving too much power to the parent with whom the child lived and as diminishing the role played by the non-residential parent. So the terms 'custody' and 'access' were replaced with the more neutral term 'residence' and the more empowering concept of 'contact'.

The welfare of children

The decrease in hostility, the emphasis on letting parents make their own decisions and taking responsibility for childcare decisions, and the encouragement of joint parenting were all seen as crucial building-blocks for creating a better environment in which the welfare of children could flourish. Naturally the legislation recognized other elements in the process of protecting children, including requiring judges and others to take cognizance of the wishes of children themselves. Safeguards were also available where one parent might have been judged to be disregarding the interests of the children.[5]

The overall tenor of the Act was therefore to be facilitative of a new style of child-centred post-divorce parenting which in turn, as we argue above, rested on the findings of influential psychological research. It also met the growing demands of fathers who felt that they deserved a greater involvement in the lives of their children after divorce. But the Act was clearly an 'experiment'. The questions which therefore arise are: has the experiment worked as anticipated?; what might be the unanticipated consequences of this social engineering?; how do parents negotiate over their children in this new context?; how are lawyers and the courts implementing the legislation?; are mothers now disadvantaged in certain ways? These were precisely some of the questions we sought to answer when we started the empirical research project which is the main substance of this book. What follows is therefore a brief outline of our research project and methods, the results of which fill the subsequent chapters.

The research project

The project identified five key objectives:

1   to apply a new conceptual framework which emphasized questions of 'moral' codes and obligations to research on households in transition

2   to accumulate new information on households in transition
    which is not dominated by the social problems framework

3   to contribute to an understanding of new forms of household
    organization and newly emergent forms of responsibilities,
    caring patterns and ethical codes

4   to achieve Aim 3 over a period of time (in which significant
    changes may occur) in order to transcend the problem of the
    'snapshot' picture produced by much research on social change
    in household organization

5   to assess, within limits, the impact of significant and radical
    policy changes in the field of family law.

Methods

Our fieldwork was located in West Yorkshire, primarily in the large
metropolitan areas of Leeds and Bradford but including the rural
areas to the north, south and east of these cities. Over a period of two
years (summer 1994 to summer 1996) we carried out two rounds of
in-depth, qualitative interviews with sixty parents, drawn from
sixty different families, who had either separated or divorced after
the implementation of the Children Act.[6] Our sampling strategy
was theoretically driven, designed to generate a sample that
would cover a relevant range of parental circumstances and experiences rather than being representative of all such circumstances
and experiences (Finch and Mason, 1990). Within these broad parameters we planned to generate a cohort of parents who had finalized
their divorces or separations since October 1991, when the Children
Act was introduced. Some of the parents had separated before this
date but had not started legal proceedings until after the introduction of the Act. This time-frame was important because part of our
aim was to explore what impact (if any) the new legislation might be
having on the negotiation of parenthood.

   Our plan was to recruit our cohort of parents through solicitors
so that we could find them as close to the conclusion of legal
proceedings as possible. To gain a spread of cases we contacted
very different types of legal firms with varied client groups. We
advised solicitors that we did not simply want to recruit bitter or
acrimonious cases but also those which were 'unremarkable'. This

method of recruitment proved to be problematic (although it had worked well in the original pilot). While we contacted a wide spread of 'cases' through the solicitors, they proved to be very tardy in establishing contacts for us and we found it difficult to pressurize them as we were reliant on their good will. We therefore developed another strategy of contacting parents through support groups for divorced parents and through advertisements in the newsletters of large organizations. Of the total sample we contacted twenty-nine parents via their solicitors, nineteen via support groups for separated parents (Gingerbread, Match[7] and F N F), seven via advertisements in works newsletters and five via snowball sampling. Among the sample twenty-two parents settled their separations or divorces with minimal legal involvement, four had been subject to court proceedings over financial settlements while thirty-four had been subject to legal proceedings under the Children Act. It is also worth noting that of the sixty parents interviewed, forty-eight had been married while twelve had separated from non-marital partnerships. Thus whenever we refer to marriage, divorce or spousal relationships in relation to our empirical data, we are also including those who had lived together in non-marital relationships and separated without a legal divorce.

In line with our ethical stance, the parents in our sample were self-selecting. This inevitably introduces a 'bias'. In our study it meant that all the parents were actively involved in parenting or wanted to develop active parenting. Even the two fathers we interviewed who had little contact with their children were attempting to establish contact through the courts. We therefore have no knowledge of the post-divorce experiences of parents who were already disengaged from their children or who might have been quite unconcerned about them.

We aimed for a gender balance as well as a wide range of social class background within our sample. We set targets for these and stopped interviewing each category once our 'cells' were completed. It was not easy to categorize social class but we interviewed a wide range of people from those living on benefit on housing estates to self-employed managing directors and professionals. Only two of the interviewees were black. Although we had used solicitors in ethnic minority areas we did not receive a response from Asian or Afro-Caribbean communities sufficient to identify the significance of ethnic differences.

Within our sample of sixty divorces/separations we interviewed thirty-one women and twenty-nine men (thirty women and twenty-seven men at the time of second interview), which enabled us to investigate differences in the way men and women approach post-divorce parenthood. For ethical and strategic reasons, however, we did not interview both mother and father from the same family. It seemed to us inevitable that former couples would have different perceptions of events and our purpose was not to compare their stories or otherwise to evaluate what they had to tell us, but to accept their stories as valid experiences. In this way we could ensure confidentiality for the parents and allow them to talk to us without inhibition about their experiences. This strategy of including only one parent from each family also allowed us to sample a much larger number of families than would otherwise have been possible. Our empirical reporting is thus based on sixty families, although seen from the perspective of only one parent in each.

The study period: changes over time

Our study covered three points in time. Time 0 was the time of separation, which we had to explore retrospectively with the parents. Time 1 was the time of first interview. This was conducted as close in time as possible to the point of legal divorce or completion of any proceedings under the Children Act, in order that these events would still be fresh in the parents' minds. Time 2 was the time of the second interview which took place between twelve and eighteen months after the first interview. Gathering data relating to these three moments meant that we covered a period in the parents' lives which varied between three and seven years depending on how long it had taken them to move from *de facto* separation to *de jure* divorce or separation.

The inclusion of this temporal dimension in our study had three objectives. First, we wanted to explore how and why different patterns of parenting arose initially, how they were experienced by parents, and we wanted to understand which factors gave rise to changes. In particular we wanted to compare circumstances at the highly pressurized point of divorce (or legal intervention) with the actuality of post-divorce life a year or so later. Evidence from previous studies (Smart, 1990; Furstenberg and Cherlin, 1991) had indicated that patterns of parenting and parental relationships following separation are not fixed but fluid, subject to negotiation and re-negotiation in line with changing life circumstances and so we wanted to capture these changes. Secondly we wanted to chart qualitative changes in relationships between the parents and between parents and children and to explore whether traditional meanings of motherhood or fatherhood were being challenged in practice. Thirdly, following Finch and Mason (1993) we wanted to explore the processes of moral reasoning behind these changes in order to find out whether negotiations over post-divorce parenthood are well served by the current legal ordering of divorce.

As we indicate above, the first interviews were as close to the end of legal proceedings as possible. At that stage we asked parents to speak about their experiences of the divorce process and then focused their attention on the decisions they made about their children, what their expectations were regarding post-divorce parenthood and how they had found the legal system and its new orientation regarding children. In the second interviews we focused their attention more directly on the children, asking them expressly about how they thought their arrangements had affected the children over time, whether they had changed or reconsidered their earlier decisions, and how matters were currently being negotiated and organized. In the second round we also introduced vignettes which focused expressly on the question of whether one should stay in a marriage for the sake of the children. Through these methods we were able to explore the kind of 'moral' thinking the parents undertook and we could see the extent to which parents were moving away from or staying close to traditional 'rules' about how to manage divorce and how to organize arrangements for their children.

Analysis

We based our analysis of our interviews on the grounded theory approach, immersing ourselves in the data and moving critically between our theoretical underpinnings and the content of the interviews and vignettes. We constantly 'checked' our conceptual and theoretical starting-points against the data, especially the data that did not and would not 'fit'. We also analysed the data in several ways, initially developing typologies which we then used to trace trends and changes, but also using case studies and 'exemplars' where we could identify cases which typified or highlighted particular theoretically significant situations. We found we had a tremendous amount of data and also that it was far harder to think about it in the context of a time dimension than in the more usual snapshot fashion. Because our approach was qualitative and because we were committed to reflecting complexity rather than simplifying processes of change, we found the analysis particularly taxing. We hope, however, that we have remained 'true' to the parents' accounts. This does not mean, of course, that we imagine that we are presenting a simple truth of these people's lives and relationships. We analysed *accounts* which were constructed histories spoken from the position of one of the parents. These accounts were reflections of the parents' lived experiences and framed the ways in which they lived their lives and negotiated with their children and former partners. These accounts were layered and textured and necessarily changed over time. They were not flat, linear descriptions of factual events. Not infrequently our subjects would be overcome with emotion and sometimes their accounts were confusing. But they all freely volunteered their time to be interviewed and we hope that we have done no disservice to any of them who proved so committed to the research that they gave us hours of their time so willingly.

3

Becoming a Post-divorce Parent

Introduction

In this chapter we focus on how divorce or separation changes parenting. This transformation clearly is not an easy one for parents and the majority in our sample did not imagine, when they first became parents, that they would have to negotiate a transformation into post-divorce parenthood some years later. There are a growing number of advice books for parents on how best to effect the transition (e.g. Cohen, 1991) but it is still the case that most parents are ill-prepared for the changes, and especially for the new parenting ethos that the Children Act has brought about. The majority of our parents simply assumed that the children would stay with their mother and that the father would have varying degrees of contact. But even though these parents were following a kind of 'tradition' it does not mean that it was problem free or without major upheavals.

The ethos behind the Children Act seems to assume that because parents have the welfare of their children at heart, they will continue to strive to be good parents. There is a presumption that parenting can continue even though the spousal relationship is at an end. This aspiration, however, is based on a partial understanding of how parenting works in intact households. We want to suggest that what works during marriage or cohabitation may be quite inappropriate after separation and that problems that arise in moving from one kind of parenting to another do not simply occur because spouses are spiteful towards one another or indifferent to the interests of their children. Pre-divorce parenting may be a poor preparation for post-divorce parenting, and the skills, qualities and infrastructural supports required for the former may be rather different to those required for the latter.

Thus far we have spoken about parenting as if it were ungendered. However it is clear that in Western cultures there are significant differences in both the responsibilities associated with mothering and with fathering, and with the meaning(s) associated with being a mother and being a father. Moreover, while motherhood may have imparted a fairly stable identity, the meaning of fatherhood has become highly contested and uncertain in Britain in the 1990s.[1] Naturally these two elements of 'responsibility' and 'identity' are closely related such that, for example, a woman who cares for and about the children may come to see herself as nurturing, maternal and as a good mother. But there may not be such a close congruence between responsibility and identity in all cases and, in any case, what defines a good mother and a good father may change over time or as individual circumstances change. In particular it may be that being a good father in an intact family entails quite different responsibilities and embraces quite a different identity to being a good post-divorce father.

We shall explore these issues of responsibility and identity through the data generated by our first round of interviews with our sixty parents (referred to hereafter as Time 1). This means that in this chapter we will present an initial picture of the situation in which parents find themselves at the point of the conclusion of legal matters. Although this may be some considerable time after a physical separation or a conscious decision to separate, the point at which an agreement over the children is legally finalized is significant because it marks the end of a process during which parents have been under formal pressure to organize and structure the shape of their post-divorce parenthood. Although some parents may return to court or may resort to solicitors again, for the majority this moment marked a point at which they could get on with their lives without legal interference. In later chapters we draw on data gathered at Time 2 in order to show the extent to which post-divorce parenting is not simply established by legal fiat but is an ongoing process subject to considerable change over time. Our aim is to build levels of complexity on the foundation of this initial analysis of our data. Here we focus on concepts of responsibility and identity and these basic concepts will reappear in later chapters so that threads will become traceable as we weave our nuanced sociological account of what it means to be post-divorce parents at a time of considerable flux and change.

Responsibility

Fathers' perspectives

Almost all of our interviewees became parents while married or cohabiting[2] and so entered into parenthood with the assumption that there would be two parents available to raise the children. Moreover the majority had settled into a form of parenting where responsibilities and duties had been allocated and become established. We found, not surprisingly, that the typical pattern was one where mothers gave up work or worked part-time in order to become primary carers (Lewis, 1986; Collier, 1995; Ferri and Smith, 1996). The fathers therefore tended to develop rather different relationships with their children because they spent less time with them and inevitably took less day-to-day responsibility for them. We found a pattern of relationships which was very similar to that described by Backett (1987a) in her study of parenting in intact households. Basically fathers were one step removed from their children and their relationship with them was sustained via their relationship with the mother. Backett argues:

> Belief in father involvement was also sustained through the relationship with the mother. This was expressed by (i) adopting a generally supportive attitude towards her child-rearing activities, (ii) relieving her of practical and psychological pressures when both parents were present and (iii) acting as substitute when she wished to have time away from home and family. (1987a: 81)

Of considerable interest in Backett's research was her discovery that fathers did not have to do equal amounts of caring in order to be regarded as good fathers (see also Backett, 1987b). Thus child-rearing was often described as being equally shared, when in fact it was nothing of the sort. In a way this is perhaps not surprising – at least in intact households. The mother may well regard the father's full-time job as an important contribution to the family's well-being and thus would hardly expect him to carry an equal responsibility for routine child-rearing. In our own sample we found that almost all the parents voiced a firm belief that there was really no difference between a 'good' mother and a 'good' father. Both were seen as good if they provided a high-quality relationship for the child. This was expressed in terms of providing love, 'being there' for the children and giving them security. At the level of rhetoric our parents seemed to suggest that mothers and fathers were interchangeable in principle – at least when they were asked a direct question about mothering and fathering. But when it came to specifics this account was modified somewhat, usually with fathers asserting that there is no difference between a mother and a father, but with mothers diverging from this account and offering what they would see as a more 'factual' account of how mother and father operate.

> **Colin Hanks**: We totally shared [the responsibility]. When we had [our daughter] we had to get rid of the car because Hilary stopped work and we'd go everywhere together. We went around on public transport. When she went shopping I always went and *helped*. During the night if one of them woke up we'd take it in turns getting up, changing the nappies, and *I was there at both births*. (Our emphasis)

Colin however had a full-time, responsible job and so it might be reasonable to assume that he could not have carried an equal share of the work of caring. This next father recognized that his job prevented him from taking equal responsibility:

> **Jim Walters**: I did cook sometimes. I bathed them sometimes. I would read them stories sometimes, but I think she would probably do more of the lion's share. The problem was that working here and living in Doncaster I was sometimes not getting home until about quarter to seven, so by then they'd tend to have had their tea. When they were very young they'd already be in the bath.

Very few of our fathers were willing to allow their careers or job prospects to suffer in order to take more responsibility for their children while they had a relationship with the mother. This does not mean that there were not exceptions of course:

Karl Fisher: I think it depends on the division of labour. When we moved from T. . . to H. . ., I lived within walking distance of work and I was home nearly every lunch time and every other evening. I do feel for fathers who have to do a job a long way away. I was there for them. In a way it was a *disastrous career move for me.* (Our emphasis)

And only one father stayed at home in a 'role-reversal' arrangement:

Matt Ford: I think what [the arrangement] was to do with really was that in terms of work, I can take it or leave it. Obviously I need the money but I'm not interested in climbing up the ladder. . . . For me it was great because I really enjoyed it and I'd stay home and look after them. . . . [My wife] was much better at taking them out and giving them treats and I was much better at coping with the day-to-day grind.

We shall say more about the significance of employment for fathers in the next section but it is clear that for most their ability to spend equal amounts of time with their children and to assume a shared responsibility at a day-to-day level was actually compromised by their paid employment.

Mothers' perspectives

The accounts of the mothers in our sample focused on two aspects of childcare, the physical work (e.g. feeding, bathing, toilet training) and the emotional care (e.g. monitoring the child's moods, anticipating needs). In some instances mothers were disappointed that fathers did relatively little of the former, or felt angry that after a 'promising start' they lapsed into a more traditional role. In other instances the mothers were not unduly concerned about the physical work, or acknowledged that the fathers had undertaken a reasonable amount of this burden, but they pointed to the fact that fathers rarely seemed to be 'in tune' with the children or that they did not notice or anticipate emotional states, illnesses or preferences. As with the mothers in Backett's study, these mothers tended to assume that they held the 'real' responsibility for the children while the fathers either helped or hindered.

Sally Burton: When we got married I thought we would both have an equal marriage. We'd both done sociology degrees, we both had the theory in our heads, really – and it just shifted back into a very chauvinistic division of labour. I did all the practical, hard work stuff . . . and he had all the fun. I would end up running from the office to the childminder while he was just free to get on with his job, get back whenever he wanted.

Ann Black: He'd do everything that I did for her but then, all of a sudden . . . he stopped doing things for her. It got to the stage where she wouldn't let him do anything for her, and it were just me all the time. So for the first eighteen months of her life, he were good, he were really good.

Christine Frost: I think I had this vision of the new man that I'm now very sceptical of. Although they may wash up, they don't see the thousand and one other things that need doing. I remember we once had a big argument because I'd been out at college all day and it was half-term and I came home and he was very upset that I didn't say 'Thank you' for looking after the children. I couldn't get across to him that I didn't see why I should. I said 'You don't say "Thank you" to me every day for the work I do'.

The fact that mothers tended to see themselves as responsible and as more experienced in childcare made the transition to post-divorce parenting hard. During their marriage or cohabitation, being a good mother meant taking this responsibility and, to some extent, taking it for granted too. But on divorce they found that they were expected to relinquish this feeling of responsibility to someone who (usually) had not actually shared it during their relationship and who might be viewed as fairly inept at the physical care work, let alone the emotional caring.

This division of labour mitigated against sharing responsibility later, especially if children were very young. Although many mothers were able to accommodate to the transition (as shown in later chapters) it was often hard for them to be told they must do this in the 'interests of the child' since the 'interests of the child' during marriage had been served by the mothers retaining this responsibility. Moreover, where fathers 'imagined' that they had really been equally responsible during marriage, they became resentful of mothers who would not accept this account *at the point of divorce*.

Tina Hurst: He kept saying, 'Well, I think I should have some responsibility for their education again'. I said, 'Why? You never cared about it when you were with them. You always said it was up to me. Well, it's up to me now, I don't see why you should have anything to do with it'.

In this scenario mothers felt undervalued and fathers felt they were losing out. These feelings were often quite intense because mothers and fathers were not simply living out 'roles' but actually had invested their identities in being mothers and fathers – albeit probably very different sorts of identity.

Identity

How parents view themselves, and how much of their personal identity is bound up with their parenthood, has an important bearing on how parenthood operates in practice. People's biographies as parents assume importance because parental identities are not made instantly or ascribed but, much like other kin relationships, are negotiated and forged over considerable periods of time (Finch and Mason, 1993). From this perspective, parenthood can be seen as part of a nexus of life commitments. It is a matter of conscious choice, which must be weighed against competing life interests such as employment, leisure pursuits, geographical mobility and, following separation, the pursuit of new intimate partnerships. How this balancing is undertaken and to what extent parents make themselves available for their children in preference to other life chances will have a strong influence on how post-divorce parenthood is negotiated and established.

Where the activities of parental care are gendered then the parental identities which arise from them are also likely to be gendered. Motherhood and fatherhood are not perceived as identical subject positions. Many of the mothers in our sample had made their parenthood a central part of their lives:

> **Felicity Lessing**: I gave up my job in order to be their mother. . . . Basically my role is to be their mother. . . . I feel as if my role disappears if I've not got something to do with them. . . . I am more available. I simply am.

> **Erica Dawson**: They are my life. My life revolves around what they do, what they need. They are my boys. . . . Where they go, I go. It was just never open to discussion.

Ann Black: I've always looked after them. . . . I've always been there. . . . I don't work. I always took it for granted that she would stay with me, no matter what. Obviously he's working and he couldn't afford to give up work. But he weren't prepared to look after 'em anyway. . . . I think they automatically go to the mother, don't they, unless there are exceptional circumstances.

The strong identity as mothers which these parents express arises in part from dominant cultural constructions which idealize motherhood (Phoenix et al., 1991). It also arises, more concretely, from their experience as full-time parents who gave up their jobs when they had children. The employment patterns of mothers have undoubtedly shifted over the past decades with a small but growing percentage returning to work within a few weeks of their child's birth[3] but even where the mothers in our sample were working full time in the early years of parenthood (nine out of thirty-one cases) they continued to take the main responsibility for the children's day-to-day care, for 'being there' when needed and for organizing substitute care. For these women, therefore, their maternal identity was (for a time at least) more significant than identities arising from their engagement in paid work.

The father's identity is less likely to be derived from such an intense focus on parenthood. As pointed out above, only one father in our sample gave up work to raise the children himself. But this does not mean that men do not have identities as fathers, but this is often linked to their work as financial providers. This work of financial provision is crucially important, yet it means deriving a sense of identity from outside the home and family. Although some fathers are now more actively involved in their children's lives, they are more likely to spend time sharing leisure pursuits with the children, rather than engaging in the basics of childcare. There is, therefore, a sense in which fathers have more freedom to opt in or out of such interactions and to choose how and when to balance fatherhood with their other commitments or interests. It is now quite acceptable for men to assume either the identity of the 'good provider' father or the 'new man' father. These fathers opted for the traditional identity:

Jim Walters: I'm a workaholic . . . [and] there's a lot of conflict in trying to follow a profession and being a parent. . . . It's a kind of balancing act, balancing my new relationship and my children . . .

because they're not my partners' kids. . . . I think I probably put me first, my partner second and the children third.

Erica Dawson: He was a financial father. He wasn't one for picking them up or cuddling them. . . . On Sundays, he'd say, 'It's my day off'.

Gordon Fenton: You don't make parents, it's not something you study at or anything. . . . *you just are a parent.* How to behave is to be yourself. . . . I think we should stop analysing how to behave in front of children. (Our emphasis)

Colin Hanks: It wouldn't have been practical [for me to have the children]. I had to work full time. She was looking after them full time because she's always been that sort of mum. I wouldn't have been able to look after them.

However, although only one father expressed his core identity as a caring parent during his marriage, we found that rather more shifted in this direction on divorce. Although we cannot generalize from our small, qualitative sample, we found that nine out of twenty-nine of our fathers were willing either to abandon their identities as earners and workers, or to reduce their commitment to their careers, in order to assume an identity as caring parent on divorce or separation. Most significantly, six of our fathers 'switched' identity at divorce either by giving up paid employment or, because they had been made redundant or taken early retirement (usually from military or police service), they decided not to seek new employment. These six fathers were all in manual or broadly working-class employment.[4]

James Grant: I knew in my own mind that I could give the children the same or better care than Paula and I thought that we're in a modern world now and everyone's talking about 'new age men'. I'm a totally modern kind of parent.

Tim Muir: I think there's a big difference between a lot of fathers than there was twenty years ago. There's a lot more fathers now who are willing and able to look after their children and bring them up, whereas twenty years ago it was just assumed that men worked and women looked after children. Now I think it's changed.

None of these six fathers had been involved in childcare to any great extent before their divorce or separation. Their wives were housewives and had taken full responsibility for the children before the separation. But what is interesting in these cases is that these men were transformed into 'new' fathers almost overnight and they had a very strong commitment to their new identities, often seeing lone fathers as far superior to lone mothers because they were more organized and less likely to be over-emotional.

The other three fathers (out of the total of nine) who made this switch of identity were in positions which enabled them to have a good deal of control over the time they spent at work or outside the home. They were either self-employed or undergoing vocational training. In our sample of twenty-nine fathers, only two who had children living with them were in full-time, inflexible employment. These had support from their extended family.

Tentatively we would suggest that men's willingness to assume an identity as a caring parent is much more likely to be related to their position in the labour market than it is for women. Women may work full or part time, be students or be outside the paid labour market, but if they are mothers, then motherhood in the form of caring parenthood is a core identity. Fathers seem to assume this identity only if they leave the labour market (or are ejected from it) or if they have some degree of flexibility or control over their hours at work. Although the findings shown in table 3.1 are hardly surprising, they do reveal in microcosm the problem that Hochschild (1997) has identified, which is particularly acute for fathers who are in full-time employment. The pressure to work long hours for a man whose identity is tied up with being

Table 3.1 The relationship between gender, employment and children's residence

| | *Women* | | *Men* | |
	Residential	*Non-residential*	*Residential*	*Non-residential*
Employed (full-time)	9	2	2	11
Unemployed	10	0	6	3
Flexible employment	9	1	3	4

a good employee or high achiever makes it virtually impossible to be involved to any great extent in his children's lives (see also Ferri and Smith, 1996). Mothers have known this for a long time and as a consequence their life-chances in the employment market have diminished because they have typically opted to give priority to their identity as mothers. But now that the traditional gender contract is subject to change (Dench, 1997) what once seemed like the 'natural' gender order becomes potentially problematic for both mothers and fathers. Fathers may be starting to make choices between the competing identities as 'new man' father and 'good provider' father. If they opt for the former then the time they are required to spend in the labour market becomes a problem which even having a new partner or help from an extended family cannot resolve. There is little point in opting to become an involved father, only to leave the children with a sister or mother. In any case the courts are still not particularly happy with this arrangement as one of the fathers (Derek Hill) in our sample discovered. He wanted to have his daughters live with him and proposed to the court that he would employ someone to collect them from school and look after them until he got home late in the evenings. But, as they had always been adequately cared for by their mother who could not work for health reasons, his proposal was frowned upon. On the other hand, fathers who gave up work or who were unemployed at the point of divorce were seen in a very favourable light as potential caring parents – at least in our sample of parents.

As we show in the next chapter, some fathers also gradually develop a new identity as fathers as a consequence of having their children living with them part of the time. In other words they did not switch identities suddenly but changed gradually as a result of spending more time with their children. Thus they became more responsible for their children and rewrote their parental script over time. But relatively few fathers[5] in our sample were either able or willing to do this, and the majority remained 'good provider' fathers (in that they paid child support and saw their children occasionally[6]) or simply fell back on the minimalist paternal identity as mere biological progenitors who had no other investment in fatherhood.[7]

Parenthood therefore still appears to have very different meanings for mothers and fathers, both before and after separation, although the meanings of both are currently subject to change. But it is important to realize that it is how motherhood and fatherhood are perceived and experienced that will have a major impact on how parents negotiate over their children after separation. Thus for some parents the traditional gender contract meets all their expectations and they continue a pattern of parenting with the mother as primary carer.[8] For others, particularly for some fathers, divorce is an opportunity to abandon one type of parental identity for another.[9] But these shifts and changes occur within the context of the demands of the labour market, the provision of welfare benefits, the formation of new relationships, the availability of support from extended families and, of course, the wishes and needs of the children in these families. Parents therefore did not simply choose how to parent after divorce, they negotiated with each other in the context of their past responsibilities and their changing parental identities but also in the context of wider social and cultural conditions which were not of their making. It was in these contexts that we felt that we could identify three types of post-divorce parenting.

Patterns of post-divorce parenthood

Studies of styles of post-divorce parenting have, as we have argued elsewhere (Neale and Smart, 1997a), tended to introduce a value judgement into the classification of modes of parenting.[10] The choice of such terms as co-operative parenting or conflicted parenting automatically conveys a sense that one is good and the other is undesirable. In any case, we found that joint parenting after divorce could be just as conflictual as instances in which one parent continued to be a primary carer. On the other hand, we did not wish to presume that an absence of conflict was necessarily a good thing or an ideal parenting arrangement. We therefore derived a typology from our interview data based on what we came to see as two vital elements in post-divorce parenting. These elements were *parental care* and *parental authority*. Parental care refers to the direct physical and emotional work of raising children. It includes practices such as bathing and dressing, providing meals and healthcare, playing games, guidance on behaviour, helping with homework, and facilitating friendships or social activities. This element focuses on the parent's relationship with the child. The element of *parental authority* refers to the degree to which parents share or monopolize the overall decision making about how a child should be raised. It encompasses, for example, long-term decisions about schooling and religion and short-term decisions about how and where children spend their time, what clothes they wear and food they eat, and how they should be disciplined. It also includes strategic decision making about how parenting should be organized and carried out and how the material and financial infrastructure for parenting should be resourced.[11] This element of *parental authority* encapsulates the relationship between the parents rather than between parents and children. It is our view that any typology of parenting practices which does not include these two sets of relationships is likely to underestimate how significant parental relationships are to post-divorce parenthood. Thus the typology we have developed is two-dimensional. However in chapter 4 we add another dimension, namely that of change over time so that we can see post-divorce parenting in its full complexity rather than as a snapshot at the point of divorce.

Our two elements of post-divorce parenting give rise to the following organization:

Sharing parental authority
> 　　Co-parenting
Sharing of parental care

No sharing of parental authority
> 　　Custodial parenting
Sharing of parental care

No sharing of parental authority
> 　　Solo parenting
No sharing of parental care

Co-parenting is a pattern of shared care and authority following separation in which the parents are both actively engaged in the rearing of their children. In our sample of parents this usually means that the children spend a lot of their time with each parent (even to the extent of having two homes[12]) and that parents make joint decisions about the lives of their children and both attend school meetings and other significant events. Ultimately neither parent can act without the agreement of the other. Custodial[13] parenting is a pattern of shared care in which children live primarily with one parent and have a visiting relationship with the other. There is no set pattern for how the child's time is shared. It may involve staying overnight with the non-residential parent on a regular basis or irregular contact for a limited number of hours at the family home. But however it is organized, parental authority is vested in the residential parent alone. Solo parenting is a pattern of care in which children live with one parent who takes sole responsibility for them. The other parent has a non-existent or highly tenuous involvement with the children, for example, through infrequent drop-in visits or occasional contact by letter or phone.

At the time of our first round of interviews (Time 1), ten of our parents were co-parenting, thirty-five were engaged in a custodial parenting arrangement, and fifteen were solo parenting. These three types of post-divorce parenting are examined below.

Co-parenting

There are several key features of this pattern of parenthood. First, each parent has a direct and active involvement in all aspects of their children's daily lives, in a way that is only indirectly mediated by the other parent. Parental responsibilities are divided on a time-share basis, not by task as they may formerly have been. Parenthood in this mode is less obviously gendered than the way that intact parenting tends to be. Second, the children have a close relationship with two parents rather than one, along with the potential to have two homes. Third, each parent is engaged in an ongoing relationship with the former partner which is bound up with their joint responsibilities. For some of our parents this meant that they made efforts to preserve a sense of their first family. They had regular discussions about the children's welfare and met frequently. There was also some flexibility around day-to-day arrangements for childcare. In short, the parents were locked into a system in which they had to take the lives of their former partners into account, not only in pursuing their parenting, but also in pursuing their other life interests or commitments. Finally, new partners were not regarded, and did not regard themselves, as step-parents and so limited their involvement with the children. What is distinctive within this pattern was the preservation of a sense of the original nuclear family, albeit spread over two households and, in some cases, intertwined with other nuclear families which were similarly dispersed.

> **Meg Johnson**: The other day, Dan [former husband] said, 'We are a family' and we try very hard for the children to understand that although we aren't partners, we don't live together any more, we are still very much, to them, the family. I never thought it would be possible for us to get on so well.

> **Felicity Lessing**: [I] get on very well [with Simon]. It's not an equal relationship but we get on fine. We discuss things . . . and make decisions together about most things.

Co-parenting is usually preceded by an explicit process of negotiation because it represents a departure from the pre-separation arrangements for childcare. It depends upon a discernible shift in the relative positions of mothers and fathers in order to become established. Fathers start to take on new caring responsibilities – often in the mother's view becoming proper parents for the first time – while the mothers accommodate to or even encourage this development. In the process these mothers have to accept some attenuation of their own sense of parental responsibility and identity.

Parents who can make these transitions would seem to be model parents doing all that the Children Act requires of them. But the challenges of co-parenting are substantial, as are the costs. Developing and sustaining co-parenting involves an enormous amount of time, emotional labour and sacrifice (Smart, 1990, 1991; Simpson et al., 1995). The needs of new partners, children and the other parent need to be juggled. It is likely to involve constant negotiations over arrangements as well as ongoing debates over children's well-being. We found a perpetual concern over the adjustment of the children to a mobile existence and two different life-styles. Parents also needed to maintain a positive image of the other parent – at least as far as the children were concerned. Painful knowledge of the activities of the other household and of new partners had to be absorbed and sometimes the individual's own needs for independence, a change of residence or career, or a new relationship had to be postponed.

Felicity Lessing: [It's] very hard to come to terms with . . . *his* girlfriend meeting *my* children from school. I feel very hard done by because there isn't anything I can do that isn't going to damage the children. I can't move house, I can't go and live somewhere where there's more work. What I'm trying to do is bring up our children together still. It's hard. It feels like the best thing. It's probably naive – it's not possible. But it's the only way I can think to bring up our children. (Our emphasis)

The co-parents are no less likely than other divorced parents to feel negatively about each other or to be in conflict over their children. Those who are co-parenting by consensus make efforts to put aside problems in their interpersonal relationship in the interests of collaboration, although they do not always succeed. But where co-parenting is the product of coercion or hard economic or legal bargaining, the arrangement may be one of conflict:

Linda Hewitt: [Our son] has half the week with each of us and alternate weekends. . . . Ivan and I don't talk when we hand over. He won't come into the house, he stands on the doorstep and refuses to look at me, and quite often at the handover point there are arguments.

In this case, Ivan was only prepared to release Linda's share of the equity on their house if she agreed to co-parent and the arrangement was based on Ivan's strict notions of equal sharing.

Three co-parents in our sample could be described as highly conflictual, with parental authority, residential status and unresolved financial and housing issues providing a focus for intense power struggles between the parents.

Gerry Marsh: I've become very powerful because I simply do not communicate. . . . I totally ignore her. . . . She knows I've got total control, there's nothing she can do or say. . . . I don't want any contact with the woman whatsoever. . . . I feel out of control and not able to make decisions unless I go through the legal process. I told her I'll pursue her through every court in the land relentlessly, and this is what she doesn't like, because she knows I'll always be on her back.

Co-parenting, then, is not necessarily the product of a shared commitment to its ethos but may represent an uneasy compromise or a deadlock in a context where neither parent has managed to assert authority over the other.

Finally, co-parenting is fragile. Given the sacrifices and difficulties that it can entail, perhaps this is not surprising. Several parents, like Gerry, regarded it as an interim arrangement, precisely because it was a manifestation of unresolved conflict over whom the residential parent should be. Others could not envisage maintaining high levels of involvement with their former partners, even where their relationship was relatively amicable:

> **Stella Drew**: We are trying to do our best for the children . . . free access, they can see their dad when they want, but I'm not sure how well that will work practically in the long term. When I move into the new house, it'll be a more formal arrangement – it's necessary to do that to split our relationship up. I can understand that the children need Nick, but I need to keep a distance or the whole of my life could be quite difficult.

The challenges of co-parenting can mean that, over time, the degree of parental collaboration tends to diminish, even where relatively high levels of shared care are maintained (Maccoby and Mnookin, 1992). This issue is explored in the next chapter.

Custodial parenting

In this type of post-divorce parenting parental authority resides with the residential parent alone, even though there may be a considerable sharing of childcare. In contrast to co-parenting arrangements, the responsibilities of the two parents within this pattern are clearly differentiated along gender lines, much as they were before separation. In this model the children clearly live with one parent and visit the other.

The dominant pattern in our sample (and across the UK and the USA; Maccoby and Mnookin, 1992; Hoggett, 1994) is that of mother-residence and father-contact. In all but one case in our sample, mothers had taken the primary responsibility for the children before separation and, except in a few cases where circumstances prevented them from doing so, they continued to take the main responsibility afterwards. Custodial parenting thus allows for continuity of care for the child and stability of living environment, but at the same time it can also accommodate the children's need for two parents. Non-residential fathers might still be very committed to an ongoing relationship with their children, but they no longer co-exist with them on a daily basis. Their parenting is reconstituted as 'contact' which is undertaken on a clearly delineated, part-time basis.

Neither parent in a custodial arrangement is disengaged from the children. But, unlike co-parents, custodial parents are more likely to be practising a 'parallel' or 'two-family' form of parenting in which they are distant or even disengaged from each other (Furstenberg and Nord, 1985; Furstenberg and Cherlin, 1991; Maccoby and Mnookin, 1992). Parents in this category rarely meet each other or discuss their children. They do not accord any priority to maintaining the first family; indeed they do not tend to think in terms of a continuing first family; it is something that is at an end. Some parents in our sample had moved to different localities as a way of starting a new life and the potential to form a new family unit was seen as important, even if it was not realized. New partners were not necessarily perceived as 'step'-parents as in a traditional reconstituted family, but they were much more likely to take on some parenting responsibilities than in co-parenting families, particularly where the children's relationship with the contact parent was limited or where the children were of a very young age.

> **Ann Black**: What I'd like is to meet somebody, somebody to be a father to them, they need a mother and a father. I'm doing both at the moment. Somebody who'd take an interest in me kids as well as me, because we all come as a package. I just want to see us all settle down.

> **Sara Birch**: I would prefer them not to see him but that is for my own personal selfishness. What they get out of seeing him I don't know. . . . I don't think he has a relationship with them. I like to think Ralph [new partner] has replaced that, if I'm totally honest, because that's the way I see our lives. The smallest one doesn't remember a time when Ralph wasn't here.

Sara shared parental authority with her new partner, whom the younger children called daddy, while parental care remained largely her responsibility. What she shared with the children's father was a small proportion of her children's time each week in exchange for his ongoing financial support.

Since custodial parenting does not rely on frequent contact

between the parents the quality of their relationship is not a crucial consideration. In our sample, the relationships between the parents ranged from cordial to overtly hostile. Among the father-residence and split-residence families,[14] which had involved abrupt reversals of the pre-separation childcare arrangements, there were high levels of conflict which, in some instances, involved the snatching of children. The degree of parental disengagement in these cases was correspondingly greater. Indeed, it was regarded as a necessity and not just an option. Some parents had volatile and unstable contact arrangements throughout the study period, but in a majority of cases the practical arrangements for care were routinized and marked by formality, or negotiated indirectly through the children. In these circumstances, whatever the feelings between the parents, conflict could be contained because there was no need for active collaboration.

Custodial parenting still requires the construction of new ways of operating as mothers and fathers, along with a sustained commitment to the children on the part of both parents. Mothers (typically) have less respite from their basic responsibilities which can only be delegated at limited times. They have to take on more of the work of disciplining children, organizing their leisure pursuits, and resourcing their basic needs through employment, and they often have to take on the work of facilitating and encouraging contact with the father. Fathers (typically) have partially to transform their parental identity so that they can develop a one-to-one relationship with their children. They also face two major challenges in having to work within the constraints of a restricted contact schedule and their limited authority to make decisions about the children.

But these constraints are offset by other advantages. Custodial parenting is a structure that is harnessed to the needs of parents to establish control over their own lives. Parents are not required to enter into co-parenting arrangements which might jeopardize their self-determination and independence. The intermittent nature of contact can also be an advantage, for it can be fitted in around other life-chances, such as new relationships or employment opportunities. These are benefits which offset the costs of what some fathers perceive to be a diminished form of parenting (Simpson et al., 1995). Thus, ironically, in conceding parental authority to one parent, both mothers and fathers could achieve a greater control over their own lives than if they attempted to co-parent.

Solo parenting

At Time 1, fifteen of our parents were engaged in solo parenting arrangements and, of these, four were solo fathers. In some cases the non-residential parent had withdrawn against the express wishes of the residential parent, and in others the non-residential parents were fighting to establish contact which they felt was being unjustly denied to them. In all, ten of the *detached* parents had instituted legal proceedings to regain contact with their children.

The parents in our study typically regarded preserving a child's relationship with both parents as normal and desirable. But there was also a pragmatic acceptance that circumstances might not always make this possible. There are two sets of circumstances that predispose towards solo parenting. The first concerns the father's commitment to his children. We know through other research that a substantial minority of non-residential fathers gradually opt out of contact arrangements because of a range of practical, financial and emotional difficulties (Backett, 1987b; Furstenberg and Cherlin, 1991; Simpson et al., 1995). In our study fathers who opted out generally retained an interest in the general well-being and development of their children but were inexperienced in dealing with them on a day-to-day basis and found it difficult to establish meaningful ways to relate to them. This was particularly so where a father's relationship with a child had been mediated by a mother in a traditional division of labour. The younger the child, the more likely this was to be the case. In several cases in our study, the early visits by the father to the family home seemed to be motivated more by hopes of a reconciliation with the mother, rather than any genuine desire to spend time with the children. When this proved impossible, contact ceased. Where contact was sustained it usually relied on paternal grandparents or other mother substitutes to carry on the work of mediating between father and child.

Some fathers also found it difficult to combine contact with other commitments particularly to their new partners and families. Some were reluctant to sustain a financial commitment to their children and they saw opting out as the only legitimate way of severing financial ties.[15] The arrangement gave such parents the potential to form reconstituted families or pursue other life-chances without being 'hindered' by past ties and commitments.

The second set of circumstances that predisposed to solo parenting was the quality of the relationship between the parents themselves and between the child and the parents. Where there were concerns over the ability to provide basic care, where parental relationships were marked by high levels of mistrust or hostility, where parental conflicts were focused upon the children, or where the mother and/or children were subject to ongoing abuse or violence, the relationship was unlikely to thrive. In these circumstances the usual presumption in favour of contact was reversed and the non-residential parent (typically the father) was redefined as a danger to the first family. In these circumstances, the residential parent (typically the mother) may well opt for solo parenting as a safeguard for herself and the children (Simpson et al., 1995).

> **Bella Tomkins**: From my point of view I think (Jean) is better off as she is . . . she's out of the conflict. . . . He was always very indifferent to her. . . . He could have given her so much, it's a shame. . . . I felt worried that I couldn't be both mother and father to her. . . . I feel sad for her sake, because she has to carry that all her life, that he's not interested.

> **Tina Hurst**: [The children] were against him anyway 'cos of the way he treated them. He were really rough. Once he grabbed hold of Sally, lifted her from the table and belted her over the head. He always took his moods out on her and I had to protect her. . . . She were terrified of him.

Solo parenting is not simply a default pattern of care that comes into play when a parent fails to sustain contact. It is an option that can be a matter of positive choice, particularly for the children and residential parent. But clearly, like co-parenting, it also brings particular challenges to the parents. Undertaking sole responsibility for a child without respite places many limitations on the lives of the residential parents. Even those who opted for this arrangement, like Bella, expressed some regrets about the loss of two parents for the child.

The parent who is disengaged from the children may also find this one of the most difficult circumstances of life to come to terms with, particularly when it is not a matter of preference. When parents withdraw or accept their forced withdrawal, they are not necessarily motivated by self-interest but may have altruistic motives. They may respect their children's wishes not to see them. Or they may wish to protect them from further conflict, court proceedings or further disruption to their lives. The 'disengaged' father should not automatically be equated with the 'deadbeat dad' (Hochschild, 1995); he may be doing what both parents feel is best for the child (Simpson et al., 1995).

Conclusion

In this chapter we have focused on the relationship between pre- and post-divorce mothering and fathering and have suggested that the usual division of labour that occurs between parents is a problematic foundation on which to build active co-parenting after divorce or separation. As noted in chapter 2, the Law Commission imagined that after the implementation of the Children Act patterns of childcare established during marriage would simply continue after divorce – but with fathers maintaining more contact and commitment. However, for some, the ideal of co-parenting after divorce has come to mean much more than this, while for others any increase in involvement by fathers raises certain difficulties. However, some of these difficulties are to do with transitions and they are not necessarily insurmountable. In the next chapter we start to look at how things can change over time.

4

Living Post-divorce Parenthood

Introduction

Leon Holt: Whatever *close arrangements* you've got for seeing the children, you've got *two separate lives* and things develop. You're always trying to *compromise* and you can't ever say 'We've got it sorted' because things *change* and you have to develop *new approaches*. (Our emphasis)

This statement captures a great deal of what is central to living the life of a divorced parent. It captures in particular the contradictions between being separate and yet being connected. Being separate means that one is subject to different experiences and different opportunities, which means that one starts to become a different person to the person one would have remained within the marital relationship. We regard it as essential to recognize the significance of this new trajectory of the self (see pp. 139–41 below). On the other hand, one is connected to one's former partner through a parenting project (at best) or simply through a triadic relationship which focuses on the children (at the least). This means that one has both a connection to a former self (the self one was during the relationship) and to a person with whom one shared the intimacy of everyday life which is no longer an appropriate context for current interactions.

In addition, what Leon said shows how fluid this relationship is and how one needs to be flexible in order to meet the kind of challenges that might never occur in married life: all this is expressed in the context of the quality of one's relationship with one's children. He is suggesting that even where this is good, there are many difficulties. These difficulties must seem much worse if one's relationship with one's children is, or always has been, strained or difficult. If the children themselves are going through a difficult 'phase', as most would at some time even in an intact marriage, then such relationships must be additionally hard to sustain.

In this chapter we want to trace these elements of separateness, connectedness and fluidity, all of which affect the quality of relationships, to try to understand how couples navigate their way through previously uncharted territory. We shall therefore explore each concept in turn as it relates to post-divorce or post-separation parenting. We suggest that it is the interplay and balance between these elements which make parenting across households particularly difficult to achieve. There are no guidelines for parents and the only certainty they have is that whatever arrangements they put in place, they will be subject to pressure to change as children start to make choices, as ex-partners remarry or as family members move away or start to voice new demands and preferences. While we start by looking at these elements in isolation, we will later explore how they 'work' in practice through an examination of three pivotal case studies. We hope that this will provide a close understanding of the difficulties inherent in such relationships and the kind of skills and qualities needed to make such parenting relationships work.

Policy discussions have emphasized the problems and harms caused by non-residential parents who disengage and disappear. But little concern has been addressed to the difficulties and problems associated with ongoing parenting relationships. It seems to be taken for granted that such relationships will thrive just so long as parents are sufficiently committed to the welfare of their children. But what we want to suggest is that, quite independently of a commitment to welfare, such relationships are hard to manage and affect very profoundly the quality of life of many thousands of children, parents, grandparents and new partners. It is increasingly important, therefore, that policy makers and politicians understand what they are asking of parents when they suggest that there is only one proper mode of post-divorce parenting, namely co-parenting.

Compromises

Being separate

When a relationship breaks down, one person in the couple is often better prepared for it than the other. One is already thinking about life beyond the current marriage and may even have definite plans. This means that the other has to face the unknown in an ill-prepared way. But it also means that both individuals must give up the intimate world they have constructed. Marriage and parenthood are usually a joint project at some stage. For the duration the couple jointly endure or enjoy experiences which affect the family as a whole (even if they are not all affected equally). The unemployment of one will affect both, the illness of one may be a tragedy for both and so on. Moreover, as Berger and Kellner (1964) have argued, couples frequently come to share an understanding of the world as they share their lives. Part of this shared understanding is located in a joint history, but also in the prospect of a joint future. Berger's and Kellner's work has been adversely criticized for ignoring gendered power relations within marriage and for over-emphasizing the unity of the couple. Nevertheless, it is important to recognize that marriage and cohabitation are collective projects at some stage and that this has consequences when the project collapses. As Morgan argues:

> It is not that individuals automatically or unthinkingly 'put the family first'; it is, rather, that family members and family obligations are seen as being an important part of an individual's moral horizons, something that they need to take into account. (1996: 195)

This means that while one is in an intimate relationship and sharing in some way the raising of children, one's life will have certain kinds of boundaries. These boundaries may be quite tailored to the specific couple and the result of painful negotiations over time, but they form a framework within which everyday life can be played out in a fairly routine way. This does not mean that family life can be planned to be perfect. Often what people accommodate to is damaging: there are all too many instances of violence, or of one partner being more prepared to give up opportunities and resources than the other. In this respect we agree with the critics of the classic Berger and Kellner stance, which ignores the extent to which the shared reality constructed within a marriage could be oppressive, damaging and exploitative. However, the central issue remains significant, that is to say that while there is an ongoing joint project, individuals are often prepared to put up with quite jarring incongruencies in order to sustain their emotional and ethical investment in a joint past and joint future.

But once a couple separates the things that could be taken for granted between them no longer operate in the same way. Both are likely to re-evaluate the previously shared biography; things will no longer have the same meanings (Brannen and Collard, 1982). Moral horizons change, separation means that fundamentally one no longer has to take account of the other. One does not have to give up the chance of a good job or promotion because it cannot accommodate one's partner's need to stay in her or his position; one does not have to give up the opportunity to meet new people, start new activities and so on, simply to spend time with one's partner. Moreover, those things which were disagreeable (or worse) become irksome in a different way. The spouse who put up with unreasonable behaviour, violence or neglect will be left wondering why s/he bothered, given that it was all for nothing. What might have seemed like a worthwhile sacrifice or endurance while the relationship lasted is transformed into an act (or series of acts) of folly after it ends. Perhaps of equal importance, although it may be less obvious, is the effect that living apart from someone has on one's own sense of self. One may start to become a different person with different points of reference. One may not stay the same person as one would have been had the relationship not ended. Couples do not simply separate and then go along parallel tracks; they are quite likely to start diverging considerably. As discussed in chapter 7, women in particular may want to become a new self once they have sloughed off the effects of a relationship which has been constraining and limiting. But while some of these things are inevitable, if only because the separated couple no longer share intimate family life on a daily basis, these divergences and the rewriting of the joint biography are perpetually constrained by the fact that – *if both want to remain engaged parents* – they have to remain in some kind of relationship with each other. There is therefore a tension for parents which means that they cannot simply leave behind a relationship – no matter how much they may wish to – in the way that couples without children can.

Being connected

The ideal model of co-operative co-parenting on divorce has a number of features: parents can set up a routine that seems fair to everyone yet can tolerate easily negotiated changes (e.g. switching weekends around at short notice); both parents are involved in the child's progress (e.g. attending school evenings); neither parent undermines the other; and children do not have to carry emotional burdens back and forth between households (e.g. secrets) and receive the same sort of care in both families (e.g. must do their homework wherever they are). Few of our parents could achieve this harmonious ideal after divorce, largely, we suspect, because few parents ever achieved it during their marriages. But the way that these differences in types and levels of care are managed in ongoing relationships cannot simply be imported into the post-divorce situation. For example, if fathers go on being 'typical' fathers (i.e. doing little more than co-residing) they will simply never get to see their children after divorce (Simpson et al., 1995). Parents therefore have to set up new 'moral horizons' and for both this often means that they have to take account of the other much more self-consciously than before but also at a time when the other is often most disliked.

> **Fred Sykes**: My [colleague] downstairs, his wife died horribly from cancer and I wouldn't wish that on anybody, but he knows how I feel because we're both without the other partner. We're both going to bed at night time with nobody there and that emptiness is there, but at least with his, he had a finality and that finality then made him arrange his life for the future. I can't go on bloody holiday without making sure it's all right with Carol and vice versa, your life is ruled still by the woman you separated from.

The idea that one's moral horizons must include one's former spouse for the foreseeable future is not easy to adjust to. But it is more than a philosophical and emotional adjustment, it also brings with it changes of substance to family life. It means no less than the end of the idea of reconstituting the exclusive nuclear family through remarriage after divorce. In the 1980s it was assumed that the best solution to divorce was remarriage and that this provided children with a substitute father on the one hand, and allowed the biological father to marry again and to start a 'new' family somewhere else. The new moral horizon created by ongoing parenting, however, makes neither of these solutions workable. If a biological father stays involved with his children, the mother's new husband or partner cannot become a substitute father. He therefore has to find a different role in relation to the children. If the biological father remarries he can hardly forget his first children if they are seeing him regularly, going on holiday with him and so on. His new wife or partner has to adjust in a way that second wives seldom had to in the past. The arrival of new children is not easy in this situation. But the mother's new husband and the father's new wife also have to contend with the ongoing relationship between their partners and their partners' former spouses. This may go so far as having to have a relationship with the ex-spouse themselves if s/he comes into their home when collecting or delivering children. Once this happens the boundaries between what were once discrete family 'units' start to dissolve. The divorced parent is in a chain of relationships, not just in a one-to-one relationship with someone he or she has fallen in love with. Collaborative parenting after divorce threatens all of the basic assumptions of the nuclear family based on (re)marriage. It has the potential to revolutionize 'family practices' (Morgan, 1996) and brings an end to the idea of the nuclear family as a concept which implies co-residence. The idea of the extended family never implied co-residence, of course, but it is quite new for the nuclear family to stretch across households (Maclean and Eekelaar, 1997). Not all divorced couples can or will tolerate the dissolution of the ideal of the nuclear family, and not all new wives and husbands will tolerate ongoing relationships between their new spouses and their ex-spouses; they cling tenaciously to their old moral horizons. This of course creates further tensions in post-divorce relationships which we shall explore below, but first it is necessary to turn briefly to the issue of fluidity.

Fluidity

As discussed in chapter 1, David Morgan (1996) has argued that rather than speaking of the family as an institution or in structural terms, we should refer to the idea of family practices. This term, he suggests, offers a degree of stability and certainty because it relies on the idea that practices are routines: they do not change suddenly and they are not random. Therefore he allows for the possibility that families have a form which can even pass from one generation to another. Thus families are not theorized as dispersed, formless or random simply because one ceases to speak of the institution of the family. But at the same time the concept of practices allows for a degree of 'open-endedness'. There can be tension between different practices, practices can change in the light of changed circumstances. In using the concept of practice one automatically imports with it the idea of the actor or agent. So one ceases to pose structure and agency as discrete entities. Practices require agents to carry them out, so to speak. But because they are fairly routine and located in culture, history and personal biography, they are not free-floating, random or serendipitous.

Most importantly, Morgan's idea of practices allows for the possibility of conceptualizing what he sees as the new fluidity in family life. People are starting to 'do' family life differently, not only differently from the way their parents might have done it, but differently in that there is now a diversity of styles of 'doing' family life. Furthermore, people may do it differently at different moments, with different partners and different children. Children too start to become actors once we adopt the idea of family practices. They can modify practices, especially if they have a choice of parents to live with or if they can compare regimes in different households. It is available to some children to learn much earlier than in the past that the way their parents do things is not the only way they can be done.

To return to the extract from Leon Holt's interview at the start of this chapter, it can be seen that he identifies the imperative to be flexible because separate lives mean that constant adjustments must be made to keep relationships working. As suggested above, this may almost mean becoming more attentive to the other parent than might have been the case during the marriage. It is impossible to take the other parent for granted, whereas married life seems to rest precisely on the presumption that one can do this. Post-divorce parenting therefore requires a lot of effort if fluidity is not to dissolve into dissociation. Because there are no longer fixed roles and fixed expectations, a huge amount of negotiation is required, but often with someone with whom communication is extremely difficult. As many of our parents discovered, it is very hard to preserve relationships which are not based on co-residence, whether these are relationships with adults or with children. There may come a point for some where the effort simply is not worth it because the quality of the relationship is not sufficiently rewarding to sustain the effort, especially if it is also impeding the formation of a more traditional relationship based on co-residence and well-established role expectations.

Quality of relationships

As discussed in chapter 3, the quality of a relationship during marriage has a great deal of influence on a parenting relationship after divorce. However, the post-divorce parenting relationship is rarely a simple continuation of what went before. New ways of relating need to be established and these, not simply the shared history of good times, are what will sustain the relationship into the future. It was possible for some of our parents to take advantage of the rupture caused by divorce or separation to establish a different (and even better) relationship with each other and with their children. As explored in the next chapter, some fathers redeemed themselves in the eyes of their former wives by becoming good, reliable fathers *after* divorce. Trust could be established afresh on a different basis, although this required tact and time. But if the non-residential parent broke trust with the children and the residential parent by, for example, breaking promises to the children, refusing to pay maintenance or providing inadequate care, then even a reasonable post-divorce parental relationship could deteriorate.

A further dimension to the issue of quality of relationships concerns relationships with wider kin and with new partners. One of the most difficult things that parents – particularly fathers – had to adjust to was the arrival of a new adult into the child's life. For some it was clearly a form of jealousy which had little to do with their relationship with their children, although it would inevitably affect the children. But for others, it was a problem of having to entrust one's children into the care of a stranger – and strange men were inevitably seen as threatening to the children. Again this issue seems linked to an understanding of what a father's role is meant to be. What most fathers seemed to dread was the thought of another man punishing their children or their children calling another man 'Dad'. Mothers seemed less worried that other women would usurp them and more concerned that the children would not get the right kind of care or that they would not properly understand their children's needs. In these cases the fragile trust that might have been built up after the divorce could quickly evaporate or come under strain.

Separateness, connectedness and fluidity, and the extent to which they affect the quality of relationships, constitute the parameters within which parenting after divorce seems to occur. Leon Holt, having eloquently identified these elements, found them difficult to negotiate even though his relationship with his former wife was not marked by extreme hostility or violence, as were many of the other relationships we researched. A refusal to be flexible, an overwhelming desire to sever contact, the arrival of a new partner or baby, or even a more subtle combination of less momentous events could mean that a custodial relationship shifted to a solo parenting arrangement, or could change co-parenting to custodial parenting. (These terms are explained in chapter 3.) Equally, similar shifts could transform a custodial arrangement into co-parenting. Over the period of our interviews with parents some moved from custodial to co-parenting and back again. Others moved from co-parenting to solo parenting. Table 4.1 gives a broad indication of change across time. Between Time 0 and Time 2 there were shifts between our categories of parenting in thirty-two out of the sixty cases we interviewed. This means that there was significant change in 53 per cent of our cases. Table 4.1 conceals some of these changes, however, because the residence of a child or children could switch from one parent to another while the actual pattern of custodial parenting remains unchanged. In some instances children decided themselves to move back to live with

Table 4.1 Changes in parenting arrangements over time

Type of arrangement	Time 0 (at separation)	Time 1 (at interview 1)	Time 2 (at interview 2)
Custodial	42	35	37
Co-parent	10	10	11
Solo	8	15	11
(Remarried)			(1)

another parent, leaving brothers or sisters behind. This would still be a custodial arrangement if the parents did not share parental responsibility for the children, but the lives of the children and parents would be considerably transformed. The following examples of six mothers and six fathers provide a more nuanced picture of the sort of changes and transformations that we discovered (the type of parenting arrangement is followed in brackets by residence arrangements across the three time zones):

MOTHERS

Meg Johnson: *Co-parenting (shared) – Co-parenting (mother) – Custodial (mother)* Initially the couple took it in turns to care for their children in the family home. After eighteen months the house was sold and the father gradually reduced his parenting and moved away.

Felicity Lessing: *Custodial (mother) – Co-parenting (mother) – Co-parenting (shared)* Felicity experienced a reduction in her mothering over time as the father gradually developed a relationship with his young children and then negotiated an equal share of their time.

Nina Hester: *Custodial (mother) – Custodial (mother) – solo (mother)* Nina fled to escape the father's continuing violence towards her and her son. The courts granted the father interim supervised contact but he then dropped his application for contact.

Kate Moore: *Co-parenting (mother) – Custodial (mother) – Co-parenting (shared)* Kate asked the court to stop contact because of the father's ongoing violence. But contact was only curtailed, and the violence continued. Kate had to stop the violence by ending her new partnership and allowing the father daily contact with her son and herself.

Sally Burton: *Co-parenting (shared) – Custodial (mother) – Custodial (split)* The father vacillated between his family and new partner until Sally regulated the arrangements. She planned to move away but the older child opted to live with her father rather than relocate. Sally lost all financial support and moved into lodgings with the younger child.

Jenny Swift: *Custodial (mother) – Solo (father) – Custodial (father)* After two years, the father received a Child Support Agency assessment, snatched his children and blocked contact for some months. By then the court had to acknowledge his *de facto* residence. He took over the family home and continued to block Jenny's contact until he found a new partner.

FATHERS

Terry Watts: *Solo (mother) – Solo (split) – Custodial (split)* The mother disappeared with the four children. Terry set out to find them and applied to the court for contact. When he located the mother he negotiated a split arrangement directly with her. The boys returned home. Contact was sporadic but eventually became established.

Jack Hood: *Custodial (mother) – Solo (father) – Custodial (father)* Jack had regular contact with his baby son and was worried about the mother's drug addiction. When the mother entered a rehabilitation unit he began caring full time for his son. The mother was able to see her son when she was well enough to do so.

Gerry Marsh: *Custodial (mother) – Co-parenting (shared) – Custodial (father)* Gerry left the family home against his will following some violent incidents. The courts ordered interim shared residence after Gerry alleged the child was being neglected, but then granted residence to the mother. Gerry then used coercive means to regain both his home and child.

Keith Minster: *Solo (father) – Custodial (father) – Custodial (mother)* When the mother found a new partner, Keith refused to leave the house and children. He blocked contact after the mother left. He obtained a residence order and then allowed minimal contact. Eventually he acquiesced to his children's wishes to live with their mother.

Tim Muir: *Solo (mother) – Custodial (mother) – Co-parenting (shared)* Tim was convicted for assault and forced to leave the house. When he was released from prison he was granted supervised contact but then negotiated flexible contact directly with the mother. Eventually he moved back into the family home with the mother.

Nathan Granger: *Co-parenting (split) – Co-parenting (mother) –*

Custodial (mother) Nathan's son stayed with him initially but then left to join his mother and sister. Nathan applied to court to obtain shared residence and to prevent the children relocating to another jurisdiction. He was unsuccessful. He has remarried and sees his children during holiday times.

We cannot of course claim that it is possible to generalize from this picture of considerable change over time. But it does seem likely that the degree of real change in parenting arrangements after divorce is distorted by impressions gained from legally disputed cases (of which there are relatively few in formal terms) or even the assumption that, if parents do not return to their solicitors, then nothing has changed. We think it is likely that arrangements change much more than policy makers might imagine and that the focus on getting an agreement at the point of divorce might be rather futile, given the pressures on parents and children to re-negotiate as their circumstances change. These nuances are best explored through an examination of three pivotal case studies.

Case Study One: Leon Holt

At separation Leon and his wife, Jill, fell almost automatically into a custodial pattern of childcare because this was largely how they had organized their married parenthood. Nevertheless, he began for the first time to establish a relationship with his two sons (then aged five and three) that was no longer mediated by their mother but relied upon him being more available for his children.

> **Leon Holt:** If we were still together I would be doing the usual stereotyped father role, come in from work, play with them, watch telly, weekends have more time to myself. . . . I'd have said, 'You look after them today, I'm going to play golf'. I was just there and I probably didn't pay them much attention at all. . . . I made a conscious decision . . . that I was going to see my children grow up and give them the best that I can. You have to think, 'Well, how do I want it to be in five years' time?' And then, 'Well, what do I need to do to make sure it happens?'

He rented a house in the same locality as the family home and spent a substantial amount of time every day driving back and forth between the two households, collecting the children and taking them to school in the mornings, or to various activities or to his home later in the day. At the weekends he made several such trips, taking the children out in the mornings, returning them to their mother for Sunday lunch, and then collecting them later in the day to visit their grandparents.

Through a process of minor adjustments and negotiations, Leon established a shared residence arrangement in which his two sons stayed at his house for three or four nights per week. This change in pattern was driven by the substantial transformation he underwent as a carer. He was able to overwrite his marital biography as 'distant' father with a new version in which he had become a 'good' father:

> **Leon Holt**: She was saying, 'What does it matter because dads don't need the custody, you can just see them as they're growing up . . . you can have the children on a weekend . . . you're always working anyway.' She had a view of what a typical father was and it wasn't a lot of contact. She didn't want me to be around too much. For her the divorce was not seeing me any more and she couldn't understand why I wanted to see them every day. I'd lost their respect and I had to win back the respect. Now her mum says, 'Oh you're a good father to them.' It was a new experience for both of us.

As with other kinds of kin responsibilities (Finch and Mason, 1993: 96) post-divorce fatherhood is not ascribed in a predetermined way but is created incrementally. Indeed, as Beck and Beck-Gernsheim argue:

> Becoming a father is not difficult, but being a divorced father certainly is. At the moment when it is too late, the family personified by the child becomes the centre of all hope and concrete effort; the child is offered time and attention in a manner which during the marriage was allegedly out of the question, 'although I really would like to spend more time with him/her'. Divorce confronts the man with his own feelings as a father; he is the one to mourn for, having realized too late what liberation means, just as its objective slips away. (1995: 154)

Leon, however, did make time for his children. Moreover, he did not take his newly constituted fatherhood for granted but recognized the need continually to negotiate it. This meant, however, that he had no space to establish a new relationship. His spare time was occupied by his children, but this gave his wife time to form another relationship.

> **Leon Holt**: I don't get a chance [to meet someone new]. . . . My priority is for the children, to see them every day and it makes it very difficult for me to have a separate life. My life away from them doesn't really exist. Everything I do, they are at the core of it and I don't want to do anything that would jeopardize the relationship with the kids.

It was not unusual for parents who were engaged in co-operative co-parenting to forgo new relationships. In fact we began to think that it was the price they had to pay for sustaining a good parental relationship with the other parent. Jill decided to marry her new partner, but their relationship collapsed when he tried to 'father' the children, who refused to accept him. Jill realized that she could not retain a close relationship with Leon and stand a chance of finding another partner because Leon was unwilling to share the children with another man. Initially she decided that she would cut Leon out of her life and drastically reduced his contact with the children. At that point many fathers would have rushed to their solicitors demanding a legal solution, but Leon went back to tactful negotiations. In any case the children would not accept the new situation and demanded to see more of their father. The co-parenting arrangement was therefore reinstated and Jill gave up the idea of a new relationship.

This case study shows how fragile a good parenting relationship can be after divorce. Leon was able to act in a caring way with Jill at a time when she was in crisis, even though it was extremely difficult for him and the children. In many respects they sustained a caring relationship beyond the divorce (an issue discussed further in chapter 6), which for many parents is quite inconceivable.

Case Study Two: Philip Laslett

When Philip left his wife Margaret their son was fourteen and their daughter ten years old. They were both in professional occupations and both in their late forties at the time. Philip felt that their relationship had been deteriorating for some time and he left to be with another woman. Margaret took it very badly and

Philip felt extremely guilty. As a consequence he tried to be kind, sending her presents on her birthday, and was as flexible as possible. But he later became resentful of his wife and felt that he began to dislike her more and more. Although they communicated over the children, Joe and Rachel, especially over important matters like schooling, he basically wanted to keep out of her way as much as possible. He saw both children regularly, but spent more time with Rachel; however, he was concerned about the superficiality of his relationship with them. This was exacerbated by his daily experience of living with a step-daughter, Fay, whom he disliked intensely.

> **Philip Laslett**: And I still have a major, major problem with that, and I suspect I always will. I've been living with the two of them for . . . more or less four years now. And, it isn't going to get any easier. I've never liked the kid. I didn't like her before – because I knew her before I married [her mother].

He resented Fay for getting in the way of his relationship with his new wife, June. At the same time, he wanted to spend more time alone with Rachel but this meant that June felt excluded.

> **Philip Laslett**: And I think June resents that, she actually feels shut out. She's a very jealous person. You know, she does her best, but for the type of person she is, it's very difficult. She's not easy-going in that department and she's very insecure herself, so she has the suspicion that I cherish being with my kids more than I do with her.

Philip's situation seemed to be deteriorating between our interviews with him. He wanted an exclusive relationship with his new wife and resented little things, for example his step-daughter doing her homework in the lounge when he wanted time alone with June. He also wanted an exclusive relationship with Rachel when she came to stay or visit and was intolerant of the friendship she developed with Fay. There was little to attract his son to visit him in his new marriage and, being around seventeen at the time, Joe was able to vote with his feet and stay away. Philip was increasingly resentful of his first wife and it seemed as if his second marriage was strained as well as his relationship with his children.

Unexpectedly, however, his relationship with Joe, which he had predicted was going to become even more distant when he went to university, actually improved. Joe had found a new way of contacting his father which was regular, but which circumvented all the emotional trauma of visits and even phone calls: he discovered electronic communication via email. Joe had easy access to the Internet and sent his father messages every day.

> **Philip Laslett**: He gets in touch with me on email all the time, which is remarkable. I am actually more in touch with him now than I was before he left home, which is quite unexpected because he communicates with me about once a day, and sometimes rings me.

What is interesting about this development is that it suggests that there may be ways of sustaining relationships which children find more satisfactory than the rather disruptive experience (for them) of having to move physically between parents and experiencing the emotional problems of two households. Perhaps virtual parenting will become a good substitute for stressful co-parenting where older children are concerned, and perhaps it will be particularly useful for fathers and sons who do not have a shared history of more personal forms of communication.

Case Study 3: Felicity Lessing

Felicity and Simon met when they were both professional performers in the same theatre company. After the birth of her second son she stopped work apart from occasional appearances as a stand-in. What was important about this decision was that it was virtually a contract between them whereby she gave up chances of a good career to be a full-time mother. Simon, however, formed another relationship and left Felicity. She was devastated but felt that it was her role to go on being the full-time carer for her small sons. Simon had the children to stay regularly, so Felicity was able to do occasional work, but she could not return to her previous status in the company, not least because Simon and his new partner were employed there. Other opportunities for work inevitably meant going to other cities, but this was virtually impossible to organize because of her childcare responsibilities. Gradually Simon began to demand more time with the children, in fact he wanted them half the time, but it was extremely difficult for Felicity to accept this.

Felicity Lessing: Well, that was last summer and we'd had a really big row. It was when he started fighting for having an equal share of the children and I was saying, *'Look, I gave up my job in order to be their mother and I do my little bit of freelance to keep ticking over but basically my role is to be their mother. And you've got not only a full-time job but various other things as well,* you've got a highly successful career and yet you're expecting to have them half the time.' We really couldn't agree about this and thumped the table and shouted and screamed for the very first time. (Our emphasis)

She then had to adjust again when Simon married his new partner and they bought a house together around the corner from the former matrimonial home. Felicity then felt that she was not simply sharing her children with Simon, but with Simon and his wife. Her relationship with Simon had deteriorated such that they could hardly speak to each other and they had to rely on the children, whom they now deemed old enough, to carry out a lot of the transactions between them. She let them answer the phone and got them to phone him.

Felicity Lessing: I feel sad because the way it was before was a kind of fantasy really that we were still bringing up our children together and this is more realistic but I don't like it. And it's because the other person is much more involved and I can't come to terms with that and we have had some big arguments about that because, of course, I can't stop her being involved. She is involved and that's the next stage, I suppose, I've got to get used to that.

But although some things were getting harder for Felicity she was prepared to put up with it for the sake of the children's best interests. And some things improved. The children became better equipped to handle the change-over and were less disruptive when they got home. Felicity too began to find it easier.

Felicity Lessing: I am getting better at it, I still feel a little bit odd if I've had three days on my own and then suddenly the house is full of children. But I'm very much better at not pouncing on them the second they get in the door and bombarding them with questions, which I've heard about somewhere else. I know I used to do that a lot and I think it was not helpful and I'm much better at just letting them be there generally. I think I'm better with the change-overs, I'm better at letting them go too.

The case of Felicity and Simon shows how difficult it is to co-parent even when both parents are committed to the welfare of the children. While the case of Leon Holt showed how difficult it could be from the point of view of the father who wants to establish a good relationship with his children *after* divorce, Felicity's case shows how hard this can be from the perspective of a mother. While Leon had to redirect some of his energies away from his work (to ensure he maintained his position as an involved father), Felicity had to relinquish her full-time job as a mother at a time when she did not have a career or a new partner. Leon's situation was made somewhat easier by Jill's decision not to repartner in the foreseeable future, but Felicity had to deal with the realization that her husband had reconstituted a family (with a new baby too) while she was a lone parent who was struggling to rekindle a career.

Philip's situation produced different dilemmas. He had remained in a relationship with his former wife out of a mixture of pity and guilt but this did not provide a very good basis for the difficulties he then encountered in trying to sustain a relationship with his children. He had been a traditional, distant father and he did not know how to become an emotionally involved post-divorce father. His former wife was not willing to help him in his attempt and he also blamed his second wife for getting in the way of establishing a new relationship with his children. While Leon and Felicity were managing the balancing act between separateness, connectedness and fluidity, thereby affecting the quality of relationships, the combination was much harder for Philip to get right. The post-divorce parenting situation was not any easier for Leon or Felicity compared with Philip, but the quality of the relationships they achieved with their children seemed to outweigh problems elsewhere – at least for most of the time. Philip's experience of post-divorce parenthood seemed a minefield of discontent and resentments.

Transformations in parenthood

The focus in this chapter has been on post-divorce parenting as a lived experience. What has emerged is a clear sense of the fluidity of such experiences over time. The notion that parenthood is in a constant state of flux is hardly surprising, of course, but following divorce the sort of changes to which parents have to accommodate take on greater significance. The fluidity of relationships is overlaid by the opposing forces of the need for parents to be separate (triggered in the main by the arrival of 'new' partners and children, and/or geographical relocations) and to remain connected (the drive to preserve 'old' familial ties and allegiances). As the three case studies show, it is not just parenting practices and relationships that may be transformed, but the relative importance that is attached to mothering and fathering. Following divorce, the very nature of parenting comes under scrutiny and can no longer be taken for granted.

The experience of living in post-divorce families forms a fluid backdrop against which parents are continually evaluating (and then negotiating, adjusting or changing) their parenting practices, identities and relationships. The widespread changes in parenting that we have alluded to can be initiated and managed in a variety of ways. The changes that we have focused on here have tended to be driven by ongoing negotiations which are bound up with the shifting reality of parental responsibilities and commitments and the quality of relationships between parents and their children. These processes of change are likely to occur over considerable periods of time, and are the very stuff of parenting, particularly following divorce. Yet they are not widely recognized or taken into account simply because they are negotiated gradually and privately. They do not tend to make their way into court nor do they involve a return to solicitors and exchanges of letters in a formal way. They are, in this sense, unrecorded and invisible.

At the other end of the spectrum the impetus for change may be primarily to do with the relationship between the parents themselves rather than their parenting *per se*. As discussed above, the quality of parental relationships may fluctuate over time, and conflicts may escalate, for example, where there are struggles over the exercise of parental authority or an abuse of power. Changes can thus be triggered which are of a different order altogether to those explored above, for example when a child is 'snatched' or contact is suddenly denied. Such changes are likely to involve the coercion of one parent by another and/ or the use of legal mechanisms to enforce a change. Rapid changes of this sort are not common but by their very nature they attract attention and consequently can give the impression that problems associated with post-divorce parenting are often of this nature. These sorts of conflicts are explored in later chapters; this chapter has aimed to cast light on the less dramatic, but very demanding, daily labour of sharing parenting across households.

5

Constructing Post-divorce Childhoods

Introduction

Jim Walters: I think what worries me most is that they don't seem to have shown any signs of it affecting them. I am almost looking for something.

The concern expressed by this non-residential father captures exactly the framework of understanding which most parents in our sample adopted when talking about children after divorce. Although a number of parents felt that their children's problems pre-dated the divorce, even these felt that they had to talk about their children in the context of harm. Many of them had read books on the damage that divorce does to children and others had experienced their parents' divorce and wanted to save their own children from similar experiences. There was therefore an anticipation that the children would not escape unscathed, and many parents whose children were still outwardly happy, involved in social activities and doing well at school, were convinced that something would 'show' later in life.

This presumption of harm was so all-pervasive that we began to think it must be an additional burden for children to carry on behalf of their parents. Many children were whisked off to psychologists; parents had discreet talks with headteachers; school nurses were asked to talk to children; and a web of anxious surveillance was set up. The aim was undoubtedly to catch the children should they fall, but its omnipresence felt more like a trap from which the children would be lucky to escape. Moreover, the knowledge that divorce might cause harm produced a huge variety of responses from parents. For a couple who were social workers it meant that they had discussions with the children and that everything was planned in advance, allowing the children a say in arrangements which were based on the principles of co-parenting. For other parents it meant that the ex-spouse could be blamed for everything, because the spouse who made the decision to go was held responsible for all the actual and anticipated harm. For yet other parents, usually mothers, it meant that they stayed in oppressive or violent relationships for far too long because they did not want to harm the children. Finally, for other parents it meant that they became almost obsessive about their children's well-being in order to make up for perceived harms.

Knowing that divorce is thought to cause harm brought forth neither a unitary nor necessarily a very satisfactory response from parents. It certainly did not stop them divorcing because few parents, save those who were bitter and angry about being 'deserted', felt that couples should stay together for the sake of the children. Parents were therefore on the horns of a dilemma. They felt sure that their children would be harmed and therefore experienced extreme guilt, but they did not always know how to translate this worry into their everyday post-divorce parenting. Some parents thought that the best thing was to ensure that children maintained a relationship with both parents to the point of sharing the children physically (Children Act ethos), while others thought that the most important thing was stability and continuity with minimal emotional conflict (pre-Children Act ethos). In this chapter we therefore want to focus on how parents managed and 'constructed' post-divorce childhood. We also want to consider the extent to which parents may have very different concepts of childhood and how to interact with children. It is, for example, often the case that the primary carer sees the child and also childhood rather differently to the contact parent, and even in co-parenting arrangements, crucial differences emerge. While these differences undoubtedly exist where marriages remain intact, they are less visible and (perhaps) more easily managed in those circumstances. Divorce highlights different styles of parenting and arguably creates new styles of childhood. These days more and more children spend time with parents in different households and are having to sustain relationships with parents who no longer live with them. Divided loyalties, which can perhaps be downplayed inside a family unit, become much more difficult to manage when a child is physically moving between her or his mother and father.

We have identified a number of key issues which seem to be an important part of post-divorce childhood and in this chapter we first explore the core question of the problem of different styles and standards of parenting. We then consider the thorny issue of the 'manipulation' of the child and how such an idea fits with a notion that children have the right to make decisions. Finally we consider situations in which a child's relationship with a parent (usually the contact parent) has worsened and the much less frequently acknowledged situation in which they have improved. In our conclusion we address a broader issue concerning what childhood means to different parents. Working through our data, we gradually came to think that the literature which focuses on the harms of divorce for children operates without a sufficiently nuanced grasp of all the different ways in which parenting (whether together or apart) operates. The myopic focus on divorce ignores the harm of certain types of parent/child relationship which are not dependent upon parents separating. We therefore came to think that it was important to understand how parents conceive of childhood. Parents do not all have the same ideas about how to raise children or how to prevent harm to children because they often have very different ideas about what a child is. They also vary in their views on whether a child experiences complex emotions and on the extent to which a child should be seen as more or less autonomous of his/her parents. This sort of complexity is not reducible to a simple judgement about 'good' and 'bad' parenting. It therefore follows that it is inappropriate to map this simple idea of 'good' parenting onto intact parents while conferring the adjective 'bad' on separated parents.

Parenting styles and standards

How to raise children 'properly' is a deeply fraught and contested issue. There is, in general, little agreement about it and there is a rapid turnover in fashionable theories and practices.

The huge range of titles in parentcraft and child development often displayed in bookshops and libraries suggests that parents are constantly in search of guidance and answers to problems. If there is no professional, political or personal agreement over something relatively straightforward like 'smacking' and physical punishment, then it is hardly surprising that there is no agreement over how to support and help a child through his or her parents' divorce.

Differences of standard and approach occur within households as well as across households. Where parents differ in approach this can itself bring about a divorce. Moreover, now that there is an emphasis on retaining the involvement of biological fathers in the care of their children after divorce, the issue of whether individual mothers and fathers have very different ideas on how children should be raised becomes much more critical. Children are now often faced with situations in which they not only have to accommodate to a new step-parent who may be living with them, but with a contact parent who also imposes a regime and set of standards and expectations on them. They may also receive care from another step-parent who lives with the non-residential parent and who also has different standards and expectations. A fairly typical picture might be a situation in which a girl is initially brought up in a two-parent household, primarily cared for by her mother with a somewhat distant father. On divorce, that father may become more involved with her if only because he spends more dedicated time with her. Her father may have repartnered and so, if she stays overnight or goes on holiday with him, she will experience care from yet another adult. Then if her mother repartners, she will be living with another adult who may adopt elements of a caring or parental role. The existence of stepbrothers or step-sisters who may be treated quite differently obviously complicates this picture further. Parenting is therefore infinitely more complex now, and as a consequence childhood is changing too. Although we cannot comment directly on how the children[1] of our sample of parents accommodated to these diverse patterns, we can identify how parents manage these new circumstances and what problems this causes them when they attempt to share responsibility for their children after divorce or separation.

With our sample of parents, some of the problems of living with different styles of parenting pre-dated the divorce and, where they were severe enough, were often part of the reason for the separation.

> **Jodie Hitchens**: The thing was, I don't believe in smacking Alice. All right, she might get a tap on her bum sometimes if she's really overwrought, but I won't smack her if I can help it, I'll do it other ways. But he believes in the way his dad brought him up, which is a good clout over the head and a good hiding and then up to bed. I don't believe in that. I think he's got more into the idea of smacking kids [since he left] because they're boys that [his new partner] has got and he took over the father role of looking after them.

> **Nina Hester**: She was twenty weeks old [and] he used to walk round the floor to scare the living daylights out of me. He used to have Jemma sat in the palm of his hand in a sitting position, legs crossed, hunched . . . and he used to have his arm outstretched and he used to walk along the kitchen floor which was tiled and he used to say, 'I've never dropped one yet.'[2]

Fathers who had been violent to their children did not necessarily lose contact with them. Sometimes mothers could not cope with children who were themselves becoming violent or who were seriously disturbed as a result of their early childhood and sent them to live with their fathers or, in one case, wished she had. In the case of Ginny Fry her son was frightened of his father, who had violent rages and would hit him and inflict severe punishment. Ginny, who was very worried about the situation, nevertheless wanted them to have some kind of relationship. She had therefore worked out an emergency code with her son so that if his father went into one of his rages, he would phone her and give the password. She would then drive over and collect him straight away. In this case the father was a solicitor. Ginny had to work very hard to sustain the relationship but not all mothers had her resources and her willingness to understand her husband's uncontrollable temper.

Differences in parenting styles and standards were not, of course, always as stark as this. They often concerned things like bedtimes, doing homework, being allowed to cross busy streets alone or to play in the street, cleanliness and things like being made to sit at table to eat rather than eating from a tray in front of the television. Delia Garrett, for example, had to tolerate her husband hiring violent videos to entertain her son. Anthony Dart insisted that when his son was with him he should be called by a name other than his given name because he was of mixed race and he did not want him to identify with his 'white' name. Even differences over the children's diet could cause considerable stress.

> **Erica Dawson**: A typical example – my eldest son is not allergic to Coca-Cola but it hypes him up. So I cut it out of his diet altogether, he can have fizzy orange or lemonade but he doesn't drink Coke. When they went to their dad's house he would buy a bottle of Coke and Steven, being four or five would say, 'I don't have Coke, it hypes me up,' and he'd say 'That's ridiculous! Your mother's picked that up off the television. She doesn't know what she's talking about, you drink it.' So he'd give him a couple of glasses of Coke and he'd come back to me and he'd be climbing up the wall!

> **James Grant**: I think the way that Paula feeds them, if it isn't too patronizing to say, [it's] the way the working class would feed their children. It's loads of chips, loads of beans, loads of eggs. I tend to buy more fresh things, it's very rarely I buy anything in a tin, it isn't any good for them and I can't stand it so there's no distinct difficulties in that I have [sic] but it's not as if they're going to drop dead by it for the weekend.

Later James added:

> I think that when you've got one system like this and one system like that, and neither of them is right or wrong, you know, that's just how it is, then I think it does make the children terribly confused in what to do and say in certain places. I mean, Paula will make Jimmy and William a sandwich and they can sit on the sofa and eat it and watch TV, I mean they don't even try it in here, you know!

Perhaps one of the most common and most frustrating things that our sample of parents faced was their children asserting that they would not do something (eat at table, do their homework, not swear) because the other parent did not make them do it. Almost all those who took a reasonable degree of responsibility for their children faced this at one time. Some parents would simply assert that they did not care what the children were allowed to do in the other house, they had to abide by the rules of whichever household they were in. Where parents were entirely co-operative they would often check with each other, and even have a joint meeting with the child if the issue was serious enough. While some parents could

different behaviour is
diff. households .

'nip this behaviour in the bud', for others it was much more difficult. If they did not see the child very often they could not really assert authority, or if the child was not merely 'trying it on' but was quite badly disturbed it became a perennial nightmare. Pete Glenn, for example, wanted to cut down on the amount of contact James was having with his mother because of the effect it was appearing to have on him.

> **Pete Glenn**: The only way is, like I say, they go on the Friday and cut the Wednesday out because James comes back on the Monday, he's boisterous but his arms are folded and he pulls a face if he doesn't get his way. Well that's [his mother], and he stamps around and I say, 'Come on, you've got to get your school work done.' 'No!', because his mum can't control him. So then Tuesday's OK, Wednesday I take him to school. He's away again till Thursday tea time, so I've got the same [thing on] Thursday. By Friday he's OK. He's away Saturday and Sunday; no wonder he wants to go, he just runs [wild], he just does what he wants.

This case is interesting because it is a residential father who is experiencing the problem of this kind of disruption. These senti- ments are more usually uttered by mothers who suffer when their children return from action-packed weekends or any other time, having been spoilt by their fathers. It became increasingly appar- ent to us that what mattered most in this kind of tension between parents was the situation of the 'most responsible' parent. This did not always have to be the parent that the child was living with, although it almost always was.[3] Thus we found that when fathers were put in the same structural position as that more commonly associated with mothers, they began to care about things like table manners and homework and bedtimes. They objected as much as mothers to children being kept up late or being taken to the pub.

> **Keith Minster**: I think I've been more loving towards them, more soft with them, probably because I know that I'm the one looking after them and I've got to get them in bed on a night because if they're not then they're tired for school the next day. It's changed in that way, but you can't avoid it because it is me who's doing it.

We need therefore to consider the structure of post-divorce parenting and hence post-divorce childhood. Moving between parents who have very different standards and expectations can clearly cause problems for children. Many of the primary carers in our sample referred to the distress children feel at 'change-over' time. Often, because of the difficulties between parents, the handover was additionally difficult for children on an emotional level. One mother would meet her ex-husband in a motorway service station. This could lead to a kind of farce with her daughters refusing to get into his car, her virtually forcing them in (because she was worried about being blamed for alienating the children) and the girls simply getting out on the other side of the car before he could drive off. In another case a mother would wait outside Marks & Spencer for her ex-husband, who had to drive 150 miles in congested traffic and who was therefore often late, causing much distress, especially in the dead of winter. But she refused to let him come to the house. Other parents were able to work out that it was best if the mother took them to school on change-over day while the father would collect them. This gave the children a neutral space between the emotional worlds of their separated parents and they could move much more easily away from one parent and towards the other.

If a child showed emotional distress at the point of transition, this too could feed into the difficulties of the parental relationship. For example, we noted that if a child cried or became clingy on leaving their father, then it would often be interpreted as a clear sign that the child wanted to be with him and not their mother. In other words, the emotional difficulty of transition became a further point of contention rather than a catalyst for developing a less stressful 'exchange'. Some parents, it would seem, could not interpret their children's distress outside the framework of their own needs and interests. Thus, for some residential parents, a child's distress on returning from a contact visit was seen as a reason to cut down on contact, while for some non-residential parents it was a clear indication that the child's residence should be changed. Rather than making the problem easier for the child, the parents' hostilities therefore increased. But it is far too simple to suggest that parents simply acted selfishly when faced with these dilemmas. Sometimes reducing contact was the sensible thing to do, and sometimes children really did want to stay with the other parent and left to do so as soon as they were old enough. So, although some situations may look like parental selfishness on the surface, it was always unwise to assume this would inevitably be the case. Indeed one of the most fraught issues between parents after divorce was the question of whether one parent was manipulating the child to suit their own interests. Because post-divorce parenting is generally assumed to be motivated by a malevolent set of interests, we found that this accusation was regularly made, regardless of the circumstances.

Manipulations

Given the assumption that after their parents have divorced, children are likely to be subject to parental manipulations, post-divorce childhood is seen as a potentially more dangerous arena for the child than that of a sustained marriage. This assumption tends to rest on the idea that, in marriage, parents work as a harmonious team and are therefore incapable of mistaking their own interests for those of their children. It also takes for granted that all children love and relate to both parents equally and that, left to their own devices, they would want to spend equal amounts of time with both parents regardless of their stage in the life cycle. The focus on manipulation obscures the extent to which children are themselves agents in the making of post-divorce childhood. It is almost automatically assumed that a child who does not wish to see her or his father (or mother) has been deliberately poisoned by the residential parent.

We found that it was much more difficult to judge this situation than these common-sense ideas allow. To a very large extent it seems easy to accuse a parent of manipulating a child while being extremely difficult to prove that this was not the case. The child does not, and cannot, exist in a completely independent emotional world. Necessarily influenced by the feelings of both parents, the child's own feelings come into play. It would seem, for example, that where a parent leaves the matrimonial home 'badly', this can damage relationships between parent and child. Molly Smith, for example, was convinced that part of the reason why her son refused to have a relationship with his father was because he left suddenly, in the middle of the night, to go and live with another woman.

Molly Smith: He has never sat Roland down and said, 'Whatever you think of me, this is why I did it,' the rights and wrongs of it, if he loves him still, that he wants to be part of his life and just some reassurance. He never has.

If a father becomes violent around the time of the break-up, a child may become very apprehensive. If he leaves to live with another woman and her children, the first set of offspring may feel deserted in favour of other children. If a father had little to do with them during the marriage, they may feel that there is no relationship to sustain when he goes. Without doubt children are able to make their own decisions and judgements; the problem is that the residential parent is too easily assumed to be planting ideas and acting maliciously.

The case of Fred Sykes is instructive. He was a residential father whose son Anthony did not want to see his mother. This case is additionally interesting because of the gender reversal. The popular stereotype of this situation inevitably portrays a vindictive mother who is using the children against the father because of her own emotional immaturity. This case shows that the problem of manipulation is not simply one of gender, but one of structural situation. It is the residential parent, mother or father, who is easily accused of manipulation, simply because the child spends more time with them. In Fred's case, his wife Carol was fighting for residence of the children. Once she dropped the case, their son Anthony felt ready to go and see her again and Fred felt vindicated as he had argued all along that the more the boy felt he was being pushed into it, the more determined he would become.

Fred Sykes: The first time Anthony fell out with mum, she thought it was me poisoning him and using him as a weapon. 'Oh, don't go and see her, she's run off with somebody else, I hate her' scenario. What she never got through her head – and I say this with a smile on my face by me having the children every weekend . . . my whole private life couldn't be run, I've got no free time whatsoever – so why would I want to keep him from going to see mum because if he had to go I could go out with somebody or do what I wanted. But she never, ever switched it round to look at it from that [point of] view.

Many parents found themselves in a really difficult catch-22 situation. If children said they did not want to go, parents would nevertheless oblige them to go because they knew they would otherwise be accused of manipulation. The more adamant or distressed the children became, the more guilty parents would feel about forcing the issue, but if they relented they did not know whether they did so for their own sakes (selfish), for the children's sakes (altruistic), or whether the children were only saying it for their parents' sake anyway (misplaced loyalty). The three cases below show just how complex it can be and how it is far too simplistic to imagine that children who refuse contact are merely doing their mother's bidding.

Case One: Selfishness?

Jean Adams: Well, as far as Joanna was concerned, she didn't want to go at all and I found myself forcing her to go to keep up this contact with the father. Then she was obviously too upset so I didn't push her any more and then I was accused of keeping her away from him. But he took all his hatred out on Joanna unfortunately. He said 'Your mother's this, your mother's that, she's a whore, a tramp. If I saw her in the street I'd thump her in the face. You can tell your mother that.' So this is what she got all the time and she didn't want to see him. Karl was his favourite and he wasn't subject[ed] to any of this at all but it split the children obviously.

Case Two: Altruism?

Ginny Fry: I say, 'Well, at the moment, John, you've got to go and if you're older then you can change your mind, but if I don't make you go now and then when you're fifteen and you think "Why haven't I seen my dad and I really want to see him." You might not like him at the moment but just take out of it what you can. I'm not going to send your sister on her own.'

(NB this father was violent towards the children, especially the son.)

Case Three: Misplaced Loyalties?

Erica Dawson: He's telephoned them a couple of times and they wouldn't speak to him on the phone. Mark is adamant he won't have anything to do with his new wife and he knows that his dad won't do anything without her being at the end of his arms, so that causes him a problem. He would like to see him. Steven I'm not sure about. He's very bitter and very angry. . . . He doesn't say anything to me because he doesn't want to upset me so it's quite a delicate subject to discuss. If we do talk he tends to say the right things rather than what he feels, whereas Mark just says what's in his mind.

What is interesting about all of these cases is that two siblings were involved. It is not uncommon for one child to be perfectly happy with contact, while a sibling does not want to go. This may be because the reluctant child never had a very good relationship with the contact parent, or because what is on offer is unattractive to that child. Oddly, it seems that parents imagine that their children owe them unconditional love and that they should want to see them and spend time with them even if it means being ignored, sat in front of a television and playing second fiddle to a new lover and a new set of step-siblings. Not infrequently, children have to give up their own space to be put into makeshift accommodation a long way away from their friends and their own independent activities. If, when they arrive they are then cross-questioned, hear criticisms of the other parent and have to fit in with everyone else's priorities, it is hardly surprising that the experience may become unappealing.

The point to make is that relationships built on contact, even if it is regular, require ongoing efforts by the contact parent, not just force applied by the residential parent to get the child to go. What we found when we looked at contact over time was that relationships could either improve or deteriorate depending to a great extent on the work that the contact parent (not just the residential parent) put into forming a close bond with the child. Often this was difficult for fathers who had not really formed much of a bond with their children in the first place, but it was not impossible. We shall therefore now explore the circumstances in which a child's relationships with a contact parent deteriorated over time and those in which they actually improved such that the contact parent became a better father (it was usually fathers) than he had been during the marriage.

Deteriorating relationships with children

As suggested above, the way a parent leaves the family can be very significant in the process of forming relationships with the children afterwards. Some parents would spend time together with their children to explain what was happening. In these circumstances almost all of the parents relied upon a common narrative to reassure their children. It usually went something like this:

> 'Your daddy (or mummy) is leaving because he does not want to live with mummy (daddy) any more. He (she) doesn't love mummy (daddy) and they are not happy living together. But this will not change in anyway his (her) relationship with you. He (she) still loves you and wants to see you.'

Of course, children remember what is said to them at this time and if elaborate promises are made about how sons will be taken off on wonderful holidays and how it will be just them with their dad and so on, they can rebound very seriously when the children find out that dad has another family and that wherever they go with him, the new partner and her children come too. But children can be even more disappointed by the father who simply vanishes or if they are told he is on a work trip from which he then never returns. Sometimes these deceits were almost unavoidable because the process of going is not always clear-cut. This arises particularly where a partner is having an affair and cannot decide whether to go or stay and thus vacillates and keeps changing his/her mind. Stella Drew faced exactly this situation when she discovered that her husband had been having an affair for years and that he had a daughter by the other woman who was the same age as her youngest son. Not only did her husband keep moving back and forth, subjecting the boys to a great deal of uncertainty and a dreadful atmosphere in the home, but once he had finally left, he took them straight round to meet their sister with whom he was then living and who, naturally, called him 'Dad' too. It was not surprising that Stella had to work hard to sustain the relationship between her sons and their father. Given that she had a virtual breakdown herself, it is hardly surprising that the children's feelings about their father fell far short of unconditional love. As Penny King suggests, a child might still love the parent who leaves, but that love might change in quality.

> **Penny King:** I don't think [the relationship has] got tensions in it but I think she treats him a bit off hand, really. Then I don't know if that's just her sort of punishing him. I think it probably is, I think

she's still – obviously it's her dad – I think she still loves him, yeah. But it's different. Love changes, doesn't it?

When relationships are fragile, little things like a contact parent arriving late to collect a child can take on huge significance. If such behaviour becomes the norm, children can become disenchanted and distrustful. While it is easy for the contact parent then to blame the residential parent for poisoning the child, it is less easy to recognize when it is the contact parent who falls short. Similarly, it is often assumed that it is the residential parent who will try to influence a child to think or feel a particular way, but it can also be the contact parent.

> **Kate Moore**: . . . and he's saying, 'Mummy doesn't love you. You'll hate living in S——, you'll hate mummy being a teacher. Mummy's doing this to make me sad.' And Jack is terrified of making his dad sad, terrified. 'Make mummy change. Make mummy let me see you every day. All mummy's friends are bad, solicitors are bad, courts are bad and police are very bad.'

(This was a case involving severe violence to Kate.)

Children can also be very disturbed by being pumped for information by parents. Such attempts can lead to children refusing to have contact or, if they are too young, to highly disturbed behaviour as their loyalties are constantly being tested.

> **Jessica Hunt**: This continued for a while but it was disrupting the children that much, because they were being grilled. He was planting ideas in their head, he had a game going with them where he was the commander, they were the little army recruits. They had to write up reports for daddy each week. They had to spy on mummy and let him know everything mummy had done. People that had come to the house, phone calls, letters and it got quite bad actually. My eldest son was just acting diabolically and he was getting totally and utterly confused.

Not infrequently parents would instruct their children to conceal something from the other parent. This put an awful responsibility on the child who, in any case, often failed to keep the matter secret and was then placed in an even more untenable position. One father instructed his sons not to tell their mother that, when they spent their very first weekend with him, his girlfriend had been there too. He did not want his ex-wife to know that he was living with this new partner so soon. It was an impossible secret to keep of course, as well as being too much of a burden for young children to carry. They were full of the illicit news that they had seen their daddy in bed with a woman on Sunday morning. One child instantly told his grandmother, saying that he had been told not to tell his mother, but it was all right to tell her. Naturally she told the mother and the whole web of relationships became even worse.

Parent-child relations were often most strained at the point where a parent entered into a new relationship. After the initial separation, relationships between parents and children could reach an equilibrium, especially if neither parent had repartnered. But once a new partner was introduced, this equilibrium could be shattered. Sometimes the children resented sharing their parent with the new lover, who might be blamed for the breakdown of the parents' marriage, sometimes it meant that the child had to abandon hope of the parents getting back together. This does not mean that all children were adversely affected by the arrival of a new partner. Yet again, what mattered was how it was managed. Some parents deliberately avoided new relationships to allow their children a period of stability. Others kept them in the background, really only spending time with their new partners while the children were away. In many other cases, parents made it clear that the new partner would not be a new mother or father. This approach was quite different to the old expectation of step-parenting. In these 'post-Children Act' arrangements a new husband or live-in partner, for example, would not automatically presume to be called 'Dad', nor would he discipline the children, rather he would co-exist and develop a certain kind of companionship with them. Men unable to adopt this new type of adult-child relationship could be given short shrift.

> **Leon Holt**: And what happened was that they got engaged and they were going to get married. . . . He never wanted to [become a father to them] but he realized he couldn't just have no relationship with the children. . . . the end result was over one bank holiday he tried to put them to bed early at half seven, when it was not a school day. They reacted, wanted to ring me up. I don't think [he could handle it]. He was sort of threatening, the children were crying. I didn't know what to do. . . . I think the children wanted me to come right over, I heard crying in the background.

In fact Leon did not go round but contacted his wife's family, who did. After that the children made it clear that they did not want a relationship with their mother's fiancé and she ended the engagement. She has since decided not to have another relationship until the children are older. Jean Adams was able to negotiate the introduction of a new relationship rather better.

Jean Adams: Karl was resentful at first, he became quite bolshy and stroppy and slamming doors. I knew it would happen. It was jealousy that someone else was taking my time away from him and I knew if I just worked through it he'd come round. We made a point of when Ewen came up for the weekend, I still gave as much time as I could to Karl. Even though I wanted to be with Ewen because I hadn't seen him for two weeks, I still spent the same amount of time with Karl and we did things together with him. It worked and he took to Ewen. I can still sense a slight resentment but he doesn't dislike him because he asked Ewen to help him build little model aeroplanes.

It is perhaps one of the most notable features of modern post-Children Act, post-divorce childhood that certain parents and children are starting to reject the old idea of the new husband becoming the father substitute.[4] Clearly where a new man insists on becoming a 'proper' father to the children this can lead to huge tensions with the biological father who wishes to remain involved with his children. Indeed we would go so far as to argue that involved ongoing fathering is quite impossible where the mother and her new partner envisage that they are reconstituting a nuclear family when they marry or cohabit. In our sample of parents we came across only one instance where a mother and her new partner were trying to reconstitute themselves into a traditional nuclear family and to deny the existence of the biological father. This was a case where the parents had never married and had had a short relationship. They separated when the child was a baby and the mother met another man whom she married. She and her husband wanted to adopt the child and give him the new family name. She was trying very hard to sever all contact between the biological father and her son. She had good reasons for wanting to exclude the biological father. We raise this case not because she was necessarily unreasonable to want to distance herself and the child from this man, but rather because she was adopting a course of action which is now seen as out of step with the ethos of the Children Act. She in fact had a daughter by another man, who had yet a different surname, and this daughter, being old enough to decide for herself, had agreed to change it by deed poll. This mother was therefore struggling to construct a traditional nuclear family in the way that family policy would have approved until the 1990s (Smart, 1997). Unfortunately her desire to constitute such a family was blocked by the biological father, who refused to allow the adoption and insisted on contact. He was fully supported in his claims to fatherhood by the new ethos of the Children Act. (Whether this was really in the best interests of the child was another matter; Hooper, 1994.)

It is clear from the instances cited above that post-divorce parenting requires many skills, not all of which are acquired through the experience of intact parenting. One of the most important challenges is the ability to deal with the new situations and emotional reactions that children will face. Childhood is no longer what it was in Britain in the 1950s or even the 1960s. Most of our sample of parents would not have been brought up in households where there was divorce. They were therefore having to deal with an unknown situation. All of our parents subscribed to the principle that children should retain contact with both parents after divorce but they were not necessarily prepared for the difficulties that this principle entailed when put into practice. The majority had had traditional parenting arrangements before divorce, with the father working full time and the mother working part time or not at all, at least while the children were young. This meant that typically the mother had been the primary carer and the father's relationship with the children was often mediated through the mother. For both to remain involved parents after divorce therefore required a great deal of effort at a time when their children's childhood was being transformed too. But it is important to recognize that, in spite of these difficulties, it would seem that some children made positive gains. In some cases the effort of becoming a real post-divorce father actually brought children and fathers closer together. It is to these more optimistic outcomes that we now turn.

Improving relationships

Sally Burton: He sees the children much more now than he saw them when we were married and the children agree with that.

Delia Garrett: He's probably better with them now than he was when we were married. He actually spends time with them which he didn't do before.

Colin Hanks: I feel more of a father now. I think the most important thing for me, anyway, is to show a healthy interest in the children and a respect for the children.

Felicity Lessing: I thought it was simply a duty that he was performing in order to do his bit as the absent father, but it wasn't at all. That's when the establishment of the relationship between him and the children really began. . . . I thought that was part of my job, to keep them out of the way, but now, being boys and being interested in the same sort of things as him, he can offer them so much now. . . . They are the most important things in his life and he has blossomed with them since we split up.

Ingrid Milton: His best interest would be to have the two of us together but I certainly think that we're better parents separate! His father is certainly a better father, there's no question of that.

Terry Watts: Since we split up me and Philip are really, really close. In fact we're like brothers now. He don't call me 'Dad' no more, he calls me 'Terry'. Me dad were telling me that they used to call their dad 'John' when they got older. I don't mind but we are really a lot closer than we used to be.

Jim Walters: I think probably I take more responsibility as a father now than I did when I lived there, in a sense. It was very much one of our sources of disagreement right from them being newborn babies. . . . But now, when I've got them on my own then I've obviously got to make decisions.

The popular emphasis on disengaging fathers and hostilities between parents can obscure the extent to which post-divorce childhood provides a unique opportunity for children to get to know their parents in a new way. After separation fathers are often for the first time having to take sole responsibility for their children even if it is only on alternate weekends. Becoming a part-time primary carer means that many fathers experience a relationship with their children which is usually available only to mothers. Structurally speaking they move into a different place in relation to their children and as a consequence their children's childhood changes and arguably becomes richer in this respect.

Of course not all fathers changed in this way. Many were able to sustain contact in the same style as they had fathered. Thus they would take the children round to the paternal grandmother's house for tea or they would leave the responsibility to their new partners. But this does not overshadow the important transformation undergone by a minority of these fathers. We might say that these fathers started to experience a different kind of love, one which carried caring responsibilities and not just distant affection. Their ideas about father/child relationships were invariably transformed and the potential for such a transformation seemed to us to be linked to parents' understanding of the meaning of childhood and the value attached to the child. It is to this issue that we now turn.

The meaning of childhood

In trying to analyse our interview data, we obviously attempted to understand why it was that some parents treated children and parenting so differently after divorce. The result was a set of issues apparently independent of the parent/parent relationship, independent of the divorce itself, but related to what parents think a child is and what childhood means (James and Prout, 1990).

Other studies which have focused more exclusively on childhood have attempted to produce models of how parents see or think about children and to relate these to child-rearing practices (Alanen, 1992). Hallden (1991), for example, refers to two metaphors with which parents work, namely the 'child-as-project' and the 'child-as-being'. She was studying twenty skilled working-class Swedish families and trying to map the relationship between the parents' practices and their understanding of child development, child welfare and the individual needs of their children. The child-as-project metaphor was one in which the parents saw their role as intervening in the child's development which could be speeded up or modified, while the child-as-being metaphor embraced the idea of the child developing at its own pace or 'unfolding' according to its own momentum. In the latter instance the parents' role was that of an 'introducer' rather than as a 'stimulator'. Although Hallden recognizes that parents could work within the boundaries of both metaphors, in her study the parents primarily saw the child-as-being.

Our study was not designed to be able to make the sort of links that Hallden can make between 'folk' psychology and child-rearing styles; however, her study lends support to our less fully formed idea that how parents see and understand childhood can be very varied and gives rise to very different reactions and types of interaction at the point of divorce or separation. There seemed to be two distinct axes along which the understanding of our sample of parents could be positioned. One axis was concerned with independence/dependence. At one end of this axis parents saw their children as dependent upon them for moral and emotional support, while parents at the other end saw them as forging an independent moral and emotional life quite apart from the sphere of parental influence. This axis is not dissimilar to the child-as-project and child-as-being metaphor, except that in our model parents felt no moral responsibility for the child-as-being, which would not be true of Hallden's parents. Our other axis was concerned with autonomy/subordination. Here some parents saw their children as having a (growing) right to autonomy and separateness, while others at the opposite end of the axis saw their children

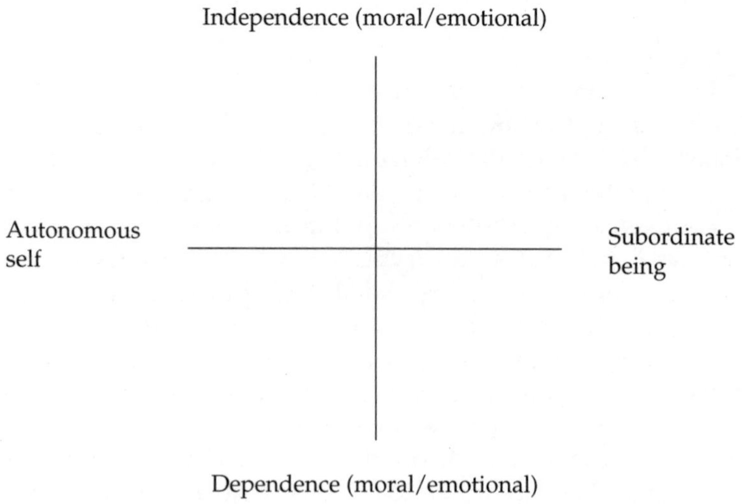

Figure 5.1 Model of parents' visions of the child

as extensions of themselves; to be told what to do until they left home. Although it seems to be a contradiction in terms, some of the parents who saw their children as their possessions also saw them as independent moral and emotional beings who were fully responsible for their actions. Other parents who saw their children as emotionally and morally dependent upon them (and therefore their parents' responsibility) also felt that the children had a right to autonomy and separateness. This may seem counter-intuitive, but the complex relationship between autonomy and dependence, and between subordination and independence, does actually seem to capture the nature of these parent/child relationships.

No doubt the model of these two axes of dependence and autonomy shown in figure 5.1 is an oversimplification but what became apparent to us in our interviews with the parents was that the ways in which children were *spoken of* varied greatly. It was therefore hardly surprising that, seemingly independent of important class differences, children's life-worlds varied greatly. Children in very similar class locations had very different childhoods. It would seem therefore that we can hardly start to understand post-divorce childhood until we ground our analysis much more in these multiple realities rather than in the two-dimensional framework of divorced (bad) and intact (good) families. We explain this more fully below.

How the parents understood childhood

To some extent a parent's perception of a child is related to gender. Thus there may be a difference of perception between mothers and fathers. But this is not inevitable and, as suggested above, typical fathers can successfully transform themselves into typical mothers in terms of how they parent their children. Another important element in the construction of childhood is the age of a child. That is to say different parents think that children become independent, culpable, intentional and so on, at very different ages. Some might see children of seven as largely responsible for themselves and their actions, while others would not hold this view until the child reached sixteen or even older. Some see a child as an extension of themselves and presume that the purpose of a child is to satisfy the adult.

Some see children as emotionally and morally autonomous beings who choose how they will behave and relate to other people from a very early age, certainly by the time they can talk. This perception of children is quite different from one which acknowledges that a child has its own personality, but which sees the way in which this is manifested as being influenced by interactions with others, particularly parents. From the former perspective the child is regarded as fully formed as a person long before he or she is capable of physical independence, being treated very much as an adult in this dimension, but as a child in every other way. So for example the child is treated as being responsible (i.e. as an adult) for 'bad' behaviour while being punished like a child.

> **Bren Neale**: Did your relationship with Patrick (aged four) change at all at the time of separation?

> **Bill Merton**: He used to wind me up. He were a little bugger for that. He was always doing stuff that he shouldn't do. He's an attention-seeking kiddie and always has been.

In this exchange it is possible to see that the child is seen as responsible for his behaviour and has been for some time even though he is only four years old. Moreover, his behaviour is seen as deliberately designed to anger or upset his father. Compare this with the following:

> **Leon Holt**: The elder one (eight years) went for about six months kicking her and it was only in anger and I would come in and Jill would say, 'Tell him off' and I said, 'No, I'm not telling him off, I'll talk to him about it.' So I would wait, take him in the car and talk to him about it. 'Do you think it's right to kick your mum?' 'Well no, but she made me angry' and then I say 'It's difficult for her.'

In this second case the father sees his role as taking his son along a path towards moral responsibility and giving him the ability to control his temper. In the first case the child would simply be smacked for being difficult, in the second the father understands why the boy is misbehaving and so does not add to his unhappiness by punishing him and appearing to reject him more. After a few months the boy's behaviour changed and he became much more settled.

The view of a child as a fully formed, separate being could have negative elements. It could mean that parents did not feel particularly responsible for what was going on in their child's lives and it was assumed that they did not need to be protected from their parents' emotions and behaviour.

> **Jodie Hitchens**: [My daughter] actually wrecked their wedding, she wrecked the reception and I knew she would because she did not want them to get married and since they've been married I've had nothing but hassle from her – from her up there – 'cos she turns round and tells me, 'Now I can do what I like, I'm her stepmother.' And I go, 'Well you're bloody not!' and I go hell for leather at them. He doesn't like it so he goes at me, she doesn't like it when we're friends, so she goes at me. It's like I'm at loggerheads at her, everybody's at me, even me own little lass. I mean, two or three weeks ago I actually felt like I was losing Alice to her dad and on Saturday gone I actually turned round to him and said, 'I'm not losing my daughter to you! I've brought her up, I've done this, that and the other with her, why the hell should she take it out on me when it's you that's bloody shouting at her?'

Jodie and her ex-husband had dreadful fights over their daughter, often in public and always in front of her. It did not seem to occur to either of them that this might be part of the reason why her behaviour was so disturbed. Compare this with Linda Hewitt's account of an occasion when she started to argue with her ex-partner in front of their son.

> **Linda Hewitt**: He'll say, 'I'm not going to talk about it now in front of David.' 'OK, well phone me.' 'I'm not going to pay for a phone call to you.' 'Fine.' We had a scene not very long ago which was awful where he picked him up and he was taking him somewhere for the weekend and I said, 'When will you be back?' and he said, 'I don't know.' I said, 'Well, that's not good enough, I need to know.' 'Well, why should you know?' 'Because I have arrangements to make and I want to know when you're bringing him back.' 'Well, I don't know.' We were standing there, David was standing there and I didn't know what to do. I thought, 'I can't just let him do this,' so I said 'You're not taking him in that case until you tell me when you're bringing him back.' Things like that are just awful because David was there, we were literally pulling him apart.

Although Linda could not always avoid these hostilities, she regretted them for the effect they must have on her son. As a result, most of the time she swallowed her anger and irritation. The child would, of course, modify his behaviour in the light of these tensions and never spoke about his father when he was with his mother. But he was not wetting the bed and setting fire to the flat, as was the case with Alice above.

Jodie made it clear that she saw her daughter as her possession: although their relationship was volatile and unstable, she claimed that Alice was all she had and that she would not give her up. This attitude towards children sits uneasily with the idea of children as emotionally and morally independent of their parents. It is almost as if the child is seen to exist to fulfil the parents' needs, while at the same time fate has moulded the child into an irascible and difficult person with whom one has to do daily battle. Sometimes the battle got too much for some parents:

> **Sylvia Ashton:** He [son aged ten] didn't want to go at the beginning but the more he's thought about it he seems keener. I said, 'You're wanting attention and I can't give you my full attention because I've three others,' and he seems to have come round. He was more worried that he would have to live in a home or go to live with foster parents, so I said, 'No, if your dad won't keep you, I'll have to persevere and keep you,' which I would.

This quotation is an interesting one. It is not that Sylvia did not care about her son and she probably made the best decision in sending him to his father's, but although she promised to 'keep' him if no one else would have him, he was treated as if he was, at the age of ten, a completely independent being who could be parcelled out among relatives. So while Sylvia loved him, she did not feel she had to go on being responsible for him on a daily basis.

This 'distance' between parents and children can be contrasted with a 'closeness' which may also be harmful. It is clear that a number of our parents became obsessed with their children on separation, and some treated them as their confidantes, keeping them up late and asking their advice. At the point of our second interviews with parents, we often found that they could reflect on what they were doing twelve months or so before and redefine their treatment of their children as inappropriate. One residential father, for example, realized that he had to get a job because his children could not be everything to him; a non-residential unmarried father had become less 'desperate' about contact and had started to have a life beyond his baby son, and a number of mothers said they had been wrong to confide too much to their children. The significance of these cases is not so much that the parents were failing their children because they made mistakes, but that they redefined their earlier relationships as inappropriate. This could mean that some children found that they were treated like adults for a while, only to be 'returned' to the status of children later. What was interesting about the way in which the parents redefined their behaviour was that many felt that it had been a mistake to share their emotions too much with their children or that it was a mistake to load too much needy emotion onto the children. Whether or not this sort of behaviour is actually harmful, certainly many of our parents came to think it had been a mistake. In other words these parents became self-reflexive and changed their behaviour.

It was very hard to identify what was different about those parents who were self-reflexive and those who were not. At times it seemed related to social class and educational differences, but this presumption really could not be supported by our data. At other times it seemed related to gender, with women being more self-reflexive in relation to children than men. But again this could not really be sustained and, as suggested above, it was often adopting the role of primary carer rather than gender *per se* which made a difference. Ultimately it seems that it was the parents' understandings of what a child was and what a child was 'for' that made the most difference to the nature of post-divorce childhood.

6

Moral Fragments?

Introduction

We have argued elsewhere (Smart and Neale, 1997a) that divorce has become identified in popular rhetoric as a moment where morality is abandoned. Patricia Morgan, for example, has stated that divorce law 'allies itself with the spouses who want to break up marriages [and] in doing so, it rewards selfishness, egoism and destructiveness over altruistic commitment' (1995: 32). It has also been consistently argued by moral absolutists in the public domain that divorce not only signifies moral decline, but heralds further future moral degeneration (Wheelan, 1995). Richard Harries, the Bishop of Oxford, has stated in relation to modern morality in general that:

> [F]undamental values are there to be recognised, not made
> up as we go along. We need to get away from a pick and
> mix attitude to morality, to acknowledge that certain fun-
> damental moral insights are inherent in the nature of
> things, and are essential for the well-being of both indi-
> viduals and society. (*Guardian*, 1 January 1997)

It is possible to argue, therefore, that we are witnessing a re-emergence of a subterranean debate on the morality of divorce and the moral values of those who opt to follow this course. This debate was given momentum by the Conservative Government's Family Law Bill in 1995, which sought, among other things, to abolish once and for all the residue of a 'fault-based' divorce law which had been bequeathed by the compromises of the Divorce Reform Act of 1969 (Law Commission, 1990). But the Bill did not revive the debate so much as give it a more public airing and new legitimacy.

The absolutist moral position on divorce needs to be distinguished from the more common set of concerns which have surrounded divorce for the last twenty years or so. The latter has focused on the harms that divorce, especially acrimonious divorce, might cause to children and more generally on the harms caused by poverty subsequent to divorce for women and children (Kelly, 1993). Such concerns may have included a sense of regret over the rise in the divorce rate over the last twenty years, but have tended to see divorce as a phenomenon to be managed and ameliorated, rather than condemned. The moral absolutist position, however, goes further: the people who divorce must be held morally accountable for any harms; they must be made fully aware that in choosing divorce they are choosing a morally reprehensible path with clearly detrimental outcomes for children and society. This symbolizes a major shift away from the idea inherent in the Law Commission's (1966) original approach to modern divorce law which was encapsulated in the expression that divorce was a misfortune which befell both parties. In the moral absolutist approach, divorce is not to be likened to a natural disaster for which no one is to blame; on the contrary, the idea that couples or delinquent spouses should be blamed is central to the argument. Indeed in the Second Reading Debate of the Family Law Bill (22 April 1996) the Pro-Family Right argued that the courts should not only be able to retain the idea of a fault-based divorce, but that they should be empowered to conduct a 'moral audit' of a marriage in order to apportion blame in a more finely tuned manner. While it was felt that the apportioning of blame by the courts would not save the marriage, it was urged that this was a necessary process in order for the innocent party to be vindicated and the guilty party to become more fully aware of his or her failings and faults in order to be better equipped for a more responsible future.

The public debate about morality and divorce in the mid-1990s has had an exceptionally narrow focus, so that it has become exceedingly difficult to talk about divorce in the context of morality or ethics without falling into – or going to extraordinary lengths to try to avoid – the intellectual and ethical strait-jacket it has created. The discursive framework set up by the absolutists makes available only two positions on divorce: the morally correct position which condemns it and the morally incorrect position which promotes divorce, human misery and national decline. The moral absolute position has also, quite expressly, rejected arguments arising from academic philosophical and sociological work which has attempted to frame questions of morality in a different light and to understand the contexts in which moral decisions are taken. Such approaches are defined as moral relativism or simply woolly, liberal thinking which, in themselves, have contributed to the perceived moral decline at the end of the twentieth century. But although it has become *dangerous* to speak of morality when dealing with divorce, it seems to us that moral questions form such a major part of people's experience of family transitions and breakdowns that we cannot grasp what is happening for them without reference to the bases on which they make decisions and choose courses of action.

We will therefore address the issue of morality but it is important to make clear what we mean by this term. We want to distance ourselves from any fundamentalist position on morality and to make it clear that we are not attempting to make judgements about whether parents make right or wrong decisions. It is not that we could not take a stance (in fact we would clearly repudiate any form of violence in the family and deprecate oppressive and manipulative behaviour) but rather than slipping into the easy pleasure of condemning others, we would rather strive to understand the conditions within which parents make their decisions and to appreciate the difficulties they face when doing so. We have argued elsewhere (Smart and Neale, 1997a) that what makes people moral agents is not whether they always make the 'right' decision but whether they reflect upon the decisions they take and weigh up the consequences of their actions.

We also feel that it is vital to move beyond orthodox ideas about the 'proper' constituent parts of a moral decision. As a consequence we take as our starting-point the work of Carol Gilligan (1982) on the ethic of care. Her ideas have been much commented upon, so we will not elaborate on them here (Tronto, 1989, 1993; Bowden, 1997; Larrabee, 1993; Hekman, 1995). Suffice it to say that Gilligan's original contribution identified the dominant ethical code of Western societies as being based on universalizable concepts such as objectivity and impartiality which she argued reflected a partial world-view more associated with masculine experience than feminine. Thus she argued that a more adequate morality required the addition of an ethic of care which was based on the desire not to harm and on the idea of connectedness which, in turn, reflect a more feminine experience. While acknowledging some of the problems in Gilligan's original thesis, we equally acknowledge that her work has been tremendously important in broadening the criteria for what passes as moral action, and that in particular her work has been vital in the re-evaluation of 'care' as a form of ethical activity and moral thinking. This broader approach is, we find, invaluable when the central issue is how parents are to care for their children after divorce or separation. Indeed we would go further and argue that one of the main problems with the way in which disputes between parents over their children are perceived and dealt with (Smart and Neale, 1997b) is precisely that such disputes are not seen as moral conflicts. Such conflicts are seen only as emotional (and hence selfish) disputes which are, by definition, assumed to be void of moral content. In fact we have almost reached a position where it is assumed that *any* disagreement over children after divorce is always already outside the moral domain (Jolly, 1995). We wish to challenge this construction of the disputes, not least because it seems to have given rise to a punitive response to separated or divorced parents, and even occasionally the astonishing resort to imprisonment to enforce agreement. By analogy, it would be inconceivable to imagine the courts sending a parent to prison where there was a dispute over the religious education of a child. Deeply held views about religion would be respected but equally deeply held views about the care of a child are rarely accorded this kind of respect, precisely because they are seen as driven (solely) by emotion rather than moral reasoning. Thus we want to use the framework for understanding moral decision making generated by Gilligan, most particularly because it allows for a consideration of moral values such as avoiding harm and sustaining connections, rather than seeking to encapsulate the 'morally correct' in the assertion of rights[1] and strict equality. In agreement with Gilligan we would like to argue 'that obligations and relations of care are genuinely moral ones, belonging to the centre and not at the margins of morality' (Benhabib, 1992: 186).

In seeking to explore the moral dimension of the decisions parents make when going through divorce we also turned to the work of Janet Finch (1989). Focusing specifically on family life and obligations owed to kin, she has argued that shared understandings about 'the proper thing to do' emerge over time and in specific contexts, albeit that the context is both social and cultural. Drawing on the work of Jack Douglas (1971) she suggests that moral philosophers have missed the point in analysing moral rules in terms of abstract principles. She argues that the key element about moral decisions is their ambiguity, which is to say that there is always more than one solution to a moral dilemma and people will routinely disagree about the right thing to do in particular circumstances. She goes on to point out that even where people agree to a principle in the abstract, they may well feel that it is inappropriate in a specific circumstance. She therefore uses the term 'social' morality to refer to the way in which people live their lives.

In talking of the way in which ideas about the proper thing to do 'emerge', Finch is not ignorant of power imbalances, particularly of gender and class, nor is she unaware of the way in which situations change such that there may be no fixed morality. She refers to 'patterned changes' which may be events like marriage or widowhood. Such patterned changes bring with them normative expectations and thus they are not experienced as a major upheaval in terms of moral actions, but even these are negotiated, not merely followed or obeyed. So, for example, on widowhood a mother might expect more support from her adult children than before, or on marriage a son or daughter might expect greater independence from their parents. How these events are negotiated may not follow strict rules, however, and specific circumstances might make traditional expectations on the right course of action quite inappropriate. Thus Finch is arguing that when faced with change in their families, people do not simply follow established 'rules' or a normative set of obligations. But this does not make them immoral or amoral.

Benhabib (1992) argues a very similar case, giving the example of a situation where a younger brother faces financial difficulties and there is an obligation on older brothers to help. She points out that refusing to help may be the 'right' moral decision. Her point is that we can know that it is right only by understanding the relationships between the brothers and their past history. Giving financial help might appear to be benevolent, but in some circumstances it might just continue an oppressive relationship of dependence. On the other hand it might simply be the result of callousness and self-interest. Benhabib, unlike Finch, tries to go beyond mapping the contours of the decisions people make, to get to a position where it is possible to make judgements on the content of their decisions. As mentioned above, we are not seeking to do this. But we would be dishonest if we did not admit that we were never appalled or exasperated (or uplifted and delighted) by the moral reasoning and the decisions made by some of the parents we interviewed. We also recognize the dilemma that Benhabib sets out in relation to an over-exclusive attention to the ethics of care. She suggests that the Mafia may be a very caring family, but that their ethic of care does not extend to people beyond their group and that by no stretch of the imagination could they be called morally exemplary. Benhabib therefore seeks to take the ethic of care seriously, but is reluctant to lose a universalizable standard against which more 'local' decisions can be measured. Benhabib's ultimate standard is the preservation of the dignity and worth of another person. While we recognize that dignity and worth are not self-evident categories, we find that this is also our ultimate standard. This point is discussed further in the conclusion of this chapter in the context of the legal processing of moral dilemmas.

To return to Finch, it must be appreciated that she is attempting to do something rather different from the usual work of moral philosophers and political theorists like Benhabib. The immense value of Finch's work (also Finch and Mason, 1993) is that she brings the moral into the realm of the sociologist as a subject of study. Of course, sociologists have always been concerned with values. But these values have tended to be dealt with as problems for the social scientist, who needs to be value-free or who needs to make clear his/her own values when doing sociology. At a different level, sociologists have spoken of *normative* values or *cultural* values, but these have always been in relation to a group, community or society. The issue of *moral* values has been much more problematic; conflicts over moral values have been typically reinterpreted by sociologists as political conflicts or cultural conflicts.

Of course part of the sociologist's reluctance to openly address the question of moral values lies in the fact that it has so clearly been the domain of the philosopher and theologian and so much the subject of philosophical games and abstract argument. Finch and also Bauman (1993) have challenged this hegemony. They both point out in different ways that 'ordinary people' do not have to be versed in the intricacies of moral philosophy in order to act morally or to form moral judgements. It follows that what is of interest to the sociologist is how people do this, rather than whether their form of justification is acceptable to the tenets of philosophical argument. So, unless sociologists are going to gloss over this important aspect of agency, it follows that we need to cease to be coy about addressing morality.[2] But it means that we do not have to address it in the way that philosophers have done. It also means that sociologists *qua* sociologists do not have to produce definitive statements on the criteria for defining the good life even though sociologists as historical and cultural subjects will inevitably import self-reflexive values into their work.

'Ordinary' people and moral action

Bauman argues that, '"To be moral" does not mean "to be good", but to exercise one's freedom of authorship and/or actorship as a choice between good and evil' (1995: 1). His use of the terms 'authorship' and 'actorship' in this sentence is significant: authorship suggests that one is making one's own history with the consequent responsibility for the consequences that will follow; actorship presumes both a will and a consciousness and is to be differentiated from the concept of behaviour which may lack intentionality. Thus for Bauman coerced rule-following could not be deemed moral action. It is for this reason that he argues that in postmodern societies we become more moral than in traditional societies because there are increasingly few straightforward rules to follow. For Bauman we are obliged to reflect upon our choices of action rather than to follow custom. His argument is therefore the complete antithesis of the moral absolutists, who seek to reimpose clear rules to make us more moral again.

Approaching this issue more empirically, Finch has shown that normative guidelines (if not hard rules) are significant to ordinary people when they are faced with difficult decisions. But she sees these as starting-points and not finishing-points; her interviewees went through a process of balancing a range of factors while conscious of traditional systems of kinship obligation and duty. She devised a normative schema which reflected the processes that people underwent as follows:

- consider who this person is; what their relationship is to you in genealogical terms

- consider whether you get on particularly well with this person

- consider the pattern of exchanges in which you and they have been involved in the past

- consider whether receiving assistance from you would disturb the balance between dependence and independence in this person's family relationships

- consider whether this is the proper time in both your lives for you to give this type of assistance to this particular person.

(1989: 178)

These normative guidelines are not exactly the ones which would apply to divorcing parents considering their children's future and so we suggest that, on the basis of our interviews, they can be modified as follows:

- consider the present quality of their relationship with their spouse/partner

- consider the nature of this relationship in the past

- consider whether the action considered would disturb family relationships (especially between children and parents but also including grandparents)

- consider whether this is the proper time to act (especially in relation to the age of the child or stage of a relationship)

- consider the degree of harm/benefit that would accrue to all those involved.

Whereas Finch's and Mason's (1993) interviewees were asked questions about the help they would give to relatives in hypothetical situations and to reflect upon moral decisions taken in the past, our interviewees were still going through very real changes in their lives which were still causing a number of dislocations. Moreover, they found themselves making decisions in the shadow of a new divorce ethos (namely the Children Act), in the context of much publicity over the harms to children of divorce, and in the context of what might be called shorthand purposes, a new project of the self. It is necessary to give some consideration to each of these factors before turning to our interviews with parents.

The new ethos of the Children Act is discussed above (p. 37f.), but it is worth underlining here that the prioritizing of joint post-divorce parenthood has meant that it has become aligned with a notion of the public good or virtue. Thus parents encounter a very clear policy on what is best for their children which is quite at odds with the former, less clearly stated principle of maternal preference. Thus the range of decisions they may make are significantly different from the sort of options which might have been taken for granted a decade ago. In addition to this they have to consider the weight of evidence which suggests that children are inevitably harmed by divorce.[3] Most parents are aware of this evidence through media representations and therefore face the classic dilemma of whether to stay together for the sake of the children with imperfect knowledge of research on these potential harms as well as anticipations about financial insecurity. In the late 1980s there was much less general awareness of the idea of psychological harms to children of divorce and so this now constitutes an added factor for parents to 'balance'. Finally, parents are making decisions about their children at a time when they are also making decisions about the direction of their own lives. The idea of having a 'life of one's own' is not new for men, but it is relatively new for women, especially mothers. Divorce often coincides with a period of profound personal change and a seeking of new goals and purposes. One option that is no longer readily available to mothers in this situation is the option of remaining a full-time mother[4] (unless they remarry quickly). While men in this situation can often just continue with their careers or jobs, women are faced with rather different choices (Joshi, 1991). If they work part time they may have to move to full time, or possibly they may have to give up a full-time job because of childcare arrangements. Of course there may be similar changes for some men too: some opt to give up work in order to become full-time fathers; others change directions in their careers to have more time for their children; some who were already unemployed or redundant decide to stay unemployed. The point is that, unlike the situations that Finch presented to her interviewees, our parents were making moral decisions in the context of major life changes and at a time when they might, quite deliberately, be becoming (or trying to become) different people. Divorce can therefore be said to be a kind of threshold to a self-conscious project of the self while at the same time being a moment when attention is focused on the fact that mothers and fathers are not actually autonomous and 'unencumbered' but deeply enmeshed in a caring relationship with a dependent child who is, in turn, enmeshed in historical family relationships which make radical transformations of the self exceedingly difficult. Balancing the needs of children with the needs of the self in this situation was one of the main moral dilemmas facing parents.

In order to explore these ideas we propose to take a number of case studies from our sample of sixty parents which exemplify most coherently the way in which parents reason morally over the post-divorce care of their children. These cases are chosen because they clearly articulate common dilemmas and because the parents were able to describe stages in their reasoning.

The case studies

Valuing the children's father: Stella Drew

Stella Drew was married to Nick and had two sons, aged six and four at the time of their separation. The thing that triggered the breakdown of their marriage was her discovery that he had been having a long-term affair with another woman with whom he had a child who was the same age as their youngest son. Nick had effectively created two families and moved between them. It is not hard to imagine how devastating the discovery was, especially as the other woman lived just around the corner. Nick had not wanted to choose between his wife and his partner and had become violent when Stella insisted on a divorce. The whole sequence of events triggered a major re-ordering of Stella's understanding of her husband, her situation and herself. Because he did not want to leave, Stella had to take the responsibility for the decision formally to end their marriage and for the disruption that it would cause their sons. A year after our first interview with Stella, Nick was still suggesting that he wanted to come back to her. This is how she dealt with the dilemma his 'offer' caused:

> **Stella**: When he first said it I got really depressed for two weeks because I thought, 'I can't afford not to consider this because of the boys and although I may want to just dismiss this, I'm actually gonna have to think about this.' I thought, 'I don't want to open all those boxes that I've dealt with and put away. I don't want to have to look at all of that again.' And I thought, 'Well, I'm going to have to,' and for a couple of weeks I got very depressed and I did open all the boxes again and look at everything and then I just thought, 'That's the best decision I ever made in my life and I'm really glad I did it.' I'm not saying it was all bad, of course it wasn't, we had some great times, but actually he's really dangerous, really aggressive and really frightening and you can't have a reasonable relationship with somebody like that and I didn't realize how submissive he'd made me.

This passage encapsulates a range of the factors that Stella had to 'balance' in order to come to the 'right' decision. She was prepared to look again at a relationship that had been very destructive for her, for the sake of the children. She acknowledged that they would probably want their father back, but she also realized that she would have to give up her new 'self' in order to go through with it. On reflection she felt that she had become a different person in the intervening period and really could not go back to accepting such a relationship. In spite of the obvious emotional problems Stella had faced on discovering that her husband had another family, she had worked hard to make contact between Nick and the boys work well. They stayed with him, his partner and their half-sister for one night every weekend and one night during the week. There were no arguments about the arrangements and they were both perfectly amicable with each other. But Stella was aware that it was 'a complete charade and it's people playing games to keep it nice for the boys and it's not reality'. She was prepared to control her anger, to be nice to his partner, and to encourage her sons to get on with their half-sister even though this was not her inclination. But in accord with her 'project of the self' she had also started to make changes. When he first moved out of the matrimonial home he used to come back when he wanted and just let himself in. He told her she was not allowed to move house and he refused to pay for the children's education unless they went to the school of his choice. In response to all of these measures, designed to continue controlling her life, she moved house and denied him casual entry, got herself a new partner and merely said that she would pay for the children's education herself. But at the same time she had decided not to live with her new partner and not to marry him because she knew that her sons (who said they would like her to remarry) might then get less of her attention and she wanted them to have complete stability for a few more years.

It was clear from her narrative that Stella had become the author of her own life and that she was constantly weighing up the moral decisions she had to take. But she was not abandoning a responsibility for her 'self' in the process of caring for her sons. Her experience of post-divorce parenting was hard but she made herself co-operate with her former husband while refusing to let him bully her. In spite of his violence and his ongoing rages, she was willing to treat him as a worthy person. In this sense she still cared about him. She did not deprecate him in front of their sons and this should be seen as a moral decision in itself. The eldest son witnessed some of the rows and the violence before his father left and he clearly had difficulties in trusting his father again. Moreover, both children were fully aware of how devastated their mother was and how ill the breakdown of the marriage had made her. It would have been both easy and understandable if she had done nothing to assist or even actively discouraged contact. It is important to recognize how much emotional and moral work went in to the way that Stella sustained contact. Terminology around the issue of contact suggests that the parent with residence merely 'permits' contact. The term 'permit' implies a passive state, as if the parent has to do nothing. But the residential parent has to do a great deal if the contact (or shared parenting) is to be at all meaningful or successful. Not only does the residential parent have to treat the other parent well, she has to overcome the fact that the other parent may have had a complete disregard for her worth and dignity as a human being. Moreover she may have to tolerate ongoing abuse of this kind.

It is for this reason that we see post-divorce parenting as comprising a number of moral elements and decisions. Within this framework it becomes perfectly possible to understand that certain circumstances are intolerable and that to insist on an ongoing joint parenting project where the moral (including caring) basis for such an enterprise is absent can be construed as mere coercion. Not all parents would balance the factors in the way that Stella did. If they took them into account and came to a different conclusion they would still be moral actors, however.

Prioritizing the Children: Jessica Hunt

Jessica Hunt had two sons, aged six and four when we first interviewed her. The children live with her and at the time of the second interview their contact with their father Alec had increased to all day each Sunday and on Monday and Tuesday evenings when they had football practice. Jessica wanted Alec to see them more often, in particular to have them to stay overnight. In fact she would have liked a shared parenting arrangement because she found the responsibility and the work of raising two boys was exhausting. She was not only working a thirty-hour week but was also studying at college to try to improve her prospects. Alec refused to pay maintenance for the boys and the Child Support Agency had become involved so their relationship was acrimonious. But although the father would not share the boys' care more, he said he would take 'full custody' of them which would allow him to give up work. At times she felt like agreeing to this.

> **Jessica**: Yeah, I mean sometimes you feel like saying, 'Yeah, you get on with it, let's see what kind of a job you can do,' because he's always having a go at me 'cos I don't do this right, I don't do that right and sometimes you just feel like, 'Right, blow it, you have the kids on a full-time basis, see how you could cope. Could you do a better job?' But then I suppose my mother instinct comes over and that's why I won't let them go.

In alluding to her 'mother instinct' Jessica was referring to her ability to care for the boys, which she believed made her a better parent than their father. Of course by referring to it as an instinct she was treating it as a natural category rather than a social or moral activity. It is precisely this tendency to treat 'caring for' others (Tronto, 1993) as instinctual behaviour rather than moral action which made Jessica's assertion seem simply self-serving. We want to argue that this is not selfishness but actually altruism, in other words she was putting the interests of her children first. Later in the interview this became clear because she had spoken seriously to the children about whether they wanted to live with their father and she had even begun to think about the transition in a practical way:

> **Jessica**: I do listen to them and sometimes I'll say to them, 'Do you want to go to live with your dad?' . . . They say, 'Yeah sometimes we'd like to live with dad because dad says that he's got to give you money now and we'd be better off if we live with him and dad wants us to live with him.'

Subsequently their father asked her to let him have 'custody' of the boys and so she thought about it. She agreed with the children that they would start by staying over at weekends and she put it to Alec that it would be best to have a trial period and to ease the children and himself into a new situation. This was because even when he had the children it was either the maternal or paternal grandmothers who cooked their teas, collected them from school, and did the basic caring work.

> **Jessica**: So I put this to Alec. I said, 'Look, if you really, really feel that you can look after these kids on a full-time basis, don't you think you ought to give yourself a weekend with them and then just see how it feels and then maybe after a weekend maybe progress to say you're having them for a full week and see how you cope with them.' He just absolutely hit the roof because he's got this thing in his head that he'd be baby-sitting for me, so he said 'No.' I said, 'Look, in that case I'm not even prepared to discuss it with you because I feel you just don't know how hard it is, you haven't had the children on a full-time basis for three years, I do feel that you're just out of it a little. [I feel you should have them] in a normal everyday routine, bringing them to school, picking them up from school, cooking, cleaning, washing and ironing for them, helping them with their homework, if they're sick, nursing them. And then we will rediscuss, reassess the situation.

In this passage Jessica was articulating the component parts of what it meant actually to 'care for' children rather than simply 'caring about' them (Smart, 1991). Moreover, she was planning a possible transition, one in which the children would have time to decide and in which both parents would have an opportunity to experience the reality of such a fundamental change. She was keeping the children's options open and it was also clear that she acknowledged how much the boys loved their father and how much she was willing to try to work with him for the sake of the children. But it was also important to recognize the quality of the relationship that she had with her husband during their marriage. She divorced her husband because of his continual sexual abuse of her. She was therefore faced with a very difficult dilemma. Because she came from a broken home she did not want her marriage to end but the marriage was destroying her.

> **Jessica**: No. I mean, I regret it that it didn't work out for the kids' sake. . . . So I have regrets that way but in my heart of hearts it would have never worked out and I know that because when I actually gave him that opportunity for that month . . . he went worse than ever. I mean, I know in my heart of hearts, that man will never change. I know and I knew if I didn't leave him, get away from him somehow, I probably would have committed suicide or something.

Jessica was clearly balancing a number of factors. She did not want to damage the children but she made the decision that the marriage was so harmful to her that she had to end it. Although her relationship with her husband was appalling (for example when she first got the injunction to have him removed from the house he would regularly phone Social Services and say she was starving the boys or mistreating them), she still worked with him as a parent. She had also embarked upon a new project of the self. This was focused on her college course, and although doing this course made her life harder in the short term, she wanted to plan for a better future. She ensured that the boys still had contact with their grandparents and she encouraged them to see more of their father.[5] If we return to the moral reasoning schema that we borrowed from Finch's work it was clear that Jessica has gone through all these stages.

- consider the present quality of their relationship with their spouse/partner
- consider the nature of this relationship in the past

- consider whether the action considered would disturb family relationships (especially between children and parents but also including grandparents)

- consider whether this is the proper time to act (especially in relation to the age of the child or stage of a relationship)

- consider the degree of harm/benefit that would accrue to all those involved.

We did of course find a number of instances where the process of balancing produced quite different decisions. Where a present and past relationship with a spouse or partner had been abusive and damaging it was often impossible for parents to allow these experiences to weigh lightly in their calculations. It is also extremely difficult to act morally if the person with whom you are interacting refuses to do the same. Moreover, these parents were on a steep learning curve. Some had come from families where there had been divorce and so had a reflexive sense of what should be done to make matters easier for their own children. But others found themselves in completely new territory and their ability to balance competing demands/needs was not fully formed. In other words they made lots of mistakes, but could often see that there had been errors of judgement.

Reflexivity: Bella Tomkins

One of the clearest examples of a mother acknowledging errors of judgement was the case of Bella Tomkins. Her husband had been violent and she left him together with their daughter, aged two at the time. The father had had occasional contact with the daughter, but was not really interested in her and had since ceased all contact. Bella was still in touch with her former mother-in-law and her daughter went to see her, in fact she named the baby after her. After her separation Bella went to live with her parents and then found her own flat and started life as a single parent.

> **Bella**: I was having various boyfriends and so on. I had a few different relationships, sort of, a few [one] after another, and a work colleague said, 'What do you think your daughter's gonna think of you? She must have an opinion on what you're doing with all these boyfriends!' I thought, 'Oh, yeah!' All of a sudden the penny dropped and I stopped and I thought, 'I'm not getting

anywhere,' 'cos I was just meeting people and having a relationship and there was no stability to it. . . . I think I was scared of being lonely actually, I was scared of being alone for the rest of my life and I was scared that when Jean grew up I would be on my own so therefore I had to get out and be with somebody.

In this instance Bella readjusted the balance between her needs and those of her daughter; she was able to see things from her daughter's point of view and change her behaviour. She also revealed another telling moment where she decided that she had to change herself.

Bella: Well like I say, I used to worry and once there was a time, I think I told you, when I really lost control and I just belted her and she flew across the room. I lost control and I knew that I'd done wrong at the time, but it's so easy to get into that and it's me, it wasn't Jean at all, I was cross with her, but it was me. But, like I say, it's difficult to see your own problems, your own reality because you're inside yourself. It's easy to blame everything but it's more difficult to actually sit and say, 'Well, it's me.' . . . But I was lucky because I went into a shop and I saw this book and I thought, 'Oh yeah,' and I read it and it clicked for me and it worked and I really understood then, I thought, 'Oh yeah, right, change your ways,' but not everyone can do that.

These re-appraisals and deliberate changes also occurred in relationships between parents. An important element in such changes was one partner's ability to see the situation from the other's point of view. But again this could be extremely difficult if only one parent was prepared to do it because there would be no reciprocity. Some parents could tolerate this lack of reciprocity and did endure it for the sake of their children, but some could not because it seemed to call for a virtual erasure of the self at a time when they were actively restructuring their selves.

Some parents were more sensitive to the fear of this kind of erasure than others. In particular it seemed to be the case that fathers feared erasure. This is not surprising, given that there is little clarity over what it means to be a father after divorce. It is generally accepted that fatherhood has tended to be part of a package which includes marriage and the removal of the marriage leaves fathers in a social vacuum. This is even more apparent where there has never been a marriage and where a relationship may have been short-lived. This seemed to give rise to a situation in which many fathers were ill-equipped to work through some of the finer points of balancing competing obligations and needs. We found that at moments of conflict many fathers reached quickly for what might be called an ethic of justice rather than an ethic of care. That is to say they invoked the principles of rights and equality combined with assertions about their social status as fathers.

Mick Jennings: I haven't got a say in which school he goes to or anything. The solicitor said to me, and he was trying to get out of telling me that I hadn't got equal rights, he says, 'You've got equal parental responsibility,' so I says 'Have I got equal rights?' He says, 'You've got equal responsibility,' so I says, 'Now come on, have I got equal rights?' He says, 'No.'

Anthony Dart: I've been discussing schools since he were two. I said 'Don't shut me out.' And I made her aware of the legal standpoint. I says, 'You have a duty as a caring parent' – which is a joke – 'to inform me of his schooling and his medical records.' I says, 'By statute.' And then I throw the law at her.

Gordon Fenton: [If] I have a complaint about the legal system it's this, they made the whole thing a heck of a lot more protracted. You see . . . if it's gonna take another four hearings to [settle] the judge ought to be prepared to put Anita in prison. . . . Now, you know, if the courts would simply do what the courts are supposed to do, which is prevent crime by punishing people who commit crime – you see society doesn't see this as a crime, to me it's legal kidnapping.

All of these fathers were involved in protracted hostilities and saw the law as a way of imposing a desired outcome, or as failing miserably to do so (this point is explored further in chapter 8). Of course there may be no other option save a resort to legally backed negotiations, but there are serious risks associated with such a strategy because of the further damage it does to future negotiations. This is most especially the case when the law is used to bludgeon the other party. There are also consequences for children in such a situation. Many of the parents we interviewed who were having difficulties over contact had to balance these competing claims. The following father was a good example:

Ron McNair: I think the only rule of thumb is that it ultimately has to be in my son's welfare. The solicitor helped me with this. But that must also take into account the parents and that's why I've hesitated from bringing any kind of legal action into it. . . . I feel as though I am ending up in a situation where I'm having to back off all the time in order for his welfare to be better looked after.

The difference between Ron and the three fathers quoted above is not simply that he came to a different decision on his ultimate approach, but that he reflected upon the consequences of different courses of action. Having weighed them up, he selected what he thought would be best for everyone in the situation. It did not occur to Mick, Anthony and Gordon that there might be a different approach and, while mothers too could be equally myopic in various ways, what seems to be clearly gendered is the idea that an appeal to objective standards and legal equality could resolve these delicate negotiations.

These fathers might have thought that their actions were entirely morally justified, but the moral code to which they would have appealed would be a long way away from Gilligan's ethic of care. Although these fathers wanted to preserve a relationship with their children, they were not the slightest bit concerned about the quality of their relationship to the mother, nor how their actions would affect the quality of their own relationship with their child and their child's relationship with their mother. It would of course be entirely misleading for us to give the impression that fathers reasoned morally in one way while mothers did it in a different (better) way. Gilligan (1982) does not essentialize moral reasoning in this way but rather talks about 'ideal types' which can be depicted as masculine and feminine, but which are available to both women and men. So we are not saying that there is a simple or clear-cut difference which can be uncovered, but we did find that mothers were more likely to articulate a clear ethic of care than fathers and that where an ethic of justice was articulated it was almost exclusively used by the fathers.

Articulating an Ethic of Care: Meg Johnson and Ingrid Milton

One of the clearest examples of an ethic of care is contained in the following extract from an interview:

Bren Neale: What would you say makes for successful parenting after divorce?

Meg Johnson: I think the very, very important thing is to respect each other and to show a commitment that you are – although you don't love one another – you care about the two children that you are bringing up together and there's that element that I think is beginning to move out of our family unit. Dan is stopping that caring for how I feel about what's happening to the children.

Bren Neale: So he's not caring for you as the children's mother any more?

Meg Johnson: Yes, and I don't think that involves, that doesn't involve love at all. And I think when you feel that you start to resent – I know I am beginning to resent his contact so that, and the communication itself, I mean, I suppose that's part of the care isn't it, because if you're communicating you're caring about how things are. . . . It's about how I see things for them and what's important to them and knowing that somebody is interested in that side of things.

This passage depicts the delicate intertwining of relationships of care after divorce. Meg was arguing that it was important that the father of her children cared about her *as a mother*. When they had initially separated they were committed to co-parenting and considered that they were still a family even though Dan had another relationship. They worked very closely in the raising of the children. But Dan eventually decided to sell his house and move further south. He saw much less of the children and started to commit much of his time to his new life. This meant that arrangements became more difficult while at the same time he stopped being involved in her mothering and in joint decision making over the children. As a consequence, as she suggested, she started to find it hard to be as positive about his fathering.

Meg distinguished between the kind of care (of a parent) that is required after divorce with the love (of a spouse) which may have existed before the estrangement. Not many of our parents could express this as clearly as Meg, although many were actively engaged in doing this sort of caring. It is interesting that there is no exact terminology which captures this kind of relationship and it would seem that where such a relationship does exist it is often seen as inappropriate by family and, in particular, by new partners. It was therefore not only difficult to form and sustain such care relationships with no name, but they come under intense pressure when they seem to spoil or prevent the formation of pure love relationships with new partners (Giddens, 1992).

While Meg's comments are a good example of one dimension of an ongoing caring relationship, Ingrid's provide a slightly different approach to the same theme. When Ingrid left her husband she decided that it would be best for her seven-year-old son to stay with him.

> **Bren Neale**: Is the relationship between Andrew [son] and John [father] any better or any worse than it was?

> **Ingrid Milton**: I think it's hard for me to say but I think it's probably quite a really close relationship, yes, and it's very important. I do not wish to deprive Andrew of it and I think probably one of the problems at the time [of separation] – which I have now worked through – was that I was thinking that he would come and live here. I think I was really quite anxious about how he would retain his contact with his father. In a sense, he's got a good relationship with his father and he's got me working very, very hard, because I'm very organized, to ensure this side [of the arrangements]. I think it wouldn't work quite that way [if the situation was reversed] because his father's much more disorganized. ... My whole week is geared around organizing to fit in with Andrew, or to see Andrew or to contact Andrew.

This passage reveals the extent to which Ingrid was working to sustain connectedness between the son and his father and between herself and the son. But this caring relationship had to take place in the face of long and unpleasant disagreements over money, 'poisonous' letters from her husband's solicitors, his refusal ever to collect Andrew from his mother's home which was an hour's drive away and his refusal to allow her to attend parent evenings at school. She also took responsibility for things like dentist and hair appointments and buying all her son's clothes. There was little active communication between Ingrid and John and so the caring that went on was not the direct kind that Meg referred to; instead, Ingrid facilitated a situation in which Andrew and John could have a good relationship, while she continued to do a great deal of the sort of caring that a residential parent might normally do. She likened her situation to that of a parent whose child was at boarding-school. Although she was not carrying out routine activities with him every day, she always had a watching brief while also doing the active caring when he was at home.

We would want to argue, along with Gilligan and Benhabib, that these are the 'obligations and relations of care [which] are genuinely moral ones, belonging to the centre and not at the margins of morality' (Benhabib, 1992: 186). But we also recognize that there are circumstances in which it is impossible to sustain such relations of care. As pointed out above, Benhabib argues that there has to be an ultimate or universalizable standard within which such 'local' relations should operate. She proposes that the preservation of the dignity and worth of the other person should be the standard. In the situation we are dealing with, this would mean the dignity and worth of the mother, father and the child(ren). If one of these is severely compromised then it might be unjustified to expect individual parents to go on caring for the other parent or facilitating the connections between child and parent. Meg's and Ingrid's comments might look rather different if we knew that the fathers involved were physically abusive. A mother who left her child with a physically abusive father would be seen as abdicating her caring role, as not acting in a morally responsible fashion. But this example is relatively easy to judge, what is more difficult to evaluate are cases where it is the dignity and worth of the parent which is at stake rather than the dignity and worth of the child.

Overriding moral considerations?

One major moral dilemma faced by our sample of parents was precisely how to balance the needs of their children with their feelings about their spouses. Such feelings are obviously complex and heightened at the time of divorce. One of the reasons why we interviewed parents twice with a gap of twelve to eighteen months between meetings was precisely to allow time for reflection on these feelings. Some parents were still very hurt and angry at the time of the divorce and we reasoned that their views of their partners might become less hostile with time (if indeed they had been hostile to start with). We assumed therefore that at the later date parents might look differently at the decisions they made and that they might be 'more reasonable'. We thought we could make a distinction between the views that (for example) a wife might have of her husband on learning of (for example) his affair with another woman, with her views of him later on when some of the immediate pain had died down. We quickly discovered that this was far too simplistic a model. As discussed in chapter 4, post-divorce parenting arrangements can change over time and what is clear is that they do not simply move from 'bad' to 'better'. We also discovered that the evaluation made of a spouse at the time of divorce would not necessarily change a year or so later. If it did change, it was often to do with how the ex-spouse was behaving in the post-divorce era rather than returning to some prior evaluation. The significance of this for our discussion of the moral dilemma faced at divorce is that it seems to suggest that people do not lose their judgement or their ability to see good and bad, or strengths and weaknesses in others. Thus, where there has been a cumulative mistreatment of a spouse throughout a relationship, the negative feelings felt at divorce were not trig-gered by the divorce nor were they likely to evaporate unless the partner changed considerably in the post-divorce period.

One of the clearest examples of this concerned a father we interviewed who had been highly critical of his wife and the care she gave to the children after they separated. When we interviewed him eighteen months later we were surprised to find that they had got back together. We expected that he might retract some of his earlier comments or at least soften them. Instead he reiterated what he saw as her weaknesses, especially in relation to the children, but pointed out that while she was hopeless as a single mother, together they made a compatible parenting team.

While it might seem self-evident that how couples relate to one another after divorce is closely linked to the quality of their relationship during a marriage, the legal management of divorce and the focus on the welfare of the child have increasingly come to disregard this issue. It is expected that parents can put these things behind them for the sake of their children. From the exam-ples quoted above, it is clear how parents strive to do this and that there are high emotional costs entailed in doing so. The problem, however, is in deciding when the costs have become too high. When would it be regarded as a moral decision (and thus one that is defensible and legitimate) to decide that the costs are too high? This is the question which forms the core of the next chapter.

Conclusion

We have argued that it is important to base an understanding of decisions about the care of children after divorce or separation in the context of a morality or ethic of care. The importance of this approach is that it avoids the long-standing debate in family law and family policy between the competing claims of rights and welfare. Care is as much about justice (the right thing to do) as are rights, but it is also part of a welfare approach in that it seeks to minimize harm and to sustain positive relationships. Through this framework we can see that parents are making difficult moral decisions when they plan how to care for their children after divorce. We have acknowledged that some take more care over these decisions than others and that sometimes, even by their own admission, they may make unwise decisions. But they are operating within a moral framework not, as the moral absolutists would argue, simply enacting 'selfishness, egoism and destructiveness'.

7

Fragments of Power and the Reconstituted Self

Introduction

In this chapter we wish to explore the extent to which divorce reflects the modern nature of marriage by focusing on how parents struggle to be free of what they see as power relations in order to reconstitute them*selves*. This rather opaque aim obviously needs clarification because there are several ideas embedded therein.[1] We will therefore need to reflect upon, albeit briefly, what we mean by the 'modern nature of marriage', how divorce can be said to 'reflect' this, what is meant by 'power relations', and finally the idea of the 'reconstituted self'.

The modern nature of marriage

Recent sociological accounts of modern marriage are discussed in chapter 1, focusing in particular on the work of Giddens (1991, 1992) and Beck and Beck-Gernsheim (1995). It will be recalled that Giddens suggests that modern marriage is now less closely associated with the 'romantic love complex', with its emphasis on fulfilment through finding the right partner and the idea of the permanence of love. He suggests that modern intimacy is marked by an emotional egalitarianism with an emphasis on becoming a whole person in one's own right (not through status) and by serial relationships if a current relationship is unsatisfactory. Thus the ideal of permanence is no longer seen as good in itself and an individual may feel quite justified in terminating an inadequate relationship. Moreover, he argues that this form of relationship, which requires each partner to reveal their whole selves to the other, is largely driven by women and their rejection of the oppressive nature of more traditional forms of intimate relationships. Although it is clear that in a multicultural society these two (and even other models of marriage and intimacy) can coincide, Giddens sees the pure relationship as in the ascendant. He then seeks to explain the rise in divorce in post-war Britain in relation to this core shift in our understanding of intimate relationships. Thus, we might argue that if marriage and intimacy are changing towards incorporating elements of the 'pure relationship', then it is likely that divorce too reflects some of these ingredients of social change.

Divorce as a reflection of the pure relationship

As argued in chapter 2, divorce policy in England and Wales did indeed embrace elements of the pure relationship for a while. By this we mean that divorce in the 1970s and 1980s increasingly facilitated the idea of the clean break on divorce and permitted husbands to cease supporting their ex-wives. Divorce became the turning over of a new leaf, and remarriage and the reconstitution of the nuclear family were seen as the solution to the ending of the first marriage and as a fresh start. The custody of children was given to one parent and, legally speaking, they could not be shared. In many cases fathers were not even required to support financially their children from a first marriage, particularly if they had more children to support from a second union. Thus divorce was the clear end of a relationship and parties could, in theory, move on unencumbered to form another relationship.[2] These policies changed dramatically in the 1990s, giving rise to the question of whether these policies still 'fit' with the modern conception of intimacy as outlined by Giddens.[3] The Children Act (1989), the Child Support Act (1991) and the Family Law Act (1996) have all challenged the idea that there can, or should, be a 'clean break' on divorce. Indeed the Family Law Act delays the process of divorce, requiring couples to reflect – and to prove that they have reflected

– upon the wisdom of the decision to divorce. Moreover, while it is clear that divorce still ends a legal relationship between a couple, since the implementation of the Children Act it no longer ends the relationship between parents and between parents and children. Thus, *if* the shift towards the pure relationship reflects, at a fairly grassroots level, changing ideas about how intimacy should be conducted in late modernity, then divorce policy is now somewhat out of step. It is therefore likely to confront couples who wish to divorce, with contradictions and difficulties that they will have to negotiate in some way.

Power relations

Although the concept of power relations is not difficult to grasp, it is important to indicate how we are using the term. Firstly we are focusing on gendered power relations as they are played out in marriage. But we do not seek to impose in an *a priori* fashion the idea that all power is 'possessed' by husbands in the marital relationship. While men still have much greater access to material resources than women, we are concerned to explore how power is deployed by both husbands/fathers and wives/mothers. Giddens suggests that in the sphere of intimacy men may be trying to hold onto a form of power which has its roots in nineteenth-century marriage. While we would agree with this in part (for example, many men resort to beating their wives when they try to leave them), the exercise of power is manifested in many more subtle ways than this, by women as well as men. Indeed, what is so interesting about the divorce process is how powerless many men *feel* themselves to be. This is perhaps related to the fact that their concept of being powerful is still associated with an outdated mode of masculinity and fatherhood. The attempt to regain this form of power may be extremely damaging to women and children, but it is also often rather futile and counter-productive. More debilitating than dangerous is another, less recognized, form of deploying power in gender relations. While we discuss both types in this chapter, this second mode, which we call 'debilitative' power, is the form of power which can be said to coincide with confluent love (while violence and brutality were often associated with, and acceptable within, more traditional forms of marriage). Giddens argues that confluent love presumes equality in emotional give and take, and that it is not an obstacle to personal growth and development. Indeed a vital element of this form of intimacy is the ability to reveal concerns and needs to the other while allowing space for autonomy. It follows therefore that debilitative power occurs when one's partner takes more than s/he gives or puts obstacles in the way of personal growth and autonomy. While this form of the deployment of power may seem trivial when compared with violence, for many of the parents we interviewed it was actually more significant. Debilitative power was seen as an attempt to stop the other from becoming a new self or from rediscovering their old selves. This brings us to the significance of the self in the divorce process.

The reconstituted self

For Giddens a prerequisite of confluent love is an engagement with the project of the self. Indeed for him, late modernity is characterized by this attention to the self and the idea that one can make and remake the self. One is not at any time a finished product because there is always room for improvement and achievement. Moreover, he argues that this project of the self is deeply enmeshed with our awareness of various phases of a lifespan. This means that the self can have a history and a future with each stage of life throwing up new challenges or opportunities for the self. Furthermore, an overriding concern becomes the desire for authenticity. This is the search for the true self, or the challenge of being oneself in difficult or varying circumstances. When it comes to intimacy, Giddens further argues that it is vital – given this emphasis on the authentic self – that individuals can allow others also to be their authentic selves and can accommodate the other's personal growth and change through the life course.

Griffiths (1995) approaches this issue from the perspective of a feminist philosopher and her focus on the self has different cadences to those apparent in Giddens which are significant to our research findings. Griffiths emphasizes that although we tend to produce a narrative of the self which presents the self as unified, it is important to recognize that the self is fragmented and that contradictions are inevitable. These contradictions are related to the fact that, as most feminist philosophers now insist, the development of the self is interactive and not a solitary activity. The point is, of course, that the development of a feminine self may proceed differently to the development of a masculine self because women are positioned differently in the material, social and emotional world. Thus feminist work which has tried to give space to women's experience has tended to identify women's connectedness to others as more significant than traditional philosophy, which has focused on men and their freedom from emotional and other encumbrances. The social agent in feminist social theory therefore tends to be a far less isolated agent than the one that Giddens seems to portray. In reading Giddens, it is hard to get away from a feeling that the self he speaks of is a very masculine self. This would not be a problem if he addressed this issue, but throughout his work on intimacy his use of the concept of self is ungendered.

This is particularly noticeable when we turn to the complex issue of autonomy and the self. Autonomy is crucial to the reflexive project of the self in Giddens' work. For him autonomy 'means the successful realisation of the reflexive project of self – the condition of relating to others in an egalitarian way'. He continues, 'The autonomous individual is able to treat others as such and to recognise that the development of their separate potentialities is not a threat' (1992: 189). Thus equality and separateness are his key words. But for feminist social theorists, the concept of equality simply does not work in familial relationships. At times people are needy or dependent, or individuals may have complementary abilities. To elevate equality in this way seems to be a misreading of how intimacy works over time. Griffiths argues:

> [F]ew of them are relations of equality in respect of neediness, power, capability, strength, knowledge, time and experience. All of them are found over all the stages of human life, in which people move from relative dependency to relative self-sufficiency and back to dependency, as a result of ageing, child-bearing, sickness and changes in earning power. (1995: 137)

The focus on separateness is also instructive. Although Giddens is obviously arguing that individuals should not be bound to others in a restrictive way and that they should be able to think differently, hold different ideas and pursue different interests while they are in a relationship, he sees this as arising from the establishment of personal boundaries which should not be transgressed. Feminist work, however, would suggest that the development of potential is based on interdependence. Thus it is often possible to pursue certain interests only because a partner is prepared to look after the children, for example, or to share the financial costs. It is inconceivable that someone could 'fulfil their full potential' unless that person had been, or is being, nurtured in such a way that this goal becomes meaningful and feasible. So potential is not simply a possession of the individual. Feminist work would therefore seek to extend and contextualize Giddens' ideas on intimacy. It is not that autonomy is not also valued by and for women, but it is always autonomy in context. For Griffiths autonomy is 'to be found in being yourself, speaking for yourself, and deciding the course of your own life, in the knowledge that a worthwhile life includes social ties which will change the self that is being, talking and deciding' (1995: 141). It is this kind of autonomy for the self that many of the women we interviewed were seeking and for which they felt that they had to struggle.

In order to reconstitute the self on divorce therefore, it was necessary for many women to disconnect themselves and to cease to be bound up with their former partners. In so doing some re-evaluated their former embeddedness in a relationship as oppressive, but even where they did not, they still had to make a difficult and careful transition. Yet the conditions under which they were making this transition was still one of connectedness – through their children. They had to construct a boundary against the husband while remaining connected to the father. The ease with which this could be attained was often linked to the degree to which the former partner was also willing to change. The more he stayed just as he was during the marriage, the harder was her task. Now, it is of course quite possible that men experience these same processes, but in our interviews there were no real examples of the husbands articulating their experiences in this way. We focus on this issue in the next section, which therefore is about the experiences of a number of key women informants.

Debilitative power and the process of finding oneself

Sally Burton is a middle-class professional woman in her early forties. Her marriage ended because her husband started another relationship. They had two daughters. When they first separated they decided that it would be best for the children if they co-parented and Graham, her husband, would come to the family home regularly to spend time with the girls and would put them to bed during the week. Sally began to find that she had not broken free of their marriage and that she was unable to move forward.

> **Sally Burton**: I think he thought that he could leave, have this new lover and I would still be at home to come back to, and he could come, have meals, spend time with the children and it's only very recently he's begun to realize that that isn't going to happen.

After two and a half years of this arrangement Sally put a stop to him coming to the house.

> **Sally Burton**: I certainly don't think he should be coming to the house, not in the foreseeable future. He's never respected the home since it's been my home. . . . He separated his life but still wanted to come into mine and I felt quite strongly that we should keep separateness. The more he respects that, the less I have to be rigid about it.

These passages show how important it was for Sally to have her own space and to start to disentangle herself from a relationship which was simply holding her back. But she did not work all this out in isolation from her children.

> **Sally Burton**: I had to make a decision that was good for me even though, on the face of it, it looked as if it was a bad decision for the children. . . . I made a good decision for myself and actually it ended up being better all round. So that's the other rule of thumb: it has to be good for the parents, the parents have to feel good about it, being motivated to make it work, otherwise it doesn't work for the children and the children know.

Thus, although Sally is talking about herself, it becomes clear that this 'self' is always in relation to the children. Moreover, this self is one she has 'worked on' and striven for since her marriage ended.

> **Sally Burton**: I don't think I had the tools that I now have, having done the therapy work and all sorts of reading, I'm now much more able to stand on my own two feet and articulate things. My understanding is better and I'm a match for him in an argument now whereas I wasn't before. I would get suppressed [*sic*] and he'd make me feel small.

In this situation it is most unlikely that her former husband would acknowledge that he was deploying what we call debilitative power, indeed Sally's decision to move from a co-parenting arrangement to a custodial one would almost certainly be seen by many as an act of wilful selfishness (see below). This is because we still seem to assume that mothers should not have selves, or certainly not selves that need to be nurtured and attended to. Yet without attending to herself and building her self-esteem, Sally was becoming a mere appendage, someone who merely regretted the ending of her marriage but who was not living her life. As she suggests, once her ex-husband started to treat her with more respect (i.e. to change himself in relation to her new self) they could start to build a more positive relationship. He had, however, tried to stop her taking control of her own space, resorting to solicitors and bitter recriminations. He was not at all happy that she was taking control of her life because it meant that he would have to make accommodations.

In the case of Meg Johnson (see pp. 130–1 above), her husband was not personally oppressive but she began to realize that the post-divorce parenting structure they had put in place was stultifying for her. Her husband had started another relationship and yet he did not want to end his marriage.

> **Meg Johnson:** I think Dan would have liked things to remain the way they were with me accommodating his needs for loving somebody else but remaining a family. So, keeping the domesticity side of things but getting the individuality as well. And I just felt then that I couldn't extend myself if . . . we remained [together].

When they separated it was decided that it would be best for their two sons if Meg lived with them in the house during the week and Dan would move back in at weekends so that he could be a proper father to them. As they lived in a village with Meg's mother nearby, she would go and stay with her mother. During the week Dan would be in his own flat and eventually moved in with his girlfriend. After a period Meg found that this was not working for her.

> **Meg Johnson:** I didn't feel that I had my independence or my space. While Dan could be away from our home and be on his own, doing his own thing, I went to live with my mother and that wasn't

enough. My mother was very accommodating and I did whatever I wanted to, but it wasn't my own home. And I don't think that I wanted to stay in our family home, it was far too large a home to run by myself and I wanted things, different things, in the home for the children.

Here again we have a situation in which the mother is at risk of being effaced while her ex-husband has both his independence and a family. Meg had not been pressured into this arrangement, she had done it because she thought it would be the least disruptive thing for her sons. But ultimately she could not live with it. She wanted her own home, not the old matrimonial home, and she wanted the space to make her own decisions and possibly have a relationship too. So, under pressure from her, it was decided that she would buy her own small house in the same village. The boys could then move between the two homes at regular intervals.

> **Meg Johnson**: Yes, I did consider their needs, but I was thinking about myself too. That I couldn't carry on being just mother and 'spouse' because I wasn't being spouse and that's when I wanted to do something about it.

Sally and Meg express very clearly the need to find themselves again after divorce and these issues of space and independence were a common theme for very many of the mothers. Many hated the way their former husbands would come into the former matrimonial home, ignoring the fact that it was now the woman's space. This seemed to symbolize a lack of respect for their independent personhood and the ability to control this space was very important in the process of rebuilding the self.

Women's sense of powerlessness therefore seemed to be embedded in their inability to become their 'own' person again. Men's sense of powerlessness was quite different; it usually manifested itself when they were unable to control others. It was other-directed rather than inwardly directed. The fathers we interviewed rarely admitted to a problem of self-identity or low self-esteem (although this does not mean that they never experienced these problems). Rather they felt powerless in relation to what they regarded as the favourable *situation* their wives or former partners occupied *vis-à-vis* the children.

Situational power and men's sense of powerlessness

In the case of Sally Burton, quoted above, it would seem that her husband felt himself to be the powerless one. What he objected to was the fact that she was, by the structure of her situation, responsible for the children and that this meant that she could exercise power.

> **Sally Burton**: Well, I know what it is, he thinks that because the children live with me I can say, 'I'd like to go away for two weeks at Christmas, therefore you can have the children.' He thinks I'm saying it suits me and he sees that as me exercising power and getting what I want. I find it very difficult to get him to understand that I don't want the *situation* I'm in. It's just making the best of the *situation* I am in. So it's as if he feels disenfranchised by the legal system and by the fact that the children are with me. (Our emphasis)

Many of the fathers in our sample experienced having to negotiate with their ex-wives as demeaning and as a tangible sign of their powerlessness:

> **Derek Hill**: The initial period was a time when Alison was wanting to wield some power over me so I had to fight over every minute.

> **Jack Hood**: They hold all the cards and you're the one who's got to crawl back. I wanted to give her a good hiding or shake her. I couldn't even upset her. You've got no choice, you've got to go by what they say.

> **Gordon Fenton**: I've nothing to lose by causing all kinds of mayhem, damage and fear, and I know that many blokes are in my position and I just simply think that if the courts don't help me . . .

> **Ben Cook**: She said if I wanted, I could make alternative arrangements to see [daughter] . . . I couldn't take the time off work, it was impossible for me to take time off work. So she basically had me by the short and curlies and there was nothing I could do about it.

> **George Daley**: I can't go up and see him any time I want to, it's got to be done through an appointment, so where does your parental rights come into it?

It is important to try to understand why these fathers felt powerless. None of those who took this confrontational stance were able to negotiate with their wives, they only wanted to make demands. They knew what they wanted and felt it was entirely unfair that there should be any obstacles placed in their way. It is fairly clear that they felt that any constraints placed on their contact with their children were unjustified. They wanted to see the children when they felt like it, they did not want mothers to complain if they took them back late or if they fed them with junk food, they wanted to see the children more but only when it suited them and not when it suited the mothers. The sense of powerlessness and anger that many of the fathers felt seemed to bear no relation at all to the amount of contact they actually had with their children. Derek Hill is a good example of this. His sense of injustice and powerlessness resulted in extreme anger. But he had wanted the divorce and he did not want to reduce his hours of work in order to have his daughters live with him. They stayed with him every weekend and overnight during the week. His wife, who had multiple sclerosis, did all the hard work of caring during the week and he acknowledged that she was a good mother. Yet he was enraged with his powerlessness. He had initially proposed that he should have the residence of the children and that he would employ a full-time carer for them, but he had had to realize that this was hardly in the girls' best interest. He would appear to have everything he wanted, yet he was still convinced that he was powerless in relation to his former wife and the legal system.

It seems possible therefore to identify two modes of exercising power and, correspondingly, two types of experience of powerlessness. In the post-divorce situation there might be a deployment of *debilitative* power, which is experienced as an effacement of the self, and on the other hand there is a *situational* power (deriving from the fact that women are mostly the primary carers of children while men are usually responsible for financial support), which is experienced as an inability to control others and a denial of rights. We want to suggest that while both of these are 'real' and are part of parents' lived experiences, it is only the latter that is socially recognized and regarded as a legitimate source of complaint. This vision of how power works in gender relations is well covered in the paper on gender and divorce mediation by Dingwall et al. (1996). They argue that mediation/conciliation is not biased against women/mothers, as some researchers have suggested. The dynamic of mediation, they argue, focuses on mothers and getting mothers to change simply because they are the ones who have the children in their charge and are therefore the ones who must be persuaded to give something up to their husbands. Husbands are defined as in deficit while mothers are defined as being in surplus, but as unwilling to share.[4] Mediation therefore, it is argued, simply equalizes this power imbalance. But this perspective acknowledges only situational power and it constitutes a rather limited understanding of the dynamics of gender power. Moreover, it continues to de-legitimate mothers' attempts to reconstitute them*selves* while supporting fathers' tendency to disparage mothers' roles as primary carers during marriage. We would further argue that any mediation or conciliation process that does ignore the interaction between these different forms of power continues to place mothers' needs below those of fathers and fails to acknowledge the importance of the mother's self-esteem to the future welfare of the children (Fineman, 1995).

Violence and the self

So far we have focused on the concept of debilitative power, which would seem to be virtually invisible to most contemporary commentators on the divorce process. It is perhaps a form of power which 'has no name' in this context, albeit it is well recognized more generally in therapeutic work and studies on the pathologies of normal family life. But there are, of course, other manifestations of gendered power: one that became particularly evident in our research was the use of physical violence. It should be noted here that when we started the project we were not looking for violence, nor was our sampling methodology organized in such a way that we were likely to find cases of violence over-represented. It is also important to note that, apart from a few cases in which the whole post-divorce process was determined by violence, most of the women in our sample who had suffered violence tended to understate what had happened. It therefore took us quite a long while to recognize the extent of incidence of violence, and even longer to understand the meaning of such events to the women.[5]

It is probably stating the obvious to remark that women who have experienced violence from men who are or have been their intimate partners cope with it in different ways. For some, because of the nature of the violence and its pervasiveness, it can be almost completely destructive of the self; for others the self remains intact or is even given greater impetus to free itself from a bad relationship. Given that we have identified the self as crucial to the divorce process, it is appropriate to use this as our framework for understanding the significance of violence to post-divorce parenthood. This framework allows us to categorize the significance of the violence in relation to the harm caused to the self as opposed to the body. Thus we are not suggesting that some types of violence are less physically harmful or even less morally culpable than others, rather we are analysing the violence in relation to how the women dealt with it. This is important for an understanding of post-divorce parenthood. Family policy in the 1990s moved towards a position in which domestic violence came to be seen as irrelevant to post-divorce parenting, the courts generally insisting that a history of violence towards women should not be a matter for consideration in deciding disputes over children (Hester et al., 1994; Hester and Radford, 1996; Mullender and Morley, 1994; Hall, 1997). But some women in our sample found that being forced to sustain contact, even indirectly through the children, was unbearable and completely distorted their attempts to make a new life for themselves. Simply being 'safe' was not enough.

Arising from both the women's and the men's accounts of the process of dissolving their relationships we identified two types of violent experience.[6] The first was the 'one-off' and the second was the violence that demolishes one's sense of self. Three of the mothers we interviewed and four of the fathers referred to incidents of violence while they were splitting up, often referred to as arising 'in the heat of the moment'. It may be possible to be a little sceptical of the men's version of these events: in one case, elsewhere in his interview, the man in question stated that he found it hard to control his temper and was clearly inclined to issue threats and to bully other people. A lot of other men also said they 'nearly' hit their wives, or that they had wanted to. But a number of the women voiced these feelings too[7] and it would seem unjustified not to recognize that there is a potential for violence by both men and women in times of stress which may not be particularly typical and which did not characterize the nature of the relationship before breakdown.

> **Jean Adams:** I think it was just his temper. He was losing control. He didn't have me doing what he wanted any more and I was standing up to him and he just couldn't cope with that.

In this case it is possible to see that the violent reaction was related to the way in which Jean was taking control of her self away from her husband. So although her experience was unpleasant, she actually saw it as part of sloughing off her old self. Her new self was not damaged. For the following mother a violent incident was the last straw which strengthened her resolve.

> **Delia Garrett**: Well, that just finished it as far as I was concerned. I think he seemed quite proud of himself, he thought he'd changed things for the better. He thought I'd learnt me lesson or something.

This mother acknowledged that the violence made her more determined, but she also felt that it was damaging for her children who witnessed it.

The sort of violence which was destructive of the self was rarely a one-off. It was the sort of violence which had a long history and which had generated physical damage as well as psychological damage. The women in this situation had lived their married lives accommodating violence. This distorted what they could do and say and it also made the divorce process dangerous. They had to take measures to avoid being victimized and this, naturally, came to determine how they could manage the process and negotiations over children.

> **Kathy Watson**: [H]e put his hand on my clothes and as I looked down he head butted me and broke my nose in two places. We weren't rowing. . . . It was about 12 o'clock in the morning and when he did it he laughed and said, 'It hurts doesn't it?' and I was absolutely hysterical. . . . I was absolutely terrified and he was calm and went back to being his normal self but even more ingratiating and I was just out of my head. He wouldn't let me out of the house, I couldn't get away from him. . . . I'd known this man for four years and he'd never done this before, he'd never even raised his voice to me before. . . . Then he started throwing me downstairs, throwing me down the steps in the front doorway, chasing me down the street when I used to try and run away.

This mother eventually got away and ultimately persuaded the court not to allow her husband to have access to their son. She was threatened with imprisonment in the process but she had decided she would rather face that than a seeming lifetime of involvement with this man. She had never experienced violence before and saw this whole episode as a nightmare in which she nearly became enmeshed, losing completely her self-esteem and her own powers of volition. She spoke of regaining her former sense of self, a thing she could not have done had she been forced to keep her husband in her life.

> **Kathy Watson:** Yes, I am [a victim] I've been intimidated by everybody but I'm not going to stand there and let my ex say, 'Look what I've made her into – nothing.' He can look at me and say, 'Look what I've made her into,' but not the pathetic person I was.

Not all women were this fortunate. Kate Moore started to endure systematic violence after she had split up with her partner. At first she had a co-parenting arrangement, with her former partner Brian having their three-year-old son Jack half the time. But Brian was becoming more and more abusive and eventually violent.

> **Kate Moore:** Plus there was a very important element of this victim cycle of abuse when Brian mentally and emotionally abused me for a long time. By the time we'd reached this point, I had absolutely no self-esteem, I had no way of knowing that there was help out there, or that I could stop the abuse. There was nothing to tell me that I could actually get this stopped, that I didn't have to go through it. Some machinery in my brain was saying, 'He's going to be your abuser for ever and there's nothing you can do about it.' That was the way I was thinking, and it only took to see Jack distressed to shake me out of that, but it took a long time to be completely free of that thought process.
>
> I fear him very much. I don't fear anything else after Brian. . . . Sometimes he accosts me in the street, and as soon as it happens I always have a panic attack. I break out into a sweat immediately at the thought of it happening and I can't speak to him. I see his eyes, and I can always tell from his eyes whether he has his nice personality or his nasty one. I'll see that, and I panic because I know exactly what's going to happen next, and know I'm going to have to endure it. So I'm going to have to live through it without dying – which would be a release. And it's that bad, it's that desperate. And I'm looking round for someone to help me and I don't even see anything, my eyes are darting about but I don't focus. And I'll just have to endure this until he decides to stop, and I've no control over when it ends or how it ends and my only thought is, 'How will I stop Jack getting involved in this?' I've got to run somewhere, and yes, I know he'll trip me up, and kick me while I'm down, but I've got to run somewhere, but it's got to be somewhere where Jack isn't.

This graphic account shows clearly the damage that systematic but also unpredictable violence can wreak on the self. But Kate was not allowed to escape her tormentor. The courts finally refused to award no contact. In an attempt to try to rebuild her life she moved to another city (in the same county) to take a postgraduate training course so that she could get a good job and perhaps form a new relationship which would be less damaging. She did find a new partner, but Brian moved to the same city and harassed them so much that the boyfriend left. Brian still has Jack half of the time, but he waits outside the school gates even on days which are not 'his'. He follows them home, talking to the boy on the way. He encourages what Kate considers to be inappropriate behaviour in their son, for example swearing and tantrums, and he undoes everything Kate tries to do. For example, Kate took her son for a haircut. The next time he came back from a few days with his father his hair had been hacked off. It appeared that Brian had given the child some scissors and told him to redesign it himself. Kate has given up struggling against Brian and has given up on her project for herself. She would like to return to her parents in Scotland but dare not because she knows that if she 'steps out of line' at all, Brian will go straight back to court. She knows that the situation is destructive for her son as well as herself, but she feels that there is absolutely nothing she can do about it.

Brian no longer needed to be violent to Kate, because she had given in to him. Sometimes, however, even where there has been prolonged and systematic violence, women are able to fight back successfully.

> **Bella Tomkins**: It was a problem, yes, and he would flare up at the slightest thing. You had to be careful what you said to him. I found myself avoiding answering truthfully, to be honest near the end because I thought 'I've got to tell him what he wants to hear or he's gonna belt me.' So I didn't want that. In fact after I'd left him I went back a couple of times for various reasons, to sort paperwork out, not to stay. He did try and hit me then and I said, 'You've got no right! I don't even live here any more, you can forget it!' And I bit his head off and after two or three times, he stopped.

Bella not only escaped the violence, she escaped the effects of victimization. But among those other mothers who left violent men, several had become so victimized that it was extremely difficult for them to cope with any kind of contact with their former husbands and equally difficult to rebuild their self-esteem. Ironically, for many of these women the start of this rebuilding process was when they decided that their husbands had to be completely excluded from their lives and the lives of their children. It was, however, exactly at that moment that they would have to confront the Children Act with its insistence on ongoing contact. Games of cat and mouse would often follow, with mothers trying to hide and fathers trying to find them. This could take the form of stalking or a mother simply failing to turn up at a Contact Centre.

> **Kathy Watson**: He'd come around and demand to be let in. I had no choice. He'd be banging on the window and [my daughter] would be terrified, his face squashed to the window. I couldn't get out without him following. He'd wait outside the nursery. I'd open the door, get round the corner and he's there, then I'd reverse back into the house and lock the door, but he just went and walked in. The police said there was nowt they could do.

Our evidence indicated that sustained and/or destructive violence occurred in at least fifteen of our sixty cases and 'one-offs' in seven. If we discount these 'one-offs', then one in four mothers were experiencing violence which could be said to be damaging to their self-esteem and sense of self before their divorce. This is an alarmingly high proportion.

Conclusion

Giddens argues that in the field of intimacy there is a move towards greater egalitarianism. This is, as discussed above, part of his idea of the pure relationship. But he argues that without a prohibition on violence and coercion, democracy in these relationships is impossible. Quite simply, men and women cannot be equal while men continue to be violent or coercive in interpersonal relationships. While it would be impossible to dissent from this view it is, we would argue, important to go further than this in understanding the significance of violence and oppressive behaviour to post-divorce parenthood. For any kind of parenting relationship to continue, not only does the woman have to cease feeling victimized (which is not always possible) but the man has to change in his behaviour also. But from the accounts we received, men who had been oppressive seemed to become more so after divorce, at least until they lost interest in their wives and/or children. For example,

Bella Tomkins (see p. 151 above), managed to stop her ex-husband being violent to her, but he lost interest in their daughter Jean after that and never saw her, although Bella and Jean remained in close contact with the paternal grandmother. Even where there is no physical violence, oppressive controlling behaviour often continues and is inescapable, as in the case of Linda Hewitt. She has a co-parenting arrangement with Ivan, her ex-partner, who has their son exactly half the time. The little boy moves between houses halfway through each week and Ivan has refused to alter the timing to accommodate Linda, who works freelance and has therefore had to turn down jobs. Every item that he buys for the boy he reclaims half from Linda. If she wants to discuss holiday plans or schools, she has to put it in writing for him to consider.

> **Linda Hewitt**: Well, he said no [to changing a day]. The pattern with Ivan, I think I probably mentioned this last time, but it's actually become even clearer now, if I ask him something he'll say no, I'll ask him again and he'll say no, I'll ask him again and he'll say, 'I'll think about it' or 'Put it on paper.' 'Please can you change a day?' has to be written down, and this goes on and on and on until I give up and then he'll suddenly say yes and this is actually what he did, by which time I didn't need to change it any more!

Linda's story is full of incidents where her ex-partner continues to exert this kind of power over her life. Ivan will not change how he relates to Linda, indeed he has said he will never change and she will have to put up with it because she left him. Because her son was only ten years old at the time of the second interview, she was looking forward to at least eight more years of such a relationship. Divorce or separation is therefore no solution to unequal relationships where parenting has to be continued. The question which therefore has to be addressed is whether the ideal of democracy in heterosexual relationships should be carried over from marriage into post-divorce parenting relationships. Few people would condone men's violence against women in ongoing relationships and men's violence – even where it is not directed towards children – is increasingly seen as indirectly harmful to children who witness it or know about it (Mullender and Morley, 1994; NCH Action for Children, 1994). Yet violence, let alone more subtle versions of oppression, tends to be ignored as far as post-divorce parenting relationships are concerned (Hall, 1997). It would seem that the focus on welfare and the concern to reinstate the father have been overzealously interpreted to the disadvantage of important moral categories of mutual respect, equality and dignity. This connects with the discussion in chapter 6 on questions of moral behaviour and the way in which the preservation of dignity and of the worth of another person can be seen as an important moral standard against which to judge individual or 'local' moral decisions (Benhabib, 1992). Our research suggests that the dignity and worth of mothers who are the victims of violence are not a consideration in the way that the Children Act is being interpreted and that these moral claims get little attention in the face of the greater concern to attach fathers to children. This is a major failing of the legislation, a topic explored in our final chapter on family law.

8

Law, Rights and Responsibilities

Introduction

The Children Act (1989) began an *ideological* process of shifting decisions about children and their care in the post-divorce context away from the courts back to the parents themselves. We suggest that it is ideological because in practice the courts rarely *decided* matters of custody and access before the Act and, in practice, there is as yet little evidence that fewer couples are resorting to court to resolve difficulties. But the Act has introduced a 'settlement culture' which emphasizes the importance of parents coming to an agreement through negotiation, rather than relying on directions from a judge. The Children Act has therefore made the role of the solicitor even more central to the divorce process. It has been well established that solicitors have been the prime actors in the legal processing of divorce since the Divorce Reform Act of 1969 and the introduction of the special procedure which dispensed with the need for parties to go to court at all (Ingleby, 1988, 1992). Mnookin (1979) introduced the idea of bargaining in the shadow of the law to explain how solicitors dealt with divorce cases. This idea captured the way in which most divorcing couples never encountered a judicial decision, but were simply told by their solicitors what a judge might make of their situation should it ever go to court. The court was, in effect, a virtual space or location which

overshadowed the divorce process but which was rarely experienced directly except as a rubber-stamping exercise. Parents/
couples may have got as close as the door of the court but typically
their disputes got no further as they would be resolved by the
barristers on the very threshold.

It is not yet clear how much the Children Act has altered this
reality. However, it would seem to be the case that solicitors are
increasingly disinclined to start formal court proceedings because,
according to the new ethos, this is a sign of failure. Solicitors are
therefore actively encouraged to negotiate rather than litigate and,
while this was preferred in the pre-Children Act era, it is now seen
as a basic principle of 'good' legal practice (Neale and Smart,
1997b). This inevitably changes the solicitor's relationship to his/
her client. The solicitor who has fully absorbed the new ethos is
more interested in a negotiated settlement than in striving to
achieve what his/her specific client may want in a unilateral sense.
As Davis (1988) has pointed out, there are core differences between
being a mediator and being a partisan, and the lawyer's role is
increasingly being reformulated into that of the mediator where
family law is concerned.

There is yet another way in which the courts are becoming less
relevant to this whole process. The Child Support Act (1991)
removed from the courts the right to make determinations about
maintenance for children and the right to enforce such agreements.
These matters have been placed with a bureaucratic agency as part
of what Maclean (1994) has described as a shift towards adminis-
trative methods away from judicial determination. This shift af-
fects solicitors too, in that they can no longer bargain with child
support in many cases and they certainly cannot litigate over it.
The role of the solicitor is therefore not only changing from that of
partisan to mediator, but it is also being reduced in some areas.
Moreover, although they do remain the main conduit for divorce,
their monopoly over matters relating to children on divorce has
been increasingly challenged by the growth of mediation and
conciliation. These services have been limited in what they can
offer divorcing parents because they have been barred from dealing with matters of finance, pensions and property. Their remit has
been focused on custody and access – now residence and contact.
Their work has therefore been supplementary to the role of the
solicitor and, for the most part, solicitors could ignore the existence
of these services if they so chose. However, this attitude is becom-

ing increasingly untenable. The desire to reduce the legal aid budget for divorce matters gave rise to the Family Law Act (1996), which may deflect resources away from traditional solicitors towards mediation 'proper'. That is to say, firms of solicitors may increasingly have to tender in advance for funds to provide mediation services rather than billing the Legal Aid Board in arrears for unlimited sums arising from solicitors' fees which have already been incurred. It is predicted that the old-style solicitor with partisan tendencies will vanish[1] as more are obliged, through this financial mechanism, to be transformed into qualified mediators rather than acting as solicitors with an inclination towards informal negotiation processes. The restriction on mediators dealing with financial and property matters will be lifted and, in effect, a new profession will be created from the ranks of legal aid solicitors and independent conciliators with the old style of solicitor being retained solely for clients who can afford private fees.

It has been argued (Cretney, 1997) that this will produce a two-tier system with wealthier clients being able to afford old-style solicitors whom they can instruct to act in certain ways, while poorer clients will be directed towards mediation. Embedded in this two-tier system is, of course, a gender dimension. It is to be expected that women clients (who currently rely on legal aid) will be more likely to be directed towards mediation, while those male clients who can afford solicitors' fees will still be able to buy partisan support. The Family Law Act will undoubtedly change quite dramatically parents' experience of the process of divorce. However, until those changes are implemented, solicitors constitute the main source of advice and guidance for divorcing and separating couples. Few of the parents in our sample had experienced conciliation and/or the intervention of the court welfare service, but all had had experience of solicitors. Relatively few had gone before a judge and these were, naturally, the most difficult of the cases, often involving violence. The parents therefore often formed a view of the operations of contemporary family law through their contact with solicitors. This often meant that they blamed their solicitors for things which were outside the solicitor's field of responsibility; it could also mean that if they found themselves with a poor solicitor they assumed that it was the legislation that was faulty rather than the solicitor. Moreover, at the time when we were interviewing parents, the Children Act had been implemented for only three years and so solicitors were still having to tell parents that the law was not as it had been. Most parents, for example, went to their solicitors expecting that one parent would be given custody of the children and were surprised to learn that this was no longer the case. In addition, many were expecting their day in court and felt let down if this did not happen or if a bargain was made at the door of the court. (Of course, those who got into court were often extremely disappointed too.) We must therefore always be cautious about how we interpret what the clients of the legal system have to say about the process as a whole. There was often a tendency for parents to make 'if only' assumptions: if only their solicitor had fought harder, things would have been better; if only they had gone to conciliation, things would have been resolved; if only they had got before a judge, he would have seen the required solution; or if only the court welfare officer had been a man (or woman), he/she would have made a less biased recommendation. This is not to say that their criticisms may not be valid, but sometimes what they saw as the *solution* was based on an inadequate knowledge of how different elements of the system actually work.

This chapter therefore explores how parents perceived the whole process of divorce in relation to decisions over the children. Although we collected basic data on ancillary matters, we focused our discussions on how decisions about the children were made. After concentrating on the role of the solicitor, we turn to the broader legal issue of rights and the more practical issue of responsibilities.

Law and the significance of gender

As stated above, we do not think that gender difference alone explains how post-divorce parenting operates. We have nevertheless found that our parents live gendered lives and attribute a great deal to gender differences. We are therefore not seeking to reject the significance of gender, but have been reluctant to deploy this concept in a simplistic way. We are also conscious of the problem of generalizing too far with a qualitative sample of sixty parents. At times, however, gender difference appears quite stark and this seems to be the case where expectations about the law are concerned. We found it appropriate to think of gender difference on a continuum, with some men clearly at one end, some women clearly at the other, and a less clearly defined grouping ranged in the centre. In the common ground in the centre of this continuum we found that men and women were equally critical of solicitors for such issues as their charges and their habit of not returning phone calls. Some were astonished to find that they had to pay for time spent on the phone or that they were individually charged for each letter that was written. Almost all those who were not on legal aid felt that the level of charges was excessive, and this view resulted in a general deprecation of the profession as consisting of people who make money out of the misfortune of others and so on. Men and women were also unanimous in their disapproval of how long the whole process took.

> **Sara Birch**: I think that solicitors are parasites and you end up paying a vast amount of money. . . . The only people who make any money are these damn solicitors, so I wish there was another system.

> **Derek Hill**: The advice I would give to people in the future is, 'Bear in mind that the solicitor is out to line his own pocket primarily. He's a business, and the suit and the office are just a front for selling cars. It's the same mentality driving it and do not be hoodwinked.'

Where there did appear to be a very noticeable gender difference, however, was in relation to what mothers and fathers expected from their solicitors. We suggest that the fathers tended towards a presumption that since they were paying for a service they should instruct the solicitor on what to do. Mothers, however, were much more likely to be looking for support, advice and someone to relieve them of a lot of worry.

Men's relationships with solicitors

> **James Grant**: In cases like this you must sit down on your own and say, 'This is what I want and what anybody tells me, whether it's the courts, solicitors, your parents, whatever they tell me, I will do what I want to do.' There were a number of times when I instructed my solicitors to do various things that they didn't want to do.

> **Tim Muir**: I think to be fair he's probably as good as most but that level's very poor. If I hadn't done most of the work myself, really sort of said to him, 'This is what I want to happen,' he wouldn't have

said to me, 'These are the options.' He'd just do nothing. I have always got to say to him, 'What if this?' and 'I'd like that to happen, how do we arrive at that point?' And then he'd say, 'We'll take this to court.'

Anthony Dart: [My solicitor] said I could be on a hiding to nothing. Usually – I know it's the Children Act – but we're still in the dark ages. Everybody tried to talk me out of it. I says, 'No, I'm not giving up.'

Gerry Marsh: I told my solicitor that I don't want a stupid woman [barrister] like that who's not interested in winning the case. . . . I'm better off representing myself.

These four fathers did not want any kind of general advice from their solicitors. They might have accepted tactical advice, but only if they were certain that their lawyers were working for the right goal. Not infrequently they read up on the law themselves and designed their own strategy; they also took advice on which solicitor would have a pro-father approach. These fathers generally felt that they were up against a conspiracy of women, especially if the court welfare officers were women. For this reason some thought it best to have a woman solicitor, while others simply thought that women solicitors would not fight for them. Interestingly, one father deliberately chose a woman solicitor because he wanted to avoid an adversarial approach, only to discover that she thought he was being far too soft and accommodating. She told him that he would feel differently once the Child Support Agency got hold of him, so he had better start fighting from the start.

If their solicitors did not achieve what they wanted, these fathers tended to assume it was because they were inadequate solicitors. One father, for example, wanted his daughters to live with him and he wanted a Residence Order. His solicitor advised him that it was worth his while to fight for this because men were likely to succeed where they were prepared to fight. So he went to court and proposed that he should have the girls although his wife, who was partly disabled, had always cared for them and was not in paid work, and although he was in a very demanding job and would have to hire a childminder or *au pair* to look after the girls each morning and evening. He made it clear that he would not reduce his work hours. The court decided that the girls should stay with their mother and he was given staying contact every weekend and during the week. He insisted that his solicitor had been useless because he had not come away with exactly what he wanted.

This tendency by fathers to instruct their solicitors was not always linked to such an adversarial stance. Interestingly, it was also used against solicitors who wanted to be adversarial when the father did not wish to be. Some fathers instructed their solicitors not to threaten and bully.

> **Colin Hanks**: I had a solicitor who led me up the garden path to a degree. He tried to point me in a direction I didn't want to go. Tried to fight for equal rights. My argument was that the girls were with her and she should have the house so that they had a decent roof over their heads and I didn't need the money that he was chasing because the most important thing at that time was to be as happy as I could be and money wasn't going to be a consideration.

The point is that, for good or ill, fathers tended to think that they should be in control of the process and that solicitors were there to do their bidding. Not infrequently fathers sacked their solicitors and represented themselves, as Colin Hanks did. They often felt that they could do a better job and in Colin's case this proved to be true, although he found it very harrowing to go to court without any representation. None of the mothers represented themselves, even if they did go as far as to change solicitors. While this might be partly explained by the fact that women were more likely to be eligible for legal aid (so they did not feel as if they were actually paying for what they saw as substandard service), this financial incentive does not fully account for the difference. It was just as likely to reflect the fact that fathers were already more used to the public arena and had greater confidence in themselves than the mothers would have.

Women's relationships with solicitors

> **Delia Garrett**: I expected the solicitor to give advice. I could never get used to them acting on your wishes when I didn't really know what I wanted or how to go about it.

> **Ann Black**: I wanted it as easy as possible. I didn't want any messing about, I just left it all in the hands of the solicitors and then signed what I had to sign and that was it. I was quite happy with that!

> **Sally Burton**: My solicitor has been excellent. I've talked wider than the immediate legal things and we've talked around it because it

hasn't been possible sometimes just to talk about legal things. . . . She is actually an incredible support to me because I had to deal with the emotional issues, at the end of the day nobody could really help me with that. She took away all the paperwork and the legal side. She took an awful lot of that burden which was very difficult for me to carry at the same time as everything else. I knew it was costing me an arm and leg but I knew it was worth it.

Diane Roper: I rang up when my friends were away, my mum and dad were on holiday, and I just felt so low. It was a really bad morning and I didn't know who to ring. I'd had a letter from her [solicitor] and I rang her up and just burst into tears and said, 'I'm sorry, I shouldn't have rung you' and she said, 'If you picked up the phone you obviously wanted to talk' and she spoke to me for twenty minutes on the phone.

These sentiments would, we feel, never have come from the fathers we interviewed. The mothers wanted a friend, a source of support and good advice. Even when they did not like the advice, they could often accept it without regarding the solicitor as a fool or a charlatan.

Sarah Birch: She was a very bright lady, switched on and totally different [to my first solicitor]. She again said, 'It's no use using the children, he has got to see them.' Then we had a meeting with Greg and myself and his solicitor, which was a total waste of time. Since then we've just been battling on about finances. Every time I flicker and say, 'I don't want the father to see the children,' she'll say, 'You've got to stick to the arrangement.' She's good.

What seems important here is that there is a degree of trust between women clients and their solicitors. Because the mothers felt completely isolated and frightened following the breakdown of their marriages (even if they had chosen to go), they really needed someone to rely on and someone who would not simply be an instrument. The mothers did not want to isolate their feelings and emotions from the legal forum because they were experiencing more than a technical process. The implications of Delia Garrett's comment above speak volumes: she says that she did not know what she wanted from her situation. Basically these women had no idea about property or tenancy transfers, about the looming problem of pensions, about how much money they would need to avoid poverty later in life. At one extreme, therefore, the men used solicitors to fight a strategic battle in a war in which they had full knowledge of the terrain and circumstances. At the other extreme, the women seemed to find themselves in a maze where the immediate local problem of finding a solution was frightening in itself, but where they had no idea of what lay outside the maze waiting for them in the future. But finding themselves in this position they, unlike the men, did not seek to know their rights and how to enforce them. The women did not construe themselves as legal subjects, rather they identified a series of needs – not necessarily their own – that had to be met. By contrast both mothers and fathers tended to see men as possessors of rights, in other words as properly constituted legal subjects who could lay claim to certain privileges through the application of a legal mechanism. In this sense men were seen to be legitimate holders and carriers of rights and justifiably angry if they were denied their rights. Because women were not construed as the legitimate holders of rights in the first place, they had no legal discourse available to them if they wanted to take issue with the way in which the legal process operated. In the legal forum a rights discourse necessarily has the greatest penetration. Although the Children Act refutes the idea of parents' rights as a mechanism for sorting out matters of residence and contact, it retains the concept of rights in defining contact as a right of the child. Moreover, in practice, the disdain for parents' rights has had no influence on how fathers articulate their position in the legal system, which is still in terms of rights. It is ironic that this apparent disdain for rights has merely confirmed that *mothers* have no legitimate claim to rights, whilst *fathers'* claims to rights are unchallenged.

The fact that mothers do not avail themselves of a rights discourse does not, of course, mean that they have no influence or power in the legal process. But it does put them at a discursive disadvantage. The person who claims their rights is seen as the good citizen who merely demands what is fair and just. Thus to construe the question of children after divorce in terms of fathers' rights is to place fathers in the position of the victim who has to strive to win what is legitimately due to him. Without a similar language of rights, the mother cannot be discursively located in this sympathetic position. Rather she is discursively constructed as the obstacle to the legitimate rights of the good citizen. In this position she is unable to frame a legitimate counter-claim. The legalization of everyday culture has meant that any apparent refusal to recognize a rights claim by another citizen is, by definition, morally suspect.

The language of rights

Not all of the parents we interviewed had been legally married to their partners and unmarried fathers were often shocked that this made a difference to their rights to the child. Often these fathers assumed, quite incorrectly, that, had they been married, they would simply have been able to take the child and raise it themselves. They therefore tended to think that there was a simple solution to their predicament which would be to give them automatic rights arising from paternity.

> **Gordon Fenton:** One of the surprising things is that unless you're married you've no legal rights, you have to apply for those rights. I said, 'Well, that's ridiculous – totally – in this day and age it is completely and utterly rubbish.' . . . Those things should be automatic. You are that child's parent, you have biological rights far beyond any human laws.

> **Ron McNair:** Why should somebody who's married have greater rights than me? . . . I feel now it's very wrong because I'm now having to fork out money to get something that should be mine by birthright.

> **Ben Cook:** It's the legal rights that I'm being – not denied – but being forced to go through. [You] have to go through the very slow legal process.

> **Alan Perkins:** I think it depends on the circumstances. If there's been aggression or violence involved, then no, or if anything's happened to the child, no. But if it's a normal couple then they should have more rights. I feel partners should have more rights – we haven't got any.

While these fathers thought that they would not have a problem if they had automatic rights, married fathers tended to think that they too were constrained, but not in the possession so much as in the exercise of their rights.

> **Anthony Dart:** We had a bit of a fight and I just got rid of him [grandfather aged sixty] as he walked into the house. The police were called, they escorted me off the premises and said there'd be an injunction, it could be assault and battery, charges could be pressed. I says, 'Legally it's wrong but morally I know I'm right, he's

my son and I'm not gonna be denied.' ... My solicitor put me straight, he says, 'Now look, let's get this straight, you've got rights.'

Anthony had legitimate concerns in that he feared that his son's grandparents were going to try to adopt him because neither he nor his wife wanted the full-time care of the boy. But Anthony was physically very imposing and frequently spoke of threatening and fighting the grandfather, who was forty years his senior. He made it plain that he wanted him dead and often told his son Drew not to rely on his grandfather because he would not be around for long. Anthony had had another son by another woman at the same time as his wife was pregnant. This unmarried mother had taken the boy back to the Caribbean and so Anthony flew over and attempted to kidnap him, being stopped at the airport with him. He wanted his own mother to raise the child. The situation was therefore extremely complicated. When put in context, Anthony's claim that he was a wronged father who was being denied his rights seems a rather partial account. But it is an account that has legitimacy because it is framed in terms of a denial of rights.

Compare Anthony's rights-based claim with the views of Leon Holt, also a married father.

> **Leon Holt**: I think at the time I felt – and probably still do – that it's still up to the father to prove that he can be a major part of the children's lives. Whatever the reality is, I know it's changed, it's still a case of having to prove. In the case of Jill, she thought, rightly or wrongly, that the law was on her side for her to do with the children what she wanted, so if we could change ideas, and it's a combination of changing the legislation but also the ideas in society, that no one has a right for custody of the children. You have to prove that you are a responsible parent and you have right of access and what you can do for them on an equal footing, then I think that will change the whole situation and actually make it more amicable in a sense that both parents realize you can talk to the other to make it work.

What is significant about Leon's position is that, while welcoming a change in the law, he recognized the need for fathers to show that they can be responsible parents and to show that they really have something to contribute. For him the change in the legislation is the platform from which fathers can start the job of showing what they have got to offer. So rights are a starting-point for the more difficult task, rather than a kind of trump card that removes the need to be responsible. This sentiment was echoed by Kate Moore:

Kate Moore: There's a very strong movement now towards fathers' rights, [about] which I used to think 'great'. But I think that they end up abusing it because it's not talking about father's responsibilities or whether this particular father is healthy for [this particular] child. It doesn't come into it.

Mothers were often inclined to think that fathers had rights (or ought to lose their rights) to their children while only one mother out of thirty-one spoke of herself in terms of rights. The linkage of fathers to children through the legal device of rights often seemed to be a kind of proxy which stood in the place of a relationship of bonding and affection that usually links mothers and children. In other words, because fathers did not have relationships which provided a lasting bond, they had to have rights instead; or because at the point of separation fathers had often not formed a direct bond with their children, they (and the mothers) often felt that the device of legal rights kept open the possibility of still forming such a relationship.

Of course, not all fathers were strangers to their children at divorce or separation. In those instances where there was already a bond the question of rights seemed superfluous.

Sally Burton: I said, 'I don't want to get in between you and the children. The children adore you. You're their father . . . and it's only natural for them to spend time with you.'

Colin Hanks: To be fair, she always had the view that while we might not love each other any more, I was their dad and I would always come first in their lives, even if she met someone else.

Felicity Lessing: If he says, 'Well, the children need their father,' then I quite agree. Why should the children see less of their father because I feel it's not fair on me? I take the point really.

These parents, and many others who expressed similar sentiments, were clearly operating more within the framework of contact being the 'right' of a child, rather than the idea that fathers have rights. As pointed out in previous chapters, many mothers agreed with this ethos even where the father had been violent towards them. But, as also pointed out above, this view could be put under considerable strain if, in the post-divorce situation, the father failed to act responsibly. As discussed in chapter 3, the idea that fathers had rights and the idea that children need their fathers could atrophy if fathers were irresponsible or if they manipulated the children.

Diane Roper: When Paul first went I felt – and all the professionals, everybody – thought that the best thing for children is to have a good relationship with an absent parent and I was all for that at the beginning. That's exactly what I wanted. Whatever animosity I felt towards him I thought, 'Well, he'll always be their father.' But having seen what he's like I really don't, and having seen the things he does and says to them. For one example, the week that he left he said to Bobby, 'Mummy's trying to steal all my money so I won't have enough money to get a place and you won't be able to come and see me.' And I thought, 'How can he tell his own children that?'. . . Since he left he's been making phone calls in the middle of the night. He's now had a verbal warning from the police. I had a monitor installed on my phone which was traced to him.

It is apparent that the idea of fathers' rights must always be put in context. A free-floating concept of rights which has no commensurate presumption about responsibilities or quality of fathering merely seems to enhance gendered power without accountability. Indeed, what a number of fathers who merely demanded rights seemed to want was precisely a freedom from accountability. It was often these fathers who were most furious with court welfare officers whose job it was to assess their relationship with their children.

James Grant: He was sticking his nose in where it wasn't wanted. It ended up where my solicitors had to go above his head and put a formal complaint in because he just wasn't handling things properly.

Gerry Marsh: Disgusted! This particular person from the court welfare office is biased towards my ex-wife, I can prove that. . . . She has no right to make a judgement on my character, performance at work or any other standard. That isn't her brief. She has contravened quite a few of her own rules and working practices and rules and regulations.

These fathers often succeeded in having the court welfare officers (CWOs) they did not like replaced (none of the mothers in our study even contemplated the possibility of doing this). What was interesting about these men's attitude not only towards CWOs but towards mediation was that they sought to transform the forums into legalistic, rule-bound proceedings. They did not like the practice of the CWOs because it seemed to entail a judgement of their abilities and worth as parents, rather than a simple acknowledgement of their rights, which were not dependent upon any kind of evaluation. The focus on correct procedures and the following of rules is telling. The fact that they were against intuitive factors entering the process explains, to a certain extent, why they were often hostile to women CWOs. They wanted measurable objectivity and exploited every opportunity to 'appeal' against any act or attitude which lay outside a rational rule-bound approach to measuring the welfare of children.

> **Derek Hill:** Yes, the welfare officer. It was another woman and I did feel that throughout the whole system I was dealing with mothers and that felt unbalanced. . . . I don't think she was very professional. . . . She talked to me afterwards, after the court case, and she'd got divorced and it was very dramatic for her and the child that was living with her because, of course, she got a Residence Order. And I just thought, 'Mm! It must be very difficult for her to put personal feelings of motherhood away from her decision making.'

The fathers who took a rights-based approach would have preferred everything to be dealt with rationally by a judge who would follow legally prescribed rules in order to allocate the children in a judicially correct fashion. When they encountered women in the system they were fearful of their apparently more emotional, less objective approach to children's welfare.

> **Keith Minster:** Or like the welfare officer. I wasn't very pleased when there were Lisa there. The welfare officer were a woman and the other welfare officer were a woman. So I knew I were half a mile behind Lisa to start with. . . . This welfare officer preferred Lisa because she's a woman. They probably try and get across that they're not biased towards one or the other but they are. It's just natural.

We have, of course, no way of knowing whether these welfare officers were *really* biased or not, but that is not the issue. They were perceived as being unprofessional and as importing the wrong sort of values. These fathers did not wish to be assessed by what they saw as a feminine code, preferring the adversarial arena of male barristers and judges. Similarly, they saw mediation as a waste of time because it 'had no teeth' and did not result in binding contracts, while the mothers were more likely to be critical of mediation because it failed to support or protect them against violence, bullying or simply being railroaded into something to which they could not agree. Once again it is clear that some fathers saw mediation as an opportunity to insist on their rights, while mothers had very different expectations.

Erica Dawson: I said to the man, 'This is my private time, I've got a lot on at work and at home. I'm not prepared to sit here and be shouted at for two hours. If he's not prepared to talk in a civil manner and treat me with some respect then I feel I should call a halt now.'

Sally Burton: I only saw her twice because I said I'd done a lot of talking and the family mediation was an awful experience, and I wasn't prepared to do that again. Unless Graham is prepared to do some work on the sessions then there isn't any point and I'm just not going to put myself at the flack end of it.

Nina Hester: She did a lot of damage with the stuff that she said. She reinforced everything and made it worse. It wouldn't have got that far if she hadn't reinforced everything he said. If you were sat there and he said, 'She provoked me to strangle her when she was holding the baby' [what would you think?] She sat there listening to that and she told me that, 'Well, occasionally people do lose control.'

Jessica Hunt: We went for mediation. It's only been recently set up has this, and it's a damned waste of time. I wouldn't say it was like two parties conflicting against one another, it was one party stooped down low – which was me – having my back broke and him throwing all this dirt at me. Maybe mediation works when you have got the two parties conflicting but when you've got one that's just got this huge paranoid obsession with me, his whole life was focused on this vendetta against me, nothing any official could say to him would stop him.

Out of the eleven parents who experienced mediation only two felt positive about their experience. The mothers felt that it just provided an opportunity for them to be harassed and the fathers felt that it was pointless if it did not lead to an enforceable contract. This of course does not allow us to draw any conclusions about mediation itself, but it does possibly lend support to the idea that there are different, gendered expectations of how disputes should be managed. Mothers felt that it was a further negation of their new and fragile selves, while fathers felt that it was an exercise without proper structure and legitimacy. In a sense, mediation could not satisfy either party. It could not satisfy the fathers who wanted to operate within a rights framework, because a rights discourse cannot operate in a mediation setting. Nor could it satisfy the mothers who felt that it paid scant attention to their role as primary carers of the children and as the parent who had carried the responsibility of child-rearing in the past.

This brings us to the question of responsibilities and the extent to which the dominant preoccupations of the divorce process with concepts of child welfare and with fathers' rights allow for the emergence of an alternative discourse of responsibility. We argue that this is a necessary prerequisite for the proper enactment of both welfare and rights.

A discourse of responsibility

Selma Sevenhuijsen (1998) argues that:

> First of all, the ethics of care involves different moral concepts: responsibilities and relationships rather than rules and rights. Secondly, it is bound to concrete situations rather than being formal and abstract. And thirdly, the ethics of care can de described as a moral activity, the 'activity of caring', rather than as a set of principles which can simply be followed. The central question in the ethics of care – *how to deal with dependency and responsibility* – differs radically from that of rights ethics: what are the highest normative principles and rights in situations of moral conflict? (1998: 107. Our emphasis)

Aspects of the ethic of care are discussed in chapter 6, which outlines the argument that caring is a moral activity in need of greater value and recognition. Here, however, we want to develop this theme in a different context. Sevenhuijsen is building on the work of Gilligan (1982) and Tronto (1989) to illustrate further how antithetical an ethic of rights is to an ethic of care. An ethic of care is based on responsibilities and relationships, is bound to concrete situations, and is an activity. To operate according to this ethic, one would have to have regard for the discharge of responsibilities, the quality of relationships, the actual situation that people find themselves in and the practice that people have been engaged in. The ethic of care allows for changes to occur in decisions because concrete situations change.

The ethic of justice, on the other hand, focuses on the application of abstract principles from an impartial stance, giving primacy to issues of equality and generalizability. Thus an ethic of justice, when deployed to decide on disputes over children, would refer to procedural rules and the possession of rights. It would not be concerned with actualities but with concepts of equality (between men and women) and/or ideals about the welfare of the child in general. It would not be concerned with who had done what in terms of providing care, but with identifying whose claim to these abstract principles is the highest. In this formulation the just outcome would be one which puts the rights of the child highest, the rights of the father (who has not had equality in childcare) next, and the welfare of children in general as its basic rule. A decision based on the ethic of justice cannot be easily changed or modified. It tends to be made once and for all, even though conditions may change at a later date.

An ethic of care might come out with a very different conclusion about a just decision. It would be concerned with who had held responsibility and established relationships, with the actuality of a specific family life and a specific child and with who had actively done the caring. In this formulation responsibility could be economic as well as nurturing, different children in the same family could be treated differently but *theoretical* claims about ability to care would not take precedence over, nor would they be regarded as being as significant as, *actual* past caring behaviour.[2] The quality of the relationship between the parents and between the parents and children would also be part of the equation[3] and the ability of parents to treat each other with dignity and respect would be considered. While the ethic of justice would almost always reach the same conclusion regardless of the circumstances – namely that the just outcome is always joint parenting after divorce – the ethic of care would have a range of different and individuated outcomes while also being just. What would be particularly significant about such a shift in basic moral philosophy would be that space would be given to a discourse of responsibility and not, as at present, solely to a discourse of rights or an abstract principle of welfare of children in general.

The mothers in our sample did not construct themselves as carriers of rights in the way that some (but not all) of the fathers did. As indicated above, the only language of rights that the mothers deployed was in relation to fathers or to the children. Mothers spoke in completely different ways, focusing much more on responsibilities (Ribbens, 1992). These responsibilities were not called upon in order to obliterate a rights claim, rather they provided a context in which most of the mothers (and some fathers) understood their relationship to their children.

Jean Adams: I think it's an *individual situation* and I think the majority are best with their mother. I really think that on the whole, but there again there are cases when it's not always so.

Sylvia Ashton: I think the mother has a lot *more love*. She shows a lot more love than the father does.

Ann Black: I don't think he wanted the *responsibility*, that was one of the reasons he left. She would always stay with me, no matter what.

George Daley: Like if the father's never in the house, so to speak, and the mother's *always had them to cope* with them, then yes, they should stop with their mothers. I can't see it's right that the father *all of a sudden* says, 'Right, she wants out, I'll have the kids.'

Bob Short: In principle [it could be either parent] but in practice it's another thing. [Bren Neale: 'Why?'] A lot of them get thrown out of their career path by having babies, they often have to be away for two or three years and they don't go back at the same level. That's one reason why they might not. It's possible they might get a part-time job because school is shorter hours than work. Those are the kind of *realities* of the current situation.

(Our emphasis in each case)

The key phrases here are 'individual situation', 'more love', 'responsibility', 'always had to cope', 'all of a sudden' and 'realities'. Put together, these utterances virtually constitute an ethic of care and not an abstract set of principles based on rights. The first highlights the actual situation, which allows for the possibility of diversity; the successive phrases reflect the quality of care, the taking of responsibility, the acknowledgement of a history of caring, the repudiation of sudden disregard for an established normative order, and finally an emphasis on the material realities within which all this takes place. We should perhaps add that many parents who followed this line of reasoning also added the rider that children too should have a voice.

Conclusion

Parents were critical of the legal system from a number of standpoints and it is clear that for some, their discontent was linked to the fact that their lawyers or the courts did not produce the 'solution' that they wanted. But it is too easy to dismiss criticisms of the way in which conflicts between parents are dealt with by assigning criticism to a category of malcontents. A core element of much of the criticism seems to be linked to the fact that the system is not sufficiently aware of individual differences and circumstances, and that clients do not feel sufficiently 'cared for'. Showing respect for individuals and acknowledging their experiences is not the same thing as agreeing that they may be right. As our interviews reveal, there are occasions when parents were willing to admit that they were wrong if they trusted their solicitors sufficiently. We therefore propose that the system of family law needs to engage more seriously with an ethic of care (this topic is developed in the next chapter).

There is evidence that some judges have started to respond to the harshness of the ethic of justice which has begun to pervade residence and contact cases since the implementation of the Children Act.[4] Mr Justice Hall, for example, has criticized an interpretation of the legislation which can result in the imprisonment of mothers for refusing to allow contact when they are in fear of the fathers of their children.[5] He is against the way in which judges see such behaviour as a form of contempt of court and argues that the welfare of the child should not be so readily divorced from the welfare of the primary carer. He argues that the fixation on father contact as the only significant criterion for determining the welfare of children is too narrow a perspective. In a different context, Mrs Justice Hale[6] has argued that the courts should take into account the fear that a mother (or it could be a father) might have in relation to a former partner and that it is not justified to imprison such a mother, nor to label her as implacably hostile, when she is genuinely afraid (see *Re D (Contact: Reasons for Refusal) CA [1997] 2 FLR 48*). In this particular case the father had a history of extreme violence and the Court of Appeal held that he should not be granted an order for contact with his child. Such shifts in the interpretation of legal policy are slight but important and they suggest that there is room for an ethic of care in the delivery of justice. In the next chapter we take forward these ideas and examine what feminist theories on an ethic of care might do to improve current policy further.

9

Family Law, Family Fragments and Feminist Thought

Introduction

One of the core issues underpinning the discussions in this book is the question of the relationship between family law and family practices. Chapter 2 explores the key legal reforms implemented in the 1990s, including the private law provisions of the Children Act (1989), the Child Support Act (1991) and the Family Law Act (1996), which were quite explicit in their aims to mould and change family practices. The point about these legislative measures is that they were imposed from the top down by a government with a clear ideological agenda about family life. In the case of the Children Act and much of the Family Law Act, provisions were initially developed by the Law Commission rather than government itself. The Law Commission may not have shared the ideological stance of the Conservative Government on family life, but the legislative context into which its proposals were put reflected the moral agenda of the ruling party. Thus the Law Commission's proposals for reforming the law of divorce were much modified as their Draft Bill moved through the various processes of official drafting and debate in the House of Commons in 1996. So the important point still stands, namely that these three legislative measures were imposed from above rather than being the result of pressure from below. The Law Commissioners were legal professionals working in the discursive framework of child protection and expert opinion about what constituted the welfare of children. The Lord Chancellor was primarily concerned with rationalizing divorce law and with reducing the size of the legal aid budget. The Conservative Party appeared to want to reduce the divorce rate and retain the concept of fault on divorce, whilst the Treasury wanted to recoup income from fathers for child support. The aims and objectives of the Conservative Government, Tory back-benchers, the Lord Chancellor and the Law Commission were therefore not all the same, but nevertheless these measures were designed to alter the practices of members of ordinary families for their own good, or for the good of their children, or for the good of a wider public morality (Smart and Neale, 1997a).

These legislative measures therefore did not come about as a response to public pressure or as a recognition of a widespread public dissatisfaction with the state of the law. On the contrary, the Child Support Act *provoked* widespread dissent rather than arising from widespread discontent (Mitchell and Goody, 1997). This is not to argue that the legislation should only be introduced as a result of popular campaigns, rather it is to make the point that, unlike the Divorce Reform Act of 1969, or even the Matrimonial and Family Proceedings Act of 1984, family legislation in the 1990s was designed to achieve a remoulding of family life, rather than being a response to wider social and economic changes which had produced public pressure for a change in the law. Most divorcing couples in 1991 (when the Children Act was first implemented) had never heard of the legislative changes it had introduced, indeed as our research has shown, few knew about it in 1995 when we first interviewed our sample of parents. But hardly anyone contemplating divorce in 1969 would not have known about the Divorce Reform Act. This Act had been the result of years of campaigning and public discussion *before* its implementation. By comparison the Child Support Act met years of campaigning and public discussion *after* its implementation, while the Children Act private law provisions are only starting to provoke public attention at the end of the 1990s.

The essential difference between important legislative changes to family law up to the 1990s and during that decade is that in the former case changes were 'from the bottom up' while more recently they have been 'from the top down'. Moreover, they have been 'from the top down' within the context of a very clear agenda about family life. Of course, having a clear agenda is no guarantee that legislation will 'work' as it is intended – indeed the unintended consequences of law reform are legion. Nevertheless, there has been a notable shift from a 'permissive' approach of the late 1960s, which basically led to governments responding to popular pressure concerning the private sphere and personal morality (Hall, 1980), towards social engineering designed to mitigate the perceived harms generated by the previous permissiveness.

This is not to say that the measures contained in legislation such as the Children Act, Child Support Act or the Family Law Act are not ambiguous or even contradictory. Moreover, further ambiguities and contradictions have emerged as the Acts have been implemented and, in the case of the Children Act, as case law has shaped and interpreted the original legislation. Notwithstanding these caveats, we can identify the following *implicit* aims:

- to prioritize first families

- to discourage 'clean breaks' on divorce

- to prioritize parenthood over spousal obligations

- to prioritize biological parenthood and descent

- to challenge the popular understanding of divorce as a solution to private problems

- to identify divorce as a social problem.

These are, as we suggest, the implicit aims. The explicit aim of these legislative measures was concerned primarily with the welfare of children. However, as Smart and Sevenhuijsen (1989) have argued, this is an empty category which is filled with different meanings and policies at different times (Clulow and Vincent, 1987; Wallerstein and Kelly, 1980; Goldstein et al., 1979). It would be true to say that family law has always taken the welfare of children as a priority; however, this has meant that very different policies have been pursued as ideas about welfare and about 'the child' have changed. We therefore need to look behind this aspiration to consider what is thought necessary in order to promote this welfare. Some of these issues are explored in chapter 2, but here we focus on yet another level of analysis: we argue that behind references to ascertaining the wishes of the child or behind presumptions about the desirability of joint parenting is buried a more general concern that divorce generates social harms and should therefore be curtailed.

In the 1950s the Royal Commission on Marriage and Divorce (Morton, 1956), which had been set up to reflect upon the need for new legislation on divorce in the light of public pressure, took the view that if the divorce rate went on increasing there might be a need to abolish divorce altogether (Smart, 1984). The Commissioners feared that once the general populace began to see divorce as an acceptable practice and solution to their marital problems, it would lead to moral decline. Moreover, they argued that there was a good case for refusing to allow divorce in individual cases, even where a matrimonial offence had been committed, if it could be shown that the divorce would harm the welfare of the children of the marriage. Some forty years later similar concerns and sentiments were expressed in the House of Commons debates on the Family Law Bill (Smart and Neale, 1997a). Naturally they were not expressed in the same terminology, but the underlying concerns had not really changed. There was consensus in the House and in the popular media that divorce harms children. There was also a consensus that the high rate of divorce was cause for concern. But in 1996, unlike in 1956, it was impossible to propose the idea that divorce should be abolished because no democratic government would have the legitimacy or authority to take such a measure. Yet because the ground had been sufficiently prepared during the 1990s it was possible to propose that divorce should be made more difficult because of the new consensus around harm. The Act therefore imposed various new obligations on couples wishing to divorce and introduced a waiting period before which it would be impossible to obtain a legal divorce.

These measures need to be considered alongside the impact of the Children Act and the Child Support Act. The latter introduced a complete shift in policy towards child support. Not only did the legislation attempt to tighten up on men's willingness to pay for their children, it shifted priorities for support from second to first families. As Maclean (1994) has argued, before this Act the courts tended to take the view that where there were limited resources, a man should be allowed to support the family he was living with (including step-children) rather than requiring him to support his first family and pushing the children he lived with into poverty. The assumption was that as an average man could support only one family, he was more likely to support the one he was living with at the time. This pragmatic policy became the focus of criticism because it was seen as permitting men to move from family to family, having more children, and then moving on again without suffering the consequences because the welfare state would be paying for the children he left behind. The Child Support Act was therefore about placing responsibility back on the individual father. At the core of this shift was the notion of the economically rational man. It was assumed that if he had to pay for his first family, he would think hard before starting a second family that he could ill afford to support. The individual harm of requiring him to part with money which was needed by his 'new' children in order to pay for his 'old' children was seen to be counterbalanced by a social benefit of generating more responsibility in fathers in general. According to this logic, it had been the old practice of allowing him to escape his early 'mistakes' which had created a generation of fathers who failed to take their responsibilities seriously enough.

The Child Support Act was a coercive piece of legislation, but it was contradicted by the Children Act, which saw fathers in a very different light. The latter held that fathers were not responsible (in the sense that they rarely remained involved with their first children after divorce) because the legal system discouraged and demoralized them by giving sole custody of children to mothers. The solution therefore was not to coerce fathers but to give them every encouragement to remain involved with their children – even if this resulted in coercing mothers. It might be only a slight exaggeration to say that the Child Support Act is about coercing fathers to be financially responsible and that the Children Act, in practice, is about coercing mothers to be responsible for maintaining father contact.[1] If we add to this the likely impact of the Family Law Act, which aims to impress upon couples the harms of divorce (both economically and in terms of child welfare) we can see the rise of explicit policies to discourage divorce and separation. The Children Act and the Family Law Act both require of parents that they collaborate over parenting after divorce. There can, therefore, be no such thing as an emotional clean break. The Child Support Act additionally abolishes the idea of a financial clean break.

Put together, these measures also have the effect of giving priority to the biological father over the social father. Under the old regime of clean breaks the biological father could move on unencumbered. The divorced mother's best option was then to remarry and to introduce a step- (or social) father into the household. This father could assume the role of the departed father both financially and in terms of socialization. Through this mechanism the nuclear family would be (apparently) reconstituted. However, there is now increasingly no place for the social *father*. The biological father is required to pay child support and is encouraged to remain involved – as a father – with the children. The social father has no place in this model and he becomes only the mother's husband or lover. The reattachment of the biological father to the first family therefore changes considerably the dynamics in that household. It also changes the dynamics in the biological father's new household. He may move in with a childless, younger woman but if they have children they must both accept that his first children have priority (Maclean and Eekelaar, 1997). This may have important consequences for second families who have to embrace the reality of previously conceived children. We obviously cannot predict what these changes will mean but they must herald the demise of the old idea of the reconstituted family. Instead we will have fragments of families spread across a number of households. Divorce will inevitably come to mean something different – less an end to a marriage and more the start of a set of relationships based on parenthood (Roche, 1991). This is not quite what the Royal Commission wanted in 1956 when it aspired to the abolition of divorce, but it is plain that divorce as it came to be understood from the 1960s is being abolished in favour of more (supposedly) indelible relationships based on biological links and parenthood. Indeed, if we consider the two cases outlined below, which took place a mere three years apart, we can see how quickly biological ties have superseded marital ties and how rapidly fatherhood has become transformed from a relationship with children which is based on marriage with the children's mother, into a direct relationship with children based on genetic links.

Re SM (A Minor) (Natural Father: Access) [1991] 2 FLR 333

In this case a woman had an illegitimate child by a man from whom she parted before the birth. He saw the child regularly for nearly two years. She then remarried her former husband and contact between the child and the biological father ceased. When the biological father applied for access under the old legislation, the magistrates granted it. The mother appealed. The case was heard by the President of the Family Division, who ruled in favour of the mother. She had argued that the child was now in a stable family unit and that to introduce the biological father would destabilize the unit and disturb the child, who now knew him only as an uncle. In this case the preservation of the married unit was seen as much more significant than the preservation of a biological link between the child and her father.

Re R (A Minor) (Contact) [1993] 2 FLR 762

This case involved a married couple but otherwise the facts are similar to those in the preceding example. That is to say, a married woman had a child by her husband, but she left him soon after the birth and went to live with another man who raised the child as his own. The child was brought up to believe that her mother's cohabitee was her father and she did not know her 'biological' father, who had not seen her for four years; indeed, she did not know of his existence. After four years the biological father applied for contact with the child. The mother argued the same case as the mother in *Re SM* (namely that the child was now in a stable unit and should not be disrupted) but was unsuccessful. Butler-Sloss LJ argued that it was the right of a child to know the truth as to the identity of its 'natural' father and that it was the right of a child to have a relationship with both 'natural' parents. Thus, against the wishes of the mother, she ordered a child psychiatrist to work with the child to overcome the trauma of discovering the truth of her parentage and she required a guardian *ad litem* to be appointed to advise the court on when contact could be resumed with the biological father. The mother reported that this would destabilize her current relationship and that the child's social father would leave, but this carried no weight with the court.

Although *Re R* did not set a precedent as such, since all family cases are treated individually, it marked a distinct change in the policy which family courts have continued to follow save in very exceptional circumstances. Contact with a biological parent as a principle has been raised to the standard of a basic human (child's) right in family law cases (Weyland, 1997). Even in cases where contact is not permitted, these are not allowed to interfere with the general principle; they are always treated as exceptions to the rule rather than modifications to the rule. What we are suggesting therefore is that family law in the UK has shifted away from treating marriage *per se* as the basis of family life (albeit that marriage is still venerated) towards treating parenthood as the basis. This means a shift away from a presumption that families co-reside or that they can be found in one spatial location. Rather fragments of families are found in various households linked by biological and economic bonds, but not necessarily by affection or shared life prospects. We might say that family law is trying to hold the fragments together through the imposition of a new normative order based on genetics and finances, but not on a state-legitimated heterosexual union with its roots in the ideal of Christian marriage (Hale, 1997).

Family fragments?

While it is probably accurate to suggest that the policy on family law pursued at the end of the 1980s and early 1990s had a conservative orientation – in that the desired aim was to return family and married life to a stable nuclear ideal – the unintended consequences of the legislation may be quite different. Rather than discouraging divorce and second unions, the impact may be to disperse the biological family across households and marriages/cohabitations. It may also generate links between grandparents and grandchildren which are no longer anchored in the marriage of the parents but which can survive various transformations in those parents' relationships because they are forged directly with the grandchildren rather than resting on the longevity of marriage. Moreover, in future these grandparents are themselves more likely to be divorced and even repartnered, introducing the possibility – for want of a better word – of *step*-grandparents. This will produce a very different spatial dimension in family connections and brings us directly back to David Morgan's (1996) concept of family practices. As Morgan (1998) has argued, we need increasingly to think in terms of 'doing' family life rather than in terms of 'being' in a family or part of an institution called the family. If co-residence ceases to be the main defining feature of a nuclear family, then it also follows that relationships need to change. As some of the fathers in our sample discovered, being a father who merely co-resides with his children is very different from being a father who has to forge a relationship based on mutual regard, shared interests, caring and so on. The same is obviously true for non-residential mothers, although the adjustments they have to make may be slightly different.

The shift away from a presumption that family life equates with biological kin co-residing has wider consequences too. Once marriage becomes less central as an anchor to automatic and legal relationships, then non-marital relationships start to be less marginalized (Kiernan, 1993). While it was almost certainly not the aim of government policy in the late 1980s and early 1990s, it is likely that the demotion of the significance of marriage (in some fora) also demotes the significance of heterosexual unions and undermines the objectionable depiction of gay and lesbian families as 'pretended family relationships'.[2] Although the refocusing on genetic links hardly gives legitimacy to, for example, a lesbian who is the non-biological mother of a child for whom she cares, it can strengthen the legal tie between a lesbian mother and her biological child and a gay father and his biological child. Moreover, the more children who are brought up outside the traditional nuclear household, the easier it becomes for other children who experience a diversity of kin relationships spread across a number of households.

It is, however, important not to overstate the degree of change and diversity that is occurring in family life. Statistics on divorce in 1994 show a small decrease when compared with 1993, although there was also a small decrease in the numbers of people marrying. Also, slightly fewer children were affected by the divorce of their parents in 1994 compared with 1993. It is, as yet, impossible to interpret these statistics. In particular it is not clear whether the rise in cohabitation heralds the demise of marriage or merely its postponement. In 1994 60 per cent of couples who married cohabited immediately before their wedding, although it is not known for how long.[3] It may be that heterosexual couples are postponing marriage until the birth of a child and, if so, this may mean that in practice, couples are also eliding marriage and parenthood and, in this sense, giving greater significance to parenthood than to matrimony. It may be that if parenthood becomes increasingly a 'free-standing' legal status, marriage will remain significant only to those with religious convictions whether Christian, Muslim, Jewish or other.

It is of course also important to recognize that while these changes are occurring in one sector of British life, in those sectors which are unlikely to have been featured in the statistics or are invisible as a specific group, there may be much less change. Where family life is differently organized, the essentially white British processes of marriage, parenthood and divorce which are measured by judicial statistics, cannot be simply superimposed on all ethnic minority communities. A secular system of divorce may simply not be relevant to religious groups and it may be immaterial in some cases where marriage does not precede childbirth. We need also to start to think differently about the relationship between ethnic minority family practices and the dominant white, secular model of family life. It is normally assumed that ethnic minority family life can be judged in terms of its nearness to or difference from the dominant model which – at least in its nuclear form – is assumed to be particularly desirable. There has also been an implicit assumption that families which are different should be encouraged to meet the ideal (e.g. the particular criticisms of black unwed mothers). But it may be that what we are witnessing is a growing diversity of white family practices which will bring them closer to the varieties of family practices found in a range of different ethnic minority communities. Thus, for example, the idea that close kin may live in different households, which has tended to be seen as deviant in black or Asian families, may start to become a more widespread and common practice.

Finally we need to give consideration to the impact of reproductive technologies on traditional understandings of parenthood and kin relationships. The disaggregation of genetic material from biological bodies means that a birth mother may no longer be the genetic mother of a child, and that neither of these may become her social mother. Men may now not only become fathers posthumously, they may also conceive children posthumously. The law remains contradictory in its dealings with these new developments, at times prioritizing marriage as the legal context for linking children with parents, and at other times insisting on a genetic link. But these contradictions cannot easily be solved because they do not arise merely out of disorganized thinking on the part of policy makers. On the contrary, they arise from the complexities of actual family practices which cannot any longer be forced into neat packages[4] wherein marriage is defined as virtuous with all other arrangements deemed beyond the pale. While it is clear that the ideal of married family life as framed in English family law since the nineteenth century never fitted the actualities of lives of the working classes, immigrant families, gays and lesbians, the infertile and so on, it is clear that until the 1960s it could impose its normative ordering on family members. But as family law began to respond to growing pressures around perceived injustices such as the legal status of illegitimacy, the obstacles to divorce and the vulnerable status of wives, it gave up – imperceptibly at first – its power to define the homogeneous family. Judges may have continued to pontificate, but not with one voice and to a less and less attentive audience.

Family law, of course, had little choice in the matter. It could hardly have remained unchanged in the light of demographic changes, the influence of social movements, changing expert ideas on childcare, the growing economic influence of women, changing patterns of employment and so on. Just as 'the family' could not remain unchanged with the process of modernization, neither could family law. Beck describes these changes thus:

> This contradiction between the requirements of a relationship and those of the labour market could only remain hidden so long as it was taken for granted that marriage meant renunciation of a career for women, responsibility for the children and 'comobility' according to the professional destiny of the husband. The contradiction bursts open where *both* spouses must or want to be free to earn a living as a salary earner. *Institutional* solutions to or ameliorations of this contradiction are quite conceivable. . . . These, however, are neither present nor in any way contemplated. Accordingly the couple must search for *private* solutions. (1992: 116–17. Emphasis in original)

The private solution for Beck is divorce or the renunciation of marriage. Or it could be that one spouse chooses to undertake the risk of economic insecurity to raise the children. But, as he points out, to undertake economic insecurity is to give up one of the basic prerequisites of modern life, it is almost a kind of civil death. In the light of this analysis we can see that family law initially attempted to paper over the cracks that were appearing in the post-war era by refusing to make divorce more widely available, by retaining strict notions of illegitimacy and by securing marital assets in the hands of husbands (Gibson, 1994). But towards the end of the 1960s it became impossible to hold this line and to ignore the growing contradictions between women's earning capacity, the newly conceived orthodoxy on children's welfare, and the unjustifiable economic power of married men.

Family law is therefore part of the change; it has not brought change about, but it has facilitated certain developments. For this reason, it seems particularly ill conceived that in the 1990s the same legal mechanism is being deployed by governments as if it were a brake on social change. Not only does it seem unlikely to work (because family law cannot work in isolation), but it risks generating harm because, as Beck points out, governments are not inclined to put in place structural or institutional reforms which would lessen the private risk involved in marriage and childrearing by offering forms of social protection or insurance. Thus, for example, current policy proposals offer parents training in parentcraft while at the same time obliging both to work full time if they want a decent standard of living. It is not, of course, that parentcraft classes are an inherently bad idea, rather it is that they are not an answer to the new problems posed by the fragmentation of family life and the rise of diverse family practices. They are, in a sense, an answer to an old dilemma – or at least to a dilemma whose contours were formed around the time of the Royal Commission on Marriage and Divorce in the mid-1950s. A crucial element of these contours was the idea that any deviation from the married nuclear family is a social and moral problem. Moreover, this formulation presumes that family life exists in the private sphere where it is subject to (supposedly) instinctual human drives such as love, sexuality and affection which are, in turn, assumed to be quite independent of the workings of the public sphere. In this formulation problems in personal life require solutions which focus on the personal rather than the social. Thus, just as the Royal Commission was keen on marriage guidance as a solution in 1950, so the current debate focuses on the solutions to be achieved by conciliation and even reconciliation.

This tendency to treat the family as essentially non-social while treating divorce as a social problem also gives succour to the idea that divorce arises from personal inadequacy or immorality and that its consequences are borne by the wider community. Thus, a one-way traffic is envisaged in which individual parents are encouraged to feel that they must carry responsibility not just explicitly for their own actions but implicitly for the negative consequences of modernity and the power of the market to delineate the lives of ordinary people. Divorced parents often feel themselves to be personal failures, just as unemployed people often feel themselves to have failed. In the field of unemployment there have, however, been counter-discourses which have pointed to government policies on inflation which deliberately drive up unemployment rates, or analyses of market deregulation which show that certain employees are made far more vulnerable to redundancy. There are, however, few voices that have articulated the way in which employment policies might drive up the divorce rate, or the way in which the uneven distribution of household labour might lead to a decline in the rates of marriage. And where there are such voices, they are rarely to be heard in popular public debate where space is more likely to be given to popular moralizers or psychologists. Divorce therefore continues to be experienced as an individual misfortune rather than part of a growing diversity in family life which mirrors other major shifts and changes in wider society.

Feminist thought

The moment has come to ask what feminism has to do with these questions. Feminist politics has, of course, a long tradition of engagement with family law and family policy, whether from the early campaigns on custody and motherhood launched by Caroline Norton in the 1850s, through to campaigns in the 1980s for financial and legal independence for women. The bases of feminist claims have naturally changed over time. Norton (1982) proclaimed the special status of motherhood arising from the natural bond a mother has for her child, while in the 1980s arguments based on special attributes were avoided, with preference being given to claims based on legal rights and equality. Family law has not been impervious to these arguments and it is possible to identify shifts in legal policy which reflect the growing social acceptability of feminist arguments which were once seen as simply outrageous or insupportable.

Feminist thought and feminist politics do not, however, have a particularly high standing in the fields of family law and family policy. Feminism is associated with a single-minded pursuit of women's interests which, it is presumed, inevitably leads to the trammelling of children's interests and – of course – the interests of men. It is hard to imagine a less accurate depiction of contemporary feminist thinking. It is, for example, mistaken to assume that feminist thinking is a unitary or homogeneous form of thought, let alone one that identifies a unitary subject called 'woman' whose interests can always be divined and represented by feminists (Riley, 1988). This perception of feminist thinking also misses completely the impact that the politics of difference has had in this area. Feminists have long given up the claim to represent women in general, since women in general are so very different, have very different needs and goals, and have different histories and cultural locations. Furthermore, this view ignores the seismic impact of postmodernist thought on feminism(s) (Butler, 1990; Ferguson and Wicke, 1994; Hekman, 1990). This subject is too large to tackle here, but it is important to remark that postmodernist ideas have transformed feminist politics but have also refocused feminist thinking on questions of values and ethics. Thus feminist work on moral philosophy has grown exponentially in the 1990s. This work in particular has so much to offer critical thinking in the field of law and justice – and hence family law – that the *a priori* rejection of feminist thought as simply a partisan expression of women's interests would constitute a very serious loss to the future formulation of fair and supportable policies. There is a sense in which it is now important for family law to take on board the latest contributions from feminist moral philosophy and to move away from the uncomfortable position that it currently straddles across the liberal presumptions of equality (or justice) and welfare.

The justice versus welfare debate is a long-standing one in legal matters concerning children and the family (James, 1992; James and Hay, 1993). Family law has never been simply about justice, but rather a mixture of concepts such as equity (in relation to matrimonial assets) and the best interests of the child. These two elements have been in a kind of tension with one another, with one gaining ascendancy at times while the other is less favoured. Thus, when married women lost the right to maintenance on divorce in 1984, the argument was focused on questions of equality and justice. It was argued that since men and women were equal in almost all areas of law, as well as in the labour market, it was an injustice to require men to give financial support to wives who should no longer benefit from special treatment. This reform was, however, mitigated by the recognition that if fathers paid a level of child support which ignored the existence and needs of a primary carer, then the children of divorced parents would, effectively, be condemned to poverty. The welfare principle (for children) therefore mitigated the equality principle (between men and women). Notwithstanding this, it was the equality/justice principle that 'won' the ideological struggle at that time. It looked as if what mattered in the question of divorce was justice rather than welfare.

More recently the equality/justice argument has resurfaced in the argument which states that mothers and fathers should be treated as equally capable of raising children and that no special consideration should be given to mothers.

> There is no presumption which requires the mother, as mother, to be considered as the primary caretaker in preference to the father. The welfare of the child is paramount, and each parent has to be looked at by the judge in order to make as best he can the assessment of each, and to choose one of them to be the custodial parent. (Butler-Sloss LJ, *Re A (A Minor) (Custody) [1991] 2 FLR 394 at 400*)

It is worth considering this quotation closely. Butler-Sloss begins by arguing that mothers and fathers should be treated equally, with no special preference to be given to the mother. But she justifies this equality argument by reference to the principle of the welfare of the child. So the welfare principle is used to support equality, just as once it was used to support absolute father right, and also to support the tender years doctrine and maternal preference. In pressing the welfare principle into use, we might underestimate the significance of the initial statement confirming equality/justice. But what we can see here is the discursive use of the welfare principle to keep alive the equality principle. In other words, the welfare principle assures equal rights for mothers and fathers. The strength of the welfare principle now – somewhat ironically – lends weight to the equality principle. But this in turn gives succour to a much more inflexible rights perspective which a number of the fathers in our study expressed. This perspective demands equal rights in the apparently certain knowledge that they alone secure the welfare of a child. Although there is a world of difference between the formulation provided by Butler-Sloss above and the argument that equal rights between mothers and fathers ensure child welfare, there is a terribly easy slippage between the two. This means that just when the Children Act welcomes the paramountcy of the welfare principle at the front door, by the back door it gives greater weight to an equality/justice/rights argument which may have little to do with the actual welfare of specific children.

The question we must pose is how to get out of this interminable binary divide between justice and welfare? How can we import the ideas emerging from feminist philosophy and political theory to try to transcend these modes of thinking, particularly when they are productive of an 'uncaring' legal system? How adequate is a system of family law which leaves mothers feeling coerced, silenced and undervalued while fathers feel powerless and aggressive? What kind of a system is it that leaves most people wishing that they had never encountered it? Moreover, how sensible a system is it, when it applies great pressure on parents to agree, without any understanding at all of the medium- or long-term 'success' of its intervention?

Turning to the possible contribution of feminist philosophy to these questions we would start with a core proposition put forward by Sevenhuijsen:

> The feminist ethics of care also offers a critical perspective on the idea that it is possible to achieve entirely just and harmonious laws in this area. The emotional bond between parents and children is, after all, often so complex that there is no single satisfactory solution. The law should pay attention precisely to the fragility of the relationships between people and to the different situations in which people need the law because they are unable to sort things out for themselves. . . . There thus needs to be a 'pluriform' law which takes account of different situations and which abstains as far as possible from positing an abstract ideal of 'good family life'. (1998: 118)

As far as family law is concerned, this would mean that it is important to challenge guiding principles once they solidify into rules which are applied rigidly regardless of the specific circumstances. As suggested at the end of chapter 8, a guiding principle which states that it is in the interest of children to maintain contact with both parents yet ends with imprisoning a residential mother[5] who has been the victim of sustained violence for failure to comply with a court order for contact seems to have gone seriously awry. Equally, a guiding principle which states that contact is the right of a child but which then imposes a contact order on an unwilling child on the grounds that it will serve the interests of the child in the *long run*, seems to want to have its cake and eat it. If contact is the right of the child, so is no contact. If the child chooses to exercise his/her rights, it is an abuse of the court's power to insist that they can only be exercised in one direction because the court actually knows what is best already (Johnston, 1993). Treated this way, the notion that contact is the right of the child does not empower the child but only the court in the pursuit of an ideal about the benefits of contact.

While we acknowledge that these new principles were introduced in order to right certain wrongs, and while we would also not dissent that in principle it is better if children do not lose contact with parents, and that children should have a voice, our difficulty with current legal practice is that, in finding a 'good enough' principle, it then applies it with all the sensitivity of a sledgehammer. The courts seem oddly incapable of 'doing the right thing' (Finch, 1989). They work *to* an abstract principle, rather than working *from* the complexities of real family relationships. Let us look at a not untypical case on contact from the court of appeal. This case is known as *Re F (Minors) (Contact: Mother's Anxiety) [1993] 2 FLR 830*. The facts of the case are as follows: A couple married when they were very young, she was approximately seventeen and he was twenty, they had two children in two years. The father was violent and was ultimately convicted of an assault on his wife and sent to prison. Contact between the father and the children ceased although the mother maintained contact between the children and their paternal grandparents who, at this point, became estranged from their son. The father then met another woman who had a small child and they subsequently had a further child of their own. At this point, it is stated that he became a reformed character and wished to resume contact with his first children. The mother however remained frightened of him and was very sceptical of the extent to which he had reformed. Because of her past experiences she suffered from panic attacks and severe headaches and these were associated with her worries about the father gaining contact. When this case was heard at County Court level, the judge accepted the evidence of the harm to the mother and the likely harm this would cause to the children. He dismissed the father's application for contact. The Court of Appeal, however, reasoned differently. The starting-point of the judges was the principle laid down in *Re H* which stated in the headnote:

> No court should deprive a child of access to either parent unless it was wholly satisfied that it was in the interests of the child that access should cease, and that was a conclusion at which the court should be extremely slow to arrive.
> (*Re H (Minors) (Access) [1992] 1 FLR 148*)

This principle is frequently cited in cases of contested contact, but it is important to note the extent to which it has altered the weighting of the welfare principle. Rather than stating that it should be presumed that contact is in the interests of the child, it requires that there should be evidence put forward that it would be in the interests of the child for contact to cease. Thus it would not be enough to show that 'no contact' would not produce any harm or that it would be neutral in its effects, rather it is required that there be some proof of *positive benefit* to the child from ceasing to have contact. But added to this condition is the rider that courts must also be very slow to come to such a conclusion. This amounts to laying down a rule to forbid courts to come to this conclusion.

The Appeal Court judges therefore adopted an initial stance which made it clear that they already knew the best solution and that this solution could be derived from established principles rather than from the facts of the case. However, when they did turn to the facts of the case they also decided that the court of first instance had balanced the competing elements incorrectly. Balcombe LJ argued:

> Miss O'Neill, who put the mother's case before us with considerable force, submitted to us that the judge was seeking to balance a real risk of injury to the mother's health, and through that, harm to the children, against the hypothetical risk that the children could be damaged by not knowing who their true father was and not knowing him at all. I think, with respect to her, that that is not the correct way of putting the case. The judge was balancing in effect two inestimable risks. There was the risk, *well documented by medical and legal literature and cases*, that the children could be damaged by not having the right to know their own father. There was the undoubted possible risk that the mother's health could be damaged and that that damage could react on the children. (*Re F (Minors) (Contact: Mother's Anxiety) [1993] 2 FLR 830: 834*) (Our emphasis)

In this passage Balcombe LJ disputes the barrister's formulation of the issues, which focused on the balancing of a real risk against a hypothetical risk. He recasts the balance of risks, basically arguing that the risks associated with loss of contact were the real risks – for which there was evidence – while the risk to the mother's health and hence to the children was demoted to a *possible* risk. The evidence of the clinical psychologist on the state of mind and health of the *actual* mother was given less weight than the evidence to be found elsewhere about the general impact of loss of contact on children *in general*. Not only did the judge not seek to doubt this 'evidence', but in readjusting the balance between these two factors he failed to acknowledge the evidence which exists in the literature on the harm of sustained domestic violence on women (Hall, 1997). He was, to put it simply, very selective in the evidence he sought to bring to bear on the case, preferring the general to the specific, and selecting only one variety of general evidence. He did this in the context of *Re H*, which indicated that his mind was virtually closed to the possibility of finding in favour of the mother.

We might speculate on how the mother might feel at the end of this appeal case. She clearly did not trust the father and she was having anxiety attacks. She did not want to become entangled with this violent man again and did not believe that he had reformed (indeed the weight of 'general' evidence on this would be on her side, since violent men do not easily or readily forgo violence). She had, however, kept the children in touch with their paternal grandparents and many other members of his family. It would not seem from this that she was, in a general sense, operating out of spite or a misplaced notion of the welfare of the children. However, the judge clearly thought that he knew better than their mother did what the interests of these children would be. He also thought that the immediate harm to them of seeing their mother in a state of panic would be outweighed by the benefits of getting to know their father, despite the fact that he had been, in the judge's words, 'a very unsatisfactory young man indeed'. Not only had he been violent, he had abused alcohol and drugs and had a criminal record.

The question then is how might such a case have been dealt with if a feminist ethic of care was deployed rather than this mixture of the welfare principle with a hint of equality and rights reasoning? Based on the core themes that emerged from our data, we would argue that four principles should be applied. These are: the principle of actuality; the principle of care; the principle of recognition of selfhood; and the principle of recognition of loss.

The principle of actuality

This is almost an anti-principle in that it argues that decisions or outcomes in difficult cases concerning parents and children should be derived from the reality of the lives of the people involved. This would mean that decisions would not be made on the basis of abstract notions of child welfare, but in relation to the needs and wishes of actual children. One of the issues that the parents in our sample raised was the way in which decisions about their children seemed to be based on what was best for children in general, which they felt to be inappropriate or insensitive as far as their actual circumstances were concerned. Decisions should also be related to a recognition of practical realities, such as who the primary carer has been, whether both parents have a relationship with the child(ren), and whether there is a climate of coercion and fear.

The principle of care

This principle would replace the principle of welfare of the child, while still being primarily focused on the children involved in a case. It would embrace notions about adequate standards of care and of maintaining the health of children and so on. But it would go further in that it would place the child in a set of relationships. Through this mechanism the child would not be completely isolated from his/her carers as if his/her interests could be legislated upon independently of the web of relationships in which the child finds himself/herself. Thus the quality of those relationships would be taken into account. This would include the valuing of different styles of parenting and would not automatically assume that the primary carer had established the only meaningful relationship with a child. But it would acknowledge the significance of a history of caring for children and would put this into the equation. Yet it would not simply be backward looking. It would not be appropriate to establish a principle which would not allow for relationships to change and develop in the future. As our data suggest, distant fathers can become highly involved fathers to the benefit of all concerned. But the principle of care would recognize that such transitions must occur with sensitivity and that there are real consequences for *both* parents which need to be acknowledged rather than dismissed. Allowing for the passage of time seems vital in cases where there is serious conflict.

The principle of care would import the concept of connectedness and would place less emphasis on rights. Thus it would lean towards maintaining contact with all family members where possible, but not at the cost of coercion. It would also import the idea of slow transitions and change over time as relationships change. The current system places great store in getting an agreement by a certain date. Yet our data show how much relationships go on changing and how they can both improve and deteriorate.[6] Those that improved were often ones where trust was re-established, but this was rarely re-established by order of the court or through the urgings of the mediators and welfare officers. Trust requires time. Issues of contact and residence therefore need to be thought about in a different time-span with more caring support given to parents through various stages of change, not just in the context of trying to find a resolution before going to court.

This principle of care therefore extends to parents as well as to children. The present system tends to want to 'knock sense' into parents to make them better carers. Take, for example, these comments from some of the solicitors we interviewed during the course of the research:[7]

> **S.H.**: The only time I lay down the law and I'm heavy handed is if I've got a mother who's not allowing contact. ... *I try to beat everybody into submission.* In those circumstances I am prepared to overstep the line a bit and upset clients sometimes. The prospect of a court ever backing [a contact order] up with [committal proceedings] is very unlikely, *but I would never tell the mum that.* What you hope is that the judge will be strong enough to *frighten the socks off mum.* ... I've got a particularly difficult case at the moment where the mother has ... been subject to what seems to be some *nasty incidences of violence and fled the area specifically to get away.* Persuading her to get contact up and running again is very, very difficult. (Male solicitor, mediator trained. Our emphasis)

> **O.H.**: The major problem, of course, is that there is no real sanction against a mother. ... I would like to see a list of judges who would put their hand up when invited to commit to prison. (Male solicitor)

> **K.A.**: I'd love to see the judge have a bit more power in effect to allow the non-custodial parent contact regardless. (Male solicitor)

> **B.O.**: One of the fundamental changes [since the introduction of the Children Act] is the flagging up of the child's right to see the absent parent. Judges in the main are taking a more *robust* approach and will not deny the absent parent contact unless the evidence is overwhelming. (Male solicitor. Our emphasis)

The principle of care would reject this kind of coercive and bullying approach, and would attempt to care for the parents as well as for the children. It is in relation to this aspect of caring for parents and in recognizing the complexity of the reality of post-divorce parenting that our final two principles are developed.

The principle of recognition of selfhood

This principle arises from the voiced experiences of many of the mothers that we interviewed, although it is not a principle that should or could be applied only for the benefit of women. As discussed in chapters 7 and 8, one of the main difficulties that women seemed to encounter at separation or divorce was the recognition that they had lost sight of their 'true' selves and that they needed to become themselves or find themselves again. Thus in the post-divorce period they needed to change and develop new goals. Often this meant getting a job and becoming more confident of their own abilities. But they frequently could not do this if their former partners refused to acknowledge this process or continued to treat them as they had during the marriage. While many of the women simply endured this ongoing eclipse of themselves, many found that it was a real obstacle to post-divorce parenting. This feeling was often exacerbated by the experience of meeting solicitors, mediators and judges who also paid no heed to the women's loss of confidence and sense of identity. If we think about how the mother in *Re F* cited above was treated by the Court of Appeal, we can get a strong sense of what it must be like to be effaced by the system. In paraphrasing Hume, Sevenhuijsen states, 'Morality is not based on respecting other people's rights, but on the ability to recognise their individuality' (Sevenhuijsen, 1998: 108). It is precisely this approach that we would like to see adopted in these cases.

The principle of recognition of loss

While it was many of the mothers we interviewed who expressed concerns about trying to find or rebuild their 'true' selves, we found that any non-residential parent might express a dreadful sense of loss, most especially if they rarely saw their children. This sense of loss might manifest itself in a form of anger and become articulated through a rights discourse (mostly in the cases of fathers) or it might take on a form of hopelessness and despair. Attention has been paid mostly to fathers' sense of loss or fear of loss because, of course, it is still more usual for fathers to be the non-residential parent. Studies of fathers in this situation have pointed to the way in which children may be coming to mean something rather different to men such that their 'loss' is becoming even more significant. Certainly a number of the fathers in our sample experienced a sense of loss and fought hard against it, often using the legal system in a rather coercive way. But we also interviewed mothers who were denied contact and suffered as well. The experience of loss is therefore not a gendered one in principle and it is quite possible that it will be an experience that increasing numbers of mothers will have to face.[8]

The experience of loss seems to call for an ethic of justice to right the wrongs that have been inflicted upon the bereaved parent. But the formal legal solution can only coerce or reallocate parental authority; it cannot repair the relationships. Moreover, there is no evidence that the application of a judicial remedy works in any meaningful way. We do not know, for example, what the consequences are for children who are in contact with fathers simply because their mothers have been threatened with imprisonment. Given the complexities of post-divorce parenthood revealed by our interviews, we can only speculate that there should be little cause for optimism about the outcome.

The application of an ethic of care might start from the assumption that wrongs cannot always be 'righted' and that they cannot be reversed by judicial utterance. It might therefore promote non-intervention in these cases rather than seeking to coerce. But it could do this in the context of recognizing the loss, supporting the parent who is excluded and providing the means of future communication when circumstances may have changed sufficiently to resume contact. In two of the cases we studied where mothers were being denied contact, we found that a year after the completion of the research they were having contact; in one case the children had moved back to live with their mother. These mothers had not used the courts, they had used time and consistency. One of these mothers had had the support of the court welfare officer, who actively persuaded the father that his young children really did need to see their mother. The other mother had had no support or recognition at all. Ironically, the only support generally available is the legal, adversarial variety which then locks these 'detached' parents into a potentially coercive and damaging engagement with the residential parent. Very few of our parents were able to devise alternative strategies without support and without any affirmation of themselves as parents which might arise from a recognition of the loss they were suffering.

Conclusion

There are rarely solutions to disputes over children, but it may be possible to treat mothers, fathers and children with more care than is currently the case. The ethic of justice promises dispute 'resolution', but the ethic of care seeks to sustain a dialogue without diminishing the sense of worth and dignity of the individuals involved. There are no simple solutions. Indeed the main lesson that must be drawn from the accounts of the parents in our study is that circumstances continue to change and that even if one problem is resolved, others arise. There can be no way that things are 'put right' once and for all. Once it is possible to see post-divorce parenting as a process rather than a contract, it becomes feasible to think in terms of flexible guidelines which emphasize the need for ethical procedures rather than final adjudications. The Children Act was conceived in such a way as to allow for flexibility and it did not promote the use of courts and judicial rulings. But it did not provide adequate principles to meet the objectives the authors hoped to achieve. The almost exclusive emphasis on the welfare of the child and the way in which this has subsequently been interpreted have given rise to a neglect of the quality of the parental relationship. As argued above, the implementation of the legislation seems ultimately to presume that parents need only to relate to the child and not to each other in order to achieve the best interests of the child. This was not how our parents saw the situation.

When asked what made for good post-divorce parenting the majority of our parents simply said communication. This term not only embraces the idea that each parent should be respected as an individual with a point of view, but also recognizes that parenting is not a static state but one which requires constant negotiation *between* parents, not just between parents and children. This emphasis on communication also signifies the extent to which these parents were reflexive moral agents. Those who emphasized communication did not adhere to fixed rules nor to the rigid enforcement of contracts. They were in many ways speaking the language of morality that Finch identified in her work on family obligations: 'The concept of negotiated commitments represents an alternative way of understanding family obligations which contrasts quite sharply with the idea of following moral rules' (1989: 181).

Finch has argued that it is a quality of family life in Britain that kinship is not governed by rules that lay down precisely how people should relate to one another. Rather there are normative guidelines which are open to interpretation and negotiation. In this context she speculates about possible government policies and laws which may increasingly attempt to coerce family members to support one another as social support is removed. It is her view that such attempts would be out of step with what most family members find acceptable because kinship obligations are not reducible to mere legal obligations. But Finch was dealing with wider kinship rather than the specifics of divorce and parenting across households. She was speculating on *possible* policy shifts which *might* try to enforce obligations. In the field of divorce there have already been *actual* policy shifts which insist that fathers maintain their obligations to children and (indirectly) former partners *regardless* of the level of commitment they may feel (the Child Support Act). Moreover, the Children Act now effectively obliges former family members to uphold mutual obligations even at a time of utmost antipathy. Finch speculated that were such conditions imposed upon a wider set of kin, most would resist. What is interesting about our sample, however, is that most have not resisted the obligations imposed by the Children Act in principle, but they do find these obligations extremely hard to sustain in practice. The majority of parents wanted to maintain the relationship between their children and both parents; many also strove to sustain relationships with wider kin, but they were not ultimately prepared to do so either as a matter of duty or simply because of legal obligations. Where relationships worked, it was because the people involved altered their behaviour: they recognized the position of the other parent and the children, and they did not take love and commitment for granted. The core problem with current policy on post-divorce parenting is that it recognizes legal status (being a father, being married) but takes little notice of the practices of parenting, which include not just the adult's relationship with the child, but also the quality of the relationship between parents. It is, in our view, time that family law freed itself from the new orthodoxy (Maclean and Eekelaar, 1997) imposed by a narrow conception of the welfare of the child and broadened its understanding of 'care' to include parents with whose welfare the future welfare of children is intimately bound.

Notes

Chapter 1   Rethinking Family Life

1 This is the subtitle of his book *Modernity and Self-identity*, first published in 1991.
2 This avoidance of the term 'family' is sensible and does allow us to be freed from perennial problems of how then to relate 'the family' to 'society' etc. However, it possibly misses something equally important, namely the ongoing significance of the ideology of the family as trenchantly identified by Barrett and McIntosh (1982).
3 Of course one problem with this depiction of modern life is that it tends to presume that 'traditional life' was less complex and stressful and that decision making was less problematic. This may be a false image and may therefore overestimate some of the newness of the problems that we now have to face.
4 'Largely involuntarily and driven by social changes, individuals are entering a searching and explorative phase' (Beck and Beck-Gernsheim, 1995: 43).
5 For further evidence of this consider the following, in which Beck and Beck-Gernsheim start to sound very similar to New Right and the Ethical Socialists, and even like the populist commentator Melanie Phillips: 'Our thesis is that the structure of industrial society which laid down gender, family and occupational roles is crumbling away, and a modern form of archaic anarchy is breaking out, with love on its banner, and a thousand delights and obstacles in its path. It is this quest for personal freedom and satisfaction here and now, which can so quickly revert into hatred, desperation and loneliness, that is leaving its mark on the divorce and remarriage figures, on overlapping and serial families, as millions of people go in search of happiness' (1995: 170). See also Dench (1996) for a further example of this type of thinking.
6 This theme of men coming to envy women and perceiving women to 'have

it all' can be found in other commentaries. Pahl has argued: 'Indeed, men may now be learning to envy women who appear more able to balance home, work and family. Man cannot manage to be fathers or grandfathers as effectively as women can be mothers and grandmothers. The child comes from the mother, and no matter how much the father shares in the birth experience, it may seem second best. .... All this may lead them to envy women at a deep level, and envy can lead to depression' (1995: 190–91).

7 It is important to recognize that the trend in legal practice to awarding mothers the custody of children in contested cases is relatively recent and arguably not fully established until after the Divorce Reform Act 1969 in England and Wales.

8 We might also want to seek alternative explanations for the rise of fathers' rights movements.

9 See Mason (1996) for a full discussion of the complexities of the concept of care and its significance to the understanding of family life.

Chapter 2 Family Policy and the Research Agenda

1 Indeed the main author of the Law Commission's report (then Professor Brenda Hoggett) has argued against the continuing presumption that marriage should form the cornerstone of family law (Hale, 1997).

2 The position of unmarried parents was different. Basically the unmarried father would not have the same rights as the married father unless the mother had agreed to share parental responsibility with him or unless he was granted this by a court.

3 The validity of these findings has subsequently been questioned; the good outcomes could have resulted less from the fact of paternal contact for the children than from the minimal conflict to which they were exposed in the collaborating families (Maccoby et al., 1990). Moreover, subsequent research, based on larger and more representative samples, has found no such correlation between the well-being of the child and the amount of contact with the father (Furstenberg et al., 1987; Zill, 1988). There is growing recognition that outcomes for children may be related less to the structure of post-divorce parenting than to its quality, including the differential impact of the parents' relationship upon a child (Maccoby et al., 1990, 1992; Dunlop and Burns, 1988; Burghes, 1994).

4 Subsequent legislation, most notably the Family Law Act of 1996, has further entrenched the importance of ongoing contact after divorce in the letter of the law, and the practice of the Court of Appeal has pursued this new policy with enthusiasm (see chapter 9 for a full discussion of this). Maclean and Eekelaar (1997) refer to this shift as the emergence of a new orthodoxy which has taken the shape of an insistence that contact with a non-residential parent must be maintained if the child of a relationship is to avoid psychological and emotional harm. Notwithstanding that, the growing evidence of research suggests that to isolate the variable of quantity of contact is grossly to oversimplify the impact of divorce on children's lives.

5 But, as we shall argue in later chapters, it is possible to identify the production of a single new orthodoxy which has taken the shape of an insistence on joint-parenting and the enforcement of contact even where

this is resisted on reasonable grounds (Smart and Neale, 1997b).

6 As a separate part of the project we also interviewed a sample of thirty-seven solicitors on the workings of the Act and the extent to which their practice had changed. The result of this element of the project can be found in Neale and Smart, 1997b.

7 Mothers Apart from Their Children.

Chapter 3 Becoming a Post-divorce Parent

1 See Burgess, A. and Ruxton, S. (1996), Burghes, L. et al. (1997), Dennis, N. and Erdos, G. (1993), Ferri, E. and Smith, K. (1996), French, S., ed. (1993), Kiernan, K. E. (1997), Lewis, C. and O'Brien, M., eds (1987), Lewis, C. (1986), Moss, P., ed. (1995), Simpson, B. et al. (1995), Smart, C. and Sevenhuijsen, S. eds (1989).

2 All of our parents had lived together at some stage but in two cases mothers had left before the birth of their first child.

3 During the second half of the 1980s 58 per cent of mothers with dependent children were in paid employment, leaving 42 per cent who were unemployed and in a state of financial dependency. But only 17 per cent of mothers worked full time and 37 per cent part time. For those with children under the age of two, only 11 per cent worked full time, compared with 30 per cent where the children were over the age of ten. This pattern is reinforced by lack of state policies to support working parents, along with differentials in employment conditions and rewards. Thus women are relatively poorly paid and there is limited provision for maternity leave and childcare provision for working mothers. (For a full review see Fox Harding, 1996.)

4 These fathers are strikingly similar to the 'pioneers' in Barker's study (1994) of working-class lone fathers. They strove to become both mother and father rather than to rely wholly on female relatives to care for the children – at least initially.

5 At Time 1 fifteen fathers, from our data on sixty families, had children living with them. By Time 2 this had risen to twenty or one-third of the total number of fathers on whom we had information. These children may not have been living with them on a full-time basis but the point is that these were not 'occasional' fathers who saw their children for treats and holidays; they were as involved in the daily routines of care as were most mothers.

6 In some instances where fathers did not provide for their children mothers felt that they forfeited their status as fathers: As Ann Black put it, 'He got paid on a Thursday so he'd come up on a Thursday with me money, then he'd see them over the weekend. . . . If he didn't pay he wouldn't see them. Whether that's wrong I don't know, but that's how I see it at the moment.'

7 Some mothers felt that fathers who came to see the children after separation were actually more interested in re-establishing a relationship with the mother. As Tina Hurst put it, 'He came to see the children for about six weeks, but he kept talking to me. He never showed any interest in them.'

8 Although many mothers wanted to remain primary carers, this did not mean that they wanted to cut fathers out, rather they wanted to preserve the kind of relationship that had been established between father and child during the marriage. Penny King said, 'They are more secure with me

because I'm here all the time but I was concerned that he wouldn't abandon them. . . . He's good at talking to them intelligently and I don't want them to lose that because I think he's a good influence on them. . . . With girls I think it's vital that they have a father figure or it can upset their whole relationship with men.'

9 In chapter 7 we discuss how mothers can also take the opportunity of rewriting their identities after divorce – however, they do not seem to rewrite their parental identity.

10 Our classification resembles that of Furstenberg and Cherlin (1991), who distinguish between co-parenting, parallel parenting and single parenting. Classifications discerned by other researchers include: harmonious co-parent, conflicted co-parent and single parent (Lund, 1987); and communicative, parallel and no-contact parent (Simpson et al., 1995). Maccoby and Mnookin pay little attention in their work to what they call single parenting, focusing instead on three categories of co-parent: co-operative, disengaged and conflicted (Maccoby et al., 1990; Maccoby and Mnookin, 1992).

11 Cf. Piper's three elements of parenting: child caretaking, decision making and financial support (1993: 34).

12 At one extreme, for example, where parents live in different geographical regions a child may change residence every few months or years, or co-parenting will be built around school terms and holidays. In one case in our sample a mother agreed that her younger son could go to live with his father and new partner in America for a three-year period. Such patterns are more widespread in the United States (Cohen, 1991), although according to our definitions these arrangements fall somewhere between co-parenting and custodial parenting, since parental care and authority are not so much shared as alternated over time, and the parents' lives do not need to be bound up with each other.

13 We have retained the terminology pre-dating the Children Act for this pattern of parenting because although it no longer has any legal validity, the concept was very much in common usage among parents (and some solicitors) at the time of our fieldwork.

14 'Split' residence means that one or more child lives with one parent, while other siblings live with the other parent.

15 However, this is not the view of the Child Support Agency .

Chapter 5   Constructing Post-divorce Childhoods

1 It should be remembered that in this project we interviewed only the parents and so we can report on only the parents' perception of post-divorce childhood. A later project has interviewed the children of these same parents and will be published later.

2 In Nina Hester's case she had to fight very hard to prevent her husband having access to the children. In the end the court acknowledged that he had abused his son, but still gave him supervised contact with his daughter. Nina could not bring herself to take the child to the Contact Centre and her mother had to do it for her: 'You have to have a degree to be a doctor, raising a child might not be so instantaneous, if you make a mistake when you're slicing someone up on the operating table, you kill them. Imagine the emotional repercussions if you get it wrong when you're raising a

child? Just how many people are affected by that child when it grows up to be an adult? It's all wrong. You should not have to go in there and prove that he's unfit. He should have to prove that he is. Give him a list now. You know what could be [more] simple? If I wrote out a questionnaire "Is this right? If a child does this, what do you do? A, B, C?" I can guarantee he wouldn't score on it.'

3 There were two notable cases where it was the parent with whom the child lived who assumed less responsibility for the overall care of the child than the non-residential parent. One was a mother who did everything for her son (such as buying clothes, taking him to the dentist and doctor, ferrying him around) and in another a case where a mother was neglecting her son but refused to give him up to his father. In this case he was forever checking up on the child and eventually persuaded social services to become involved until he ultimately got the child living with him.

4 It would be false to suggest that the idea of a father substitute was widely rejected. Some mothers in our sample felt that it was very important for their children to have father substitutes, especially where biological fathers were seen as inadequate or uncaring. Many solo mothers also wanted to find father substitutes for their children.

Chapter 6   Moral Fragments?

1 Contact with parents after divorce is now taken to be a 'right' of the child rather than of parents. While this is an important shift in thinking – because it makes it clear that the child is not the property of the parents – it simply obfuscates the moral dilemma inherent in disputes between parents over contact. This so-called right tends to be used as a sledgehammer to resolve sensitive issues and to render disputes inaudible and illegitimate. Again, using an analogy to make this point clear, imagine a dispute between an employer and an employee where the employer is insisting that the employee should work a seven-day week or lose her or his job. Then supposing he or she went to arbitration and the panel stated that what was paramount was the right of the consumer to buy the product made by the firm seven days a week. The arbitrators would be saying that they were not at all interested in the content of the argument between the parties because there was a higher interest, that of the consumer. As a consequence, the employee would have to agree to work a seven-day week or lump it (possibly going to prison in the case of parental disputes!). Would this be the appropriate (i.e. moral) decision? How would the employee feel?

2 Feminism has not been so coy of course, but then feminist scholarship has been interdisciplinary and thus much more willing to cross boundaries between subjects like philosophy, psychology and sociology.

3 One of our parents was reading *The Exeter Family Study* (Cockett and Tripp, 1994) at the time of the second interviews. This study compares outcomes for children in 'intact' and 'split' families.

4 Although mothers can live on state benefits, we are referring here to the fact that husbands no longer have a legal duty to maintain their wives after divorce, only their children. It is now expected that women will take up work, even if they have not taken paid employment during their marriage.

5 This latter desire has two elements and we discovered that this is very

common among post-divorce parents. Residential parents often want their children to see more of the other parent for two reasons, the first is for the children and their relationship with the other parent, and the second is to give the primary carer more space for themselves.

Chapter 7   Fragments of Power and the Reconstituted Self

1 It was not our original intention to develop this chapter in this way. We had thought we would concentrate on how power relations within marriage spill over into post-divorce relationships and parenting. While this is still a core element of this chapter, as is often the case with empirical work, we found that a one-dimensional concentration on power hardly did justice to what our parents had been telling us. Certainly they spoke quite a lot about power in a variety of ways, but this concept alone could not capture the experiences that many of the parents in our study were relaying to us.

2 Of course men were much more able to move on in an unencumbered fashion because while freed of financial obligation they were also freed of the problem of raising children. Of course many may not have welcomed this 'freedom' but this was nevertheless the pattern that emerged in the 1980s.

3 Or conversely we might ponder whether Giddens' theory of intimacy and pure relationships is any longer an adequate analysis of modern heterosexual marriage and cohabitation.

4 The way that Dingwall et al. (1996) describe the relationship between mothers and fathers in mediation is very close to our understanding, but the main difference is that they only recognize what we have called situational power as power, and they disregard other issues in exactly the same way that the mediators do. It is worth quoting their work at some length: 'This gender-linked difference is closely related to the bargaining positions of male and female disputants. In the majority of cases, women are defending the status quo: holding out against requests for increased contact or, less commonly, demands that the children be removed from their day-to-day care. By the same token, men are usually in the position of seeking changes to the current situation, increasing their contact with the children at the mother's expense. The tendency of men to be more specific than women in linking "expressive" and "instrumental" issues is related to the (structural) positions of men and women within divorce cases. . . . Both male and female mediators tend to focus more on instrumental than expressive issues. In the majority of the sessions the mediators tend to try and exclude consideration of expressive issues concerning the relationship between the disputants and to focus on the formulation of proposals for contact and residence' (1996: 4–5).

5 A few of the men said that they had experienced violence. One mother acknowledged that she and her husband hit each other, one father said that he had had things thrown at him and he had been hit with a frying pan, another said that he had been stabbed and wanted to reveal his wound. In this last case, however, he freely admitted that this was totally out of character for his partner but that it had really strengthened his case in getting a Residence Order and restricting almost all contact between her and the children.

6 We are aware that this is something of a simplistic typology when compared with the more sophisticated ones deriving from dedicated studies of spousal violence. Johnston and Campbell (1993) have, for example, produced a complex typology which is designed to predict the likely seriousness of a violent attack, particularly in the post-separation period. However, although our typology is much more limited in scope, the basic premise is supported by other studies which have found essentially similar dimensions.

7 Sarah Birch: 'I could honestly have taken a knife to him and stabbed him. I could understand crimes of passion. I threw a hair brush at him once and cut his face and I was getting progressively worse. I just wished him dead. I'd never felt like that before. That and my odd behaviour were enough to say that I had got to do it otherwise the children wouldn't have a mother. I'm certainly not proud of myself for the way I reacted and wouldn't want to go through it again.'

Chapter 8   Law, Rights and Responsibilities

1 But see Piper (1997).

2 In this respect the ethic of care approach would come close to the more established principle deployed in some states in the USA and Canada which is the primary carer principle (Neely, 1984; Sandberg, 1989; Ziff, 1990). This presumption in favour of the parent who has been the primary carer for a child gives legal recognition to the value of the care that has been provided and also recognizes the value of continuity of care. However, it is not as flexible as the guidelines we are suggesting based on the ethic of care.

3 This would mean that solicitors would enquire into who had provided most of the care for the children and what kinds of arrangements had been established during the marriage/cohabitation, rather than merely assuming that equal rights must prevail.

4 It is of course a great irony that this Act heralded such a powerful ethic of justice when its aim was to improve the welfare of children.

5 See, for example, such cases as *Re H (A Minor)(Contact) [1994] 2 FLR 776, Re O (Contact: Imposition of Conditions) [1995] 2 FLR 124, Re P (Contact: Implacable Hostility) [The Times, 9 May 1996] and Re P (Contact: Supervision) [1996] 2 FLR 314.* Moreover, in the cases of *Z v Z (1996) Fam Law 225* and *RvN (Committal Refusal of Contact) [1997] 1 FLR 533,* the mothers, who had both been victims of violence, were imprisoned for refusing to facilitate contact. See Willbourne and Geddes (1995) and Rosenblatt and Scragg (1995) for examples of how keen the legal profession has been to vilify mothers who want to curtail contact.

6 It is important to note that Mrs Justice Hale was formerly Professor Brenda Hoggett, who was the leading Law Commissioner when the Children Act was formulated and drafted. It is in many ways her Act. Now that she is a judge she is in the position of influencing directly how it is interpreted.

Chapter 9   Family Law, Family Fragments and Feminist Thought

1 In remarking that coercion has been inflicted upon mothers, we are not

suggesting that this was the aim of the original legislation. Indeed this seems most unlikely. However, case law in the mid-1990s moved directly towards a policy of coercing 'implacably hostile' mothers, even if they were hostile for very good reasons. Interestingly, the main architect of the Children Act, then Professor Brenda Hoggett, on becoming a high court judge set about trying to challenge the courts' enthusiasm for branding and punishing the 'implacably hostile' mother. *See Re D (Contact: Reasons for Refusal) [1997] 2 FLR 48.*

2 The Conservative Government in the mid-1980s was so opposed to the idea that lesbian and gay unions should become socially acceptable that they introduced a clause into the Local Government Act (1986) which stated that a local authority shall not: '(a) intentionally promote homosexuality or publish material with the intention of promoting homosexuality; (b) promote the teaching in any maintained school of the acceptability of homosexuality as a pretended family relationship.' It is from this legislation that the notorious phrase 'pretended family relationship' comes.

3 '1994 Divorce Statistics', *Family Law*, 1997, 25: 630.

4 Elsewhere Smart has discussed some of the legal fictions that accompanied the desire to impose order on family life. In particular the nonsense of the legal presumption of legitimacy where any child born to a married woman was presumed to be the biological child of her husband (Smart, 1987).

5 *A v N (Committal: Refusal of Contact) [1997] 1FLR 533.*

6 It is interesting to note that in two of our cases where fathers had residence and were blocking contact between the children and their mothers, we discovered through telephone calls a year after our second interviews with them, that in one case residence had switched back to the mother and in the other the father had started to encourage contact because he had formed a new relationship with a woman whose children lived with her former husband. In the latter case she was able to explain to him what it felt like to be denied contact. In the former case, the father had become somewhat jaded with being a lone parent and the children had started to make it clear that they wanted their mother (who had been their full-time carer before the separation).

7 See chapter 2, note 6, p. 202.

8 One of the mothers we interviewed had lived with her children for two years before her former husband decided to 'snatch' them. He made various allegations against her which were shown to be unfounded, but he created a *status quo* effect and by the time the case went to court he was able to win the residence of the children. He then prevented her from seeing them. To quote from Jenny Swift's interview: 'I just can't understand why he's being so vindictive. I could have understood it if I'd run off with somebody or done something but with it being the other way round I don't know why he's still so vindictive. He wants to cut me out of the children's lives completely and he's just about done it. . . . I have to put my energy into different things, that was the only way to survive – so I put a lot of energy into my work and hobbies and things. The worst thing for me is I'll be looking forward all week to seeing them and then it gets to an hour before and instead of sending them, he's cancelled, which he does deliberately, knowing then that it's too late for me to ring anybody up and go out.' We contacted Jenny again a year after the research had concluded and

discovered that the father had had a change of heart. He was living with a woman whose own children were with her former husband. It seems that he had become less focused on the children and better able to understand Jenny's position.

Bibliography

Alanen, L. (1992) *Modern Childhood?* Research Report 50, Institute for Educational Research: University of Jyväskylä

Allen, G. (1985) *Family Life*, Oxford: Blackwell

Archbishop of Canterbury's Group (1966) *Putting Asunder: A Divorce Law for Contemporary Society*, London: SPCK

Backett, K. (1987a) 'The Negotiation of Fatherhood', in C. Lewis and M. O'Brien, eds, *Reassessing Fatherhood*, London: Sage

Backett, K. (1987b) *Mothers and Fathers*, London: Macmillan

Bainham, A. (1989) 'When is a Parent not a Parent? Reflections on the Unmarried Father and his Child in English Law', *International Journal of Law and the Family*, 3(2): 208–39

Barker, R. (1994) *Lone Fathers and Masculinities*, Aldershot: Avebury Press

Barrett, M. and McIntosh, M. (1982) *The Anti-social Family*, London: Verso

Bauman, Z. (1993) *Postmodern Ethics*, Cambridge: Polity Press

Bauman, Z. (1995) *Life in Fragments*, Oxford: Blackwell

Beck, U. (1992) *Risk Society: Towards a New Modernity*, London: Sage

Beck, U. and Beck-Gernsheim, E. (1995) *The Normal Chaos of Love*, Cambridge: Polity Press

Benhabib, S. (1992) *Situating the Self*, Cambridge: Polity Press

Berger, P. and Kellner, H. (1964) 'Marriage and the Construction of Reality', *Diogenes*, 46: 1–24

Bowden, P. (1997) *Caring: Gender-sensitive Ethics*, London: Routledge

Bowlby, J. (1965) *Childcare and the Growth of Love*, Harmondsworth: Penguin

Brannen, J. and Collard, J. (1982) *Marriages in Trouble: The Process of Seeking Help*, London: Tavistock

Brophy, J. (1982) 'Parental Rights and Children's Welfare: Some Problems of Feminists' Strategy in the 1920s', *International Journal of the Sociology of Law*, 7(2): 149–68

Brophy, J. (1989) 'Custody Law, Child Care and Inequality in Britain', in C.

Smart and S. Sevenhuijsen, eds, *Child Custody and the Politics of Gender*, London: Routledge

Burgess, A. and Ruxton, S. (1996) *Men and their Children: Proposals for Public Policy*, London: Institute for Public Policy Research

Burghes, L. (1994) *Lone Parenthood and Family Disruption: The Outcomes for Children*, London: Family Policy Studies Centre

Burghes, L., Clarke, L. and Cronin, N. (1997) *Fathers and Fatherhood in Britain*, London: Family Policy Studies Centre

Butler, J. (1990) *Gender Trouble: Feminism and the Subversion of Identity*, London: Routledge

Cheal, D. (1991) *Family and the State of Theory*, New York: Harvester Wheatsheaf

Clulow, C. and Vincent, C. (1987) *In the Child's Best Interests*, London: Tavistock

Cockett, M. and Tripp, J. (1994) *The Exeter Family Study: Family Breakdown and its Impact upon Children*, Exeter: Exeter University Press

Cohen, M. (1991) *The Joint Custody Handbook: Creating Arrangements that Work*, Philadelphia: Running Press

Collier, R. (1995) *Masculinity, Law and the Family*, London: Routledge

Cretney, S. (1997) 'Lawyers under the Family Law Act', *Family Law*, 27 (June): 405–12

Davis, G. (1988) *Partisans and Mediators*, Oxford: Clarendon Press

Delphy, C. (1976) 'Continuities and Discontinuities in Marriage and Divorce', in D. Leonard Barker and S. Allen, eds, *Sexual Divisions and Society*, London: Tavistock

Dench, G. (1996) 'Men without a Mission', *Times Higher Education Supplement*, 28 June

Dench, G. (1997) *Rewriting the Sexual Contract*, London: Institute of Community Studies

Dennis, N. and Erdos, G. (1993) *Families without Fatherhood*, 2nd edition, London: Institute of Economic Affairs

Dingwall, R. and Eekelaar, J. (1988) *Divorce Mediation and the Legal Process*, Oxford: Clarendon Press

Dingwall, R., Greatbatch, D. and Ruggerone, L. (1996) 'Divorce Mediation: Micro-studies and Macro-issues', paper delivered to the Joint LSA/RCSL Conference, Glasgow: 10–13 July

Douglas, J. (1971) *American Social Order*, New York: Free Press

Dunlop, R. and Burns, A. (1988) *Don't Feel the World is Caving In: Adolescents in Divorcing Families*, Monograph 6, Melbourne: Australian Institute of Family Studies

Dunne, G. A. (1997) *Lesbian Lifestyles: Women's Work and the Politics of Sexuality*, Basingstoke and London: Macmillan

Eekelaar, J. (1991) 'Parental Responsibility: State of Nature or Nature of the State?', *Journal of Social Welfare and Family Law*, 1: 37–50

Eekelaar, J. and Clive, E. (1977) *Custody after Divorce*, Oxford: Centre for Socio-legal Studies

Eekelaar, J. and Maclean, M. (1986) *Maintenance after Divorce*, Oxford: Oxford University Press

Eekelaar, J. and Sarcevic, P., eds (1993) *Parenthood in Modern Society: Legal and Social Issues for the Twenty-first Century*, Dordrecht: Martinus Nijhoff

Etzioni, A. (1993) *The Parenting Deficit*, London: Demos

Everingham, C. (1994) *Motherhood and Modernity*, Milton Keynes: Open University Press

Ferguson, M. and Wicke, J., eds (1994) *Feminism and Postmodernism*, London: Duke University Press

Ferri, E. and Smith, K. (1996) *Parenting in the 1990s*, London: Family Policy Studies Centre

Finch, J. (1989) *Family Obligations and Social Change*, Cambridge: Polity Press

Finch, J. (1993) 'Problems and Issues in Studying the Family', in A. Leira, ed., *Family Sociology: Developing the Field*, Oslo: Institute for Social Research: 16–33

Finch, J. (1997) *The State and the Family*, lecture to inaugurate the Institute's annual theme for 1996–7, 30 October 1996, Edinburgh: International Social Sciences Institute

Finch, J. and Groves, D., eds (1983) *A Labour of Love*, London: Routledge and Kegan Paul

Finch, J. and Mason, J. (1990) 'Decision Taking in the Fieldwork Process', *Studies in Qualitative Methodology*, 2: 25–50

Finch, J. and Mason, J. (1993) *Negotiating Family Responsibilities*, London: Routledge

Fineman, M. (1995) *The Neutered Mother, the Sexual Family and other Twentieth Century Tragedies*, London: Routledge

Finer, M. (1974), *Report of the Committee on One-Parent Families*, vols I and II, London: HMSO, Cmnd 5629

Fletcher, R. (1966) *Family and Marriage in Britain*, Harmondsworth: Penguin

Fox Harding, L. (1996) *Family, State and Social Policy*, London: Macmillan

French, S., ed. (1993) *Fatherhood*, London: Virago

Furstenberg, F. and Cherlin, A. (1991) *Divided Families: What Happens to Children when Parents Part?*, Cambridge, Mass.: Harvard University Press

Furstenberg, F. and Nord, C. (1985) 'Parenting Apart: Patterns of Child Rearing after Marital Disruption', *Journal of Marriage and the Family*, 47: 893–904

Furstenberg, F., Morgan, S. and Allison, P. (1987) 'Paternal Participation and Children's Well-being after Marital Dissolution', *American Sociological Review*, 52: 695–701

Gibson, C. (1994) *Dissolving Wedlock*, London: Routledge

Giddens, A. (1991) *Modernity and Self-identity: Self and Society in the Late Modern Age*, Cambridge: Polity Press

Giddens, A. (1992) *The Transformation of Intimacy*, Cambridge: Polity Press

Gilligan, C. (1982) *In a Different Voice*, London: Harvard University Press

Gingerbread and Families Need Fathers (1982) *Divided Children: A Survey of Access to Children after Divorce*, London: Gingerbread and FNF

Goldstein, J., Freud, A. and Solnit, A. (1979) *Beyond the Best Interests of the Child*, 2nd edition, New York: Free Press

Goode, W. (1965) *Women in Divorce*, New York: Free Press

Griffiths, M. (1995) *Feminisms and the Self: The Web of Identity*, London: Routledge

Hale, Mrs Justice (1997) 'Private Lives and Public Duties: What is family law for?', The Eighth ESRC Annual Lecture, London, 23 October

Hall, Mr Justice (1997) 'Domestic Violence and Contact', *Family Law*, 27: 813–18

Hall, S. (1980) 'Reformism and the Legislation of Consent' in National Deviancy Conference, ed., *Permissiveness and Control*, London: Macmillan

Hallden, G. (1991) 'The Child as Project and the Child as Being: Parents' Ideas as Frames of Reference', *Children & Society*, 5(4): 334–46

Haskey, J. (1996) 'Divorce Statistics', *Family Law*, 26: 301–4

Hekman, S. (1990) *Gender and Knowledge: Elements of a Postmodern Feminism*, Boston: Northeastern University Press

Hekman, S. (1995) *Moral Voices, Moral Selves*, Cambridge: Polity Press

Hester, M., Humphries, J., Pearson, C., et al. (1994) 'Domestic Violence and Child Contact', in A. Mullender and R. Morley, eds, *Children Living with Domestic Violence*, London: Whiting & Birch: 102–21

Hester, M. and Radford, L. (1996) *Domestic Violence and Child Contact Arrangements in England and Denmark*, University of Bristol: Policy Press

Hetherington, E., Cox, M. and Cox, R. (1978) 'The Aftermath of Divorce', in J. Stevens and M. Matthews, eds, *Mother-Child, Father-Child Relations*, Washington, DC: National Association for the Education of Young Children

Hetherington, E., Cox, M. and Cox, R. (1982) 'Effects of Divorce on Parents and Children', in M. Lamb, ed., *Non-traditional Families*, Hillsdale, NJ: Lawrence Erlbaum Associates

Hochschild, A. (1995) 'Understanding the Future of Fatherhood', in M. van Dongen, G. Frinking and M. Jacobs, eds, *Changing Fatherhood*, Amsterdam: Thesis Publishers: 219–30

Hochschild, A. (1997) *The Time Bind: When Work Becomes Home and Home Becomes Work*, New York: Metropolitan Books

Hoggett, B. (1989) 'The Children Bill: The Aim', *Family Law*, 19: 217–21

Hoggett, B. (1994) 'Joint Parenting Systems: The English Experiment', *Journal of Child Law*, 6(1): 8–12

Hooper, C. (1994) 'Do Families need Fathers?: The Impact of Divorce upon Children', in A. Mullender and R. Morley, eds, *Children Living with Domestic Violence*, London: Whiting & Birch: 86–101

Humphrey, R. (1996) *Families behind the Headlines*, Newcastle: British Association for the Advancement of Science/University of Newcastle

Ingleby, R. (1988) 'The Solicitor as Intermediary', in R. Dingwall and J. Eekelaar, eds, *Divorce Mediation and the Legal Process*, Oxford: Clarendon Press

Ingleby, R. (1992) *Solicitors and Divorce*, Oxford: Clarendon Press

James, A. (1992) 'An Open or Shut Case? Law as an Autopoietic System', *Journal of Law and Society*, 19 (2): 271–83

James, A. and Hay, W. (1993) *Court Welfare in Action*, Hemel Hempstead: Harvester Wheatsheaf

James, A. and Prout, A., eds (1990) *Constructing and Reconstructing Childhood*, Brighton: Falmer Press

Johnston, J. (1993) 'Children of Divorce who Refuse Visitation', in C. Depner and J. Bray, eds, *Non-residential Parenting*, London: Sage

Johnston, J. and Campbell, E. G. (1993) 'A Clinical Typology of Interparental Violence in Disputed-custody Divorces', *American Journal of Orthopsychiatry*, 63(2): 190–99

Jolly, S. (1995) 'Implacable Hostility, Contact and the Limits of the Law', *Child and Family Law Quarterly*, 7 (4): 228–35

Joshi, H. (1991) 'Sex and Motherhood as Handicaps in the Labour Market', in M. Maclean and D. Groves, eds, *Women's Issues in Social Policy*, London: Routledge

Kaganas, F. and Piper, C. (1994) 'Domestic Violence and Divorce Mediation', *Journal of Social Welfare and Family Law*, 3: 265–78

Kelly, J. (1993) 'Current Research on Children's Post Divorce Adjustment', *Family and Conciliation Courts Review*, 31(1): 29–49

Kiernan, K. E. (1993) *Cohabitation: Extra-marital Childbearing and Social Policy*, London: Family Policy Studies Centre

Kiernan, K. E. (1997) *The Legacy of Parental Divorce*, CASE paper 1, London: London School of Economics

Laing, R. D. (1971) *The Politics of the Family*, London: Tavistock

Land, H. (1976) 'Women: Supporters or Supported', in D. Leonard Barker and S. Allen, eds, *Sexual Divisions in Society*, London: Tavistock

Larrabee, M. J., ed. (1993) *An Ethic of Care*, London: Routledge

Law Commission (1966) *Report on the Reform of the Grounds of Divorce: The Field of Choice*, 6, London: HMSO

Law Commission (1986) *Family Law Review of Child Law: Custody*, working paper 96, London: HMSO

Law Commission (1988) *Review of Child Law: Guardianship and Custody*, Law Commission Report, 172, London: HMSO

Law Commission (1990) *The Grounds for Divorce*, Law Commission Report, 192, London: HMSO

Leonard, D. (1978) 'The Regulation of Marriage: Repressive Benevolence', in G. Littlejohn et al., eds, *Power and the State*, London: Croom Helm

Lewis, C. (1986) *Becoming a Father*, Milton Keynes: Open University Press

Lewis, C. and O'Brien, M., eds (1987) *Reassessing Fatherhood*, London: Sage

Lord Chancellor's Department (1995) *Looking to the Future*, London: HMSO, Cm 2799

Lund, M. (1987) 'The Non-custodial Father: Common Challenges in Parenting after Divorce', in C. Lewis and M. O'Brien, (eds), *Reassessing Fatherhood*, London: Sage

McCant, J. (1987) 'The Cultural Contradiction of Fathers as Nonparents', *Family Law Quarterly*, 21(1): 127–43

Maccoby, E. and Mnookin, R. (1992) *Dividing the Child: Social and Legal Dilemmas of Custody*, Cambridge, Mass.: Harvard University Press

Maccoby, E., Depner, C. and Mnookin, R. (1990) 'Co-parenting in the Second Year after Divorce', *Journal of Marriage and the Family*, 52: 141–55

McGregor, O. R. (1957) *Divorce in England*, London: Heinemann

Mackintosh, M. (1979) 'Domestic Labour and the Household', in S. Burman, ed., *Fit Work for Women*, London: Croom Helm

Maclean, M. (1994) 'The Making of the Child Support Act of 1991: Policy Making at the Intersection of Law and Social Policy', *Journal of Law and Society*, 21 (4): 505–19

Maclean, M. and Eekelaar, J. (1997) *The Parental Obligation: A Study of Parenthood across Households*, Oxford: Hart Publishing

Maidment, S. (1981) *Child Custody: What Chance for Fathers?*, London: National Council for One-Parent Families

Marcuse, H. (1955) *Eros and Civilisation*, Boston: Beacon Press

Mason, J. (1996) 'Gender, Care and Sensibility in Family and Kin Relationships', in J. Holland and L. Atkins, eds, *Sex, Sensibility and the Gendered Body*, Basingstoke and London: Macmillan

Mason, M. A. (1994) *From Father's Property to Children's Rights*, New York: Columbia University Press

Miller, A. (1987) *For your own Good*, London: Virago

Mitchell, A. (1985) *Children in the Middle: Living with Divorce*, London: Tavistock

Mitchell, J. and Goody, J. (1997) 'Feminism, Fatherhood and the Family in Britain', in A. Oakley and J. Mitchell, eds, *Who's Afraid of Feminism?*, New York: New Press

Mnookin, R. (1979) *Bargaining in the Shadow of the Law*, working paper 5, Oxford: Centre for Socio-legal Studies

Morgan, D. (1991) 'Ideologies of Marriage and Family Life', in D. Clark, ed., *Marriage, Domestic Life and Social Change*, London: Routledge

Morgan, D. (1996) *Family Connections*, Cambridge: Polity Press

Morgan, D. (1999) 'Risk and Family Practices: Accounting for Change and Fluidity in Family Life', in E. B. Silva and C. Smart, eds, *The 'New' Family?*, London: Sage, chapter 2, pp. 13–30

Morgan, P. (1995) *Farewell to the Family?*, London: Institute of Economic Affairs

Morton, Lord (1956) *Royal Commission on Marriage and Divorce 1951–1955 Report*, London: HMSO, Cmd 9678

Moss, P., ed. (1995) *Father Figures: Fathers in the Families of the 1990s*, Edinburgh: HMSO

Mullender, A. and Morley, R., eds (1994) *Children Living with Domestic Violence*, London: Whiting & Birch

Murch, M. (1980) *Justice and Welfare in Divorce*, London: Sweet & Maxwell

NCH Action for Children (1994) *The Hidden Victims: Children and Domestic Violence*, London: National Children's Homes Action for Children

Neale, B. and Smart, C. (1997a) 'Experiments with Parenthood?', *Sociology*, 31 (2): 201–19

Neale, B. and Smart, C. (1997b) '"Good" and "Bad" Lawyers?: Struggling in the Shadow of the New Law', *Journal of Social Welfare and Family Law*, 19(4): 377–402

Neely, R. (1984) 'The Primary Caretaker Parent Rule: Child Custody and the Dynamics of Greed', *Yale Law & Policy Review*, 3: 168–85

Nicholson, L. (1997) 'The Myth of the Traditional Family', in H. L. Nelson, ed., *Feminism and Families*, London: Routledge

Norton, C. (1982) *Caroline Norton's Defence*, Chicago: Academy, 1st edition, 1854

Oakley, A. (1974) *The Sociology of Housework*, Oxford: Martin Robertson

Pahl, R. (1995) *After Success*, Cambridge: Polity Press

Phillips, M. (1997) *The Sex Change State*, London: Social Market Foundation, Memorandum 30, October

Phoenix, A., Woollett, A. and Lloyd, E. (1991) *Motherhood: Meanings, Practices, Ideologies*, London: Sage

Piper, C. (1993) *The Responsible Parent*, Hemel Hempstead: Harvester Wheatsheaf

Piper, C. (1997) 'Ascertaining the Wishes and Feelings of the Child', *Family Law*, 27: 796–800

Ribbens, J. (1992) 'Mothers with Young Children: Responsibility with or without Authority?', paper presented to the British Sociological Association Annual Conference, University of Kent, April 1993

Ribbens, J. (1994) *Mothers and their Children: A Feminist Sociology of Childrearing*, London: Sage

Rich, A. (1985) 'Anger and Tenderness: The Experience of Motherhood', in E.

Whitelegg et al., eds, *The Changing Experience of Women*, Oxford: Blackwell

Richards, M. (1982) 'Post-divorce Arrangements for Children: A Psychological Perspective', *Journal of Social Welfare Law*, 69: 133–51

Richards, M. (1993) 'Children and Parents and Divorce', in Eekelaar and Sarcevic, eds, *Parenthood in Modern Society: Legal and Social Issues for the Twenty-first Century*, Dordrecht: Martinus Nijhoff: 307–15

Riley, D. (1988) *'Am I That Name?': Feminism and the Category of 'Woman' in History*, London: Macmillan

Roche, J. (1991) 'The Children Act: Once a Parent, Always a Parent?', *Journal of Social Welfare Law*, 5: 345–61

Rosenblatt, J. and Scragg, P. (1995) 'The Hostile Parent: A Clinical Analysis', *Family Law*, 25: 152–3

Sandberg, K. (1989) 'Best Interests and Justice', in C. Smart and S. Sevenhuijsen, eds, *Child Custody and the Politics of Gender*, London: Routledge: 100–25

Sevenhuijsen, S. (1998) *Citizenship and the Ethics of Care: Feminist Considerations about Justice, Morality and Politics*, London: Routledge

Silva, E. and Smart, C., eds (1998) *The New Family?* London: Sage

Simpson, B., McCarthy, P. and Walker, J. (1995) *Being There: Fathers after Divorce*, Newcastle: Relate Centre for Family Studies

Smart, C. (1984) *The Ties that Bind*, London: Routledge and Kegan Paul

Smart, C. (1987) '"There is of course the distinction dictated by nature": Law and the Problem of Paternity', in M. Stanworth, ed., *Reproductive Technologies*, Oxford: Polity Press: 98–117

Smart, C. (1990) *The Legal and Moral Ordering of Child Custody*, Report to the Nuffield Foundation, University of Warwick

Smart, C. (1991) 'The Legal and Moral Ordering of Child Custody', *Journal of Law and Society*, 18(4): 485–500

Smart, C. (1996) 'Deconstructing Motherhood', in Silva, E. ed., *Good Enough Mothering: Feminist Perspectives on Lone Mothering*, London: Routledge

Smart, C. (1997) 'Wishful Thinking and Harmful Tinkering? Sociological Reflection on Family Policy', *Journal of Social Policy*, 26 (3): 1–21

Smart, C. and Neale, B. (1997a) 'Good Enough Morality?: Divorce and Postmodernity', *Critical Social Policy*, 53: 3–27

Smart, C. and Neale, B. (1997b) 'Arguments against Virtue: Must Contact be Enforced?', *Family Law*, 28: 332–6

Smart, C. and Sevenhuijsen, S., eds (1989) *Child Custody and the Politics of Gender*, London: Routledge

Théry, I. (1989) 'The "interests of the child" and the Regulation of the Post Divorce Family', in C. Smart and S. Sevenhuijsen, eds, *Child Custody and the Politics of Gender*, London: Routledge: 78–99

Tronto, J. C. (1989) 'Women and Caring: What can Feminists Learn about Morality from Caring?', in A. Jaggar and S. Bordo, eds, *Gender, Body, Knowledge*, New Brunswick: Rutgers University Press

Tronto, J. C. (1993) *Moral Boundaries*, London: Routledge

Walker, J. (1993) 'Parenting after Separation', unpublished paper presented at the Joseph Rowntree Foundation Seminar: Relationship Breakdown and the Management of Change, London, November

Wallerstein, J. and Kelly, J. (1980) *Surviving the Breakup*, New York: Basic Books

Weeks, J., Donovan, C. and Heaphy, B. (1998) 'Everyday Experiments:

Narratives of Non-heterosexual Relationships', in E. Silva and C. Smart, eds, *The New Family?* London: Sage

Weston, K. (1991) *Families we Choose: Lesbian, Gays and Kinship*, New York: Columbia University Press

Weyland, I. (1997) 'The Blood Tie: Raised to the Status of a Presumption', *Journal of Social Welfare & Family Law*, 19(2): 173–88

Wheelan, R., ed. (1995) *Just a Piece of Paper? Divorce Reform and the Undermining of Marriage*, London: Institute of Economic Affairs

Willbourne, C. and Geddes, J. (1995) 'Presumption of Contact: What Presumption?', *Family Law*, 25: 87–9

Winnicott, D. W. (1971) *The Child, the Family, and the Outside World*, Harmondsworth, Penguin

Young, M. and Willmott, P. (1973) *The Symmetrical Family*, London: Routledge and Kegan Paul

Ziff, B. (1990) 'The Primary Caretaker Presumption: Canadian Perspectives on an American Development', *International Journal of Law and the Family*, 4: 186–200

Zill, N. (1988) 'Behaviour, Achievement and Health Problems among Children in Step-families : Findings from a National Survey of Child Health', in E. Hetherington and J. Arasteh, eds, *The Impact of Divorce, Single Parenting and Step-parenting on Children*, Hillsdale, NJ: Lawrence Erlbaum Associates

Index

$\mathcal{P}$lant more flowers
than you pick.

$\mathcal{F}$ollow your own star.

$\mathcal{R}$emember the ones
who love you.

Love, respect,
and home-grown
tomatoes are all
that really matter
in the end.

—ROBERT WALLER

*R*emember the three
powerful resources you
always have available
to you:

LOVE
PRAYER
FORGIVENESS

I long to accomplish a great
and noble task, but it is my
chief duty to accomplish
humble tasks as though they
were great and noble.
The world is moved along,
not only by the mighty shoves
of its heroes, but also by the
aggregate of the tiny pushes
of each honest worker.

—HELEN KELLER

How wonderful it is
that nobody need wait a
single moment before starting
to improve their world.

—ANNE FRANK

The real things haven't changed.

It is still best to be honest
and truthful;

to make the most of what
we have;

to be happy with simple
pleasures;

and to have courage when
things go wrong.

—Laura Ingalls Wilder

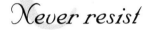

Never resist

a generous

impulse.

$\mathcal{D}$ream big.
There is little power
in little plans.

$\mathscr{I}$'ve learned that…

. . . if you want your children to be good readers, let them see you read.

—AGE 31

. . . the quality of my life is enhanced by volunteering.

—AGE 36

$\mathcal{B}$e bold and courageous.
When you look back on
your life, you'll regret the
things you didn't do more
than the ones you did.

Remember that you can almost always improve your performance by improving your attitude.

When you were born,
you cried and the world
rejoiced. Live your life
in such a manner that
when you die the world
cries and you rejoice.

—OLD INDIAN PROVERB

$\mathcal{I}$'ve learned that...

. . . the best way to have friends is to be the kind of friend you'd like to have.

—AGE 62

. . . love never grows old when you grow old with the one you love.

—AGE 71

in the noisy confusion of life, keep peace with your soul.

With all its sham, drudgery, and broken dreams, it is still a beautiful world. Be careful. Strive to be happy.

—ANONYMOUS

It is one of the most beautiful compensations of life that no man can sincerely try to help another without helping himself.

—RALPH WALDO EMERSON

Exercise caution in your business affairs for the world is full of trickery. But let this not blind you to what virtue there is. Many persons strive for high ideals and everywhere life is full of heroism. . . .

You are a child of the universe, no less than the trees and the stars; you have a right to be here. And whether or not it is clear to you, no doubt the universe is unfolding as it should.

Therefore, be at peace with God, whatever you conceive Him to be, and whatever your labors and aspirations

$\mathcal{B}$ecome an example of
what you want to see
more of in the world.

$\mathcal{R}$emember that no one
deserves your best behavior
more than your family.

What is the use
in living if not to strive
for noble causes and
to make this muddled world
a better place for those
who will live in it after
you are gone?

—WINSTON CHURCHILL

I've learned that…

. . . I don't need more to be
thankful for; I need to be
thankful more.

—AGE 46

. . . when someone forgives
you, they give you a gift; when
you forgive someone else,
you give a gift to yourself.

—AGE 32

Treat people as if they
were what they ought to be
and you can help them
to become what they are
capable of becoming.

—Johann Wolfgang von Goethe

A man's
accomplishments
in life are the
cumulative effect
of his attention
to detail.

—JOHN FOSTER DULLES

$\mathcal{N}$ever be too busy to
meet someone new.

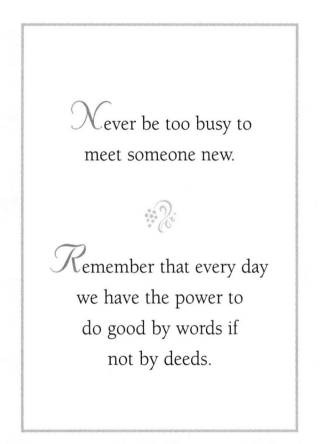

$\mathcal{R}$emember that every day
we have the power to
do good by words if
not by deeds.

In matters of style,
swim with the current;
in matters of principle,
stand like a rock.

—THOMAS JEFFERSON

*L*et your children observe
you being generous
to those in need.

I would like to have
engraved inside every
wedding band BE KIND TO
ONE ANOTHER. This is the
Golden Rule of marriage
and the secret of making
love last through the years.

—RUDOLPH RAY

Do not care overly much
for wealth or power or fame,
or one day you will meet
someone who cares for
none of these things, and
you will realize how
poor you have become.

—RUDYARD KIPLING

$\mathcal{W}$hen facing a difficult
task, act as though it is
impossible to fail. If you're
going after Moby Dick,
take along the tartar sauce.

*Don't forget that
what you are
thinking about,
you are becoming.*

I've learned that…

. . . a torch loses no heat by lighting a thousand torches.

—AGE 59

. . . people will remember how you treated them long after they have forgotten what you were wearing.

—AGE 42

*A reputation for
a thousand years
may depend upon
the conduct of
a single moment.*

—ERNEST BRAMAH

You and I cannot determine what other men shall think and say about us. We can only determine what they ought to think of us and say about us.

—Josiah Gilbert Holland

$\mathcal{R}$emember that when
you take inventory
of the things in life
you treasure most,
you'll find that none
of them was purchased
with money.

The people on our
planet are not standing
in a line single file.
Everyone is really standing
in a circle, holding hands.
Whatever you give to
the person standing next
to you eventually comes
back to you.

15. Don't overlook life's small joys while searching for the big ones.

16. Discover the power of prayer.

17. Discover the power of forgiveness.

18. Love people more than things.

19. Look for the good.

20. Search for the truth.

21. Hope for the best.

9. Be devoted to your spouse and dedicated to your children.

10. Be of service to your community and to your country.

11. Have courage when things go wrong.

12. Tell the truth.

13. Maintain a grateful heart.

14. Manage your resources wisely.

5. Take family vacations whether you can afford them or not.

6. Stand up for your principles even if you stand alone.

7. Judge your success by the degree that you're enjoying peace, health, and love.

8. Be there when people need you.

21 Suggestions for Living Wisely and Well

1. Teach by example.

2. Bless every day with a generous act.

3. Never waste an opportunity to tell someone you love them.

4. Do something every day that maintains your good health.

$\mathcal{I}$'ve learned that...

. . . old friends and laugh
lines are life's finest trophies.

—AGE 78

. . . an old Bible falling apart
usually belongs to someone
who isn't.

—AGE 62

A happy home

is a glimpse

of heaven.

$\mathcal{R}$ekindle old friendships.

❧

$\mathcal{N}$ever underestimate
the power of a kind word
or deed.

❧

$\mathcal{S}$hare your knowledge
and experience.

We—all of us, but especially the young—need around us individuals who possess a certain nobility, a language of soul, and qualities of human excellence worth imitating and striving for. Every parent knows this, which is why parents are concerned with both the company their children keep and the role models they choose. Children watch what we do as well as what we say, and if we expect them to take morality seriously, they must see adults taking it seriously.

—WILLIAM J. BENNETT

This is our purpose:
to make as meaningful as
possible this life that has been
bestowed upon us; to live
in such a way that we may be
proud of ourselves; to act
in such a way that some part
of us lives on.

—OSWALD SPENGLER

I've learned that...

...the older I get, the more
I appreciate the times my
parents said no.

—AGE 17

...your conscience will
sometimes hurt when
everything else feels good.

—AGE 52

$\mathcal{R}$egardless of the situation,
react with class.

$\mathcal{C}$herish your children for
what they are, not for what
you want them to be.

Compliment three
people every day.

Take care of your
reputation; it's your
most valuable asset.

Choose a charity in your community and support it generously with your time and money.

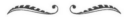

Never deprive someone of hope; it might be all they have.

Resolve to be tender with
the young, compassionate with
the aged, sympathetic with the
striving, tolerant with the weak,
and forgiving with the wrong.
Sometime in your life you will
have been all of these.

—Lloyd Shearer

$\mathcal{R}$emember that no situation is so bad that losing your temper won't make it worse.

$\mathcal{A}$pply this simple rule to your conversations: If you wouldn't write it down and sign it, don't say it.

He who passively accepts evil is as much involved in it as he who helps to perpetuate it.

—Martin Luther King Jr.

Speak only well of
people and you'll never
have to whisper.

Be modest. Much was
accomplished before
you were born.

Never ignore evil.

$\mathcal{I}$'ve learned that…

. . . pain is inevitable;
misery is optional.

—AGE 100

. . . there's no greater
resource when you're
a new mother than
your mother.

—AGE 29

Never esteem anything
as of advantage to you that
will make you break your word
or lose your self-respect.

—MARCUS AURELIUS

Honor is like an island,
rugged and without a beach;
once we have left it,
we can never return.

—NICHOLAS BOILEAU-DESPREAUX

If we discovered that we had
only five minutes left
to say all that we wanted
to say, every telephone booth
would be occupied
by people calling other
people to stammer that
they loved them.

—CHRISTOPHER MORLEY

That best portion of a
good man's life—His little,
nameless, unremembered acts
of kindness and of love.

—WILLIAM WORDSWORTH

Be ashamed to die until
you have won some
victory for humanity.

—HORACE MANN

You are not here merely to
make a living. You are here in
order to enable the world to live
more amply, with greater vision,
with a finer spirit of hope and
achievement. You are here to
enrich the world, and you
impoverish yourself
if you forget the errand.

—WOODROW WILSON

ROTARY INTERNATIONAL'S FOUR-WAY TEST

1. Is it the TRUTH?

2. Is it FAIR to all concerned?

3. Will it build GOODWILL and BETTER FRIENDSHIPS?

4. Will it be BENEFICIAL to all concerned?

$\mathcal{B}$e open and accessible. The next person you meet could become your best friend.

$\mathcal{N}$ever watch a video or movie with your children or take them to a live performance that involves activities and language that you don't want them to imitate.

A thousand words will not
leave so deep an
impression as one deed.

—HENRIK IBSEN

I agree . . . that there is a
natural aristocracy among men.
The grounds of this are
virtue and talents.

—THOMAS JEFFERSON

Let your hand feel for the afflictions and distress of everyone, and let your hand give in proportion to your purse, remembering always the estimation of the widow's mite. Not everyone that asketh deserveth charity; all however, are worthy of the inquiry or the deserving may suffer.

—GEORGE WASHINGTON

$\mathcal{W}$hen a friend is in need,
help him without his
having to ask.

$\mathcal{B}$ecome the most
positive and enthusiastic
person you know.

$\mathcal{L}$eave everything
a little better than
you found it.

$\mathcal{H}$ave courage when
things go wrong.

$\mathcal{N}$ever give up
on what you really
want to do.
The person with
big dreams is more
powerful than one
with all the facts.

Many of the things you
can count, don't count.
Many of the things you can't
count, really count.

—ALBERT EINSTEIN

You have a lifetime to work,
but children are young once.

—POLISH PROVERB

$\mathcal{B}$e happy with what you have while working for what you want.

$\mathcal{L}$ook for opportunities to make people feel important.

$\mathcal{N}$ever underestimate the
influence of the people you
have allowed into your life.

We are what we repeatedly do.
Excellence, then,
is not an art but a habit.

—ARISTOTLE

He did it with all
his heart,
and prospered.

—2 CHRONICLES 31:21 (KJV)

The most important
handshake of your life
will happen when your
newborn infant's tiny
hand grabs hold
of your index finger.

—ANONYMOUS

$\mathcal{G}$et involved at your
child's school.

$\mathcal{L}$ove people more
than things.

$\mathcal{L}$et your life be
your sermon.

Do not consider anything
for your interest which
makes you break your word,
quiet your modesty, or
incline you to any
practice which will not
bear the light or look the
world in the face.

—MARCUS AURELIUS

I've learned that...

. . . if you let your integrity slip just a little, it can have lasting consequences.

—Age 51

. . . a happy person is not a person with a certain set of circumstances but rather a person with a certain set of attitudes.

—Age 19

Let love be genuine; hate
what is evil, hold fast to what
is good; love one another with
brotherly affection; outdo one
another in showing honor. . . .
Rejoice in your hope,
be patient in tribulation,
be constant in prayer.

—ROMANS 12:9-12 (RSV)

*D*onate two pints of
blood every year.

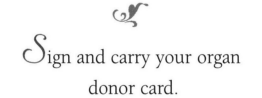

*S*ign and carry your organ
donor card.

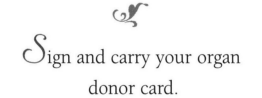

*C*ommit yourself to
constant self-improvement.

Do not pray for easy lives.
Pray to be stronger men!
Do not pray for tasks equal
to your powers. Pray for
powers equal to your tasks.
Then the doing of your
work will be no miracle,
but you shall be the miracle.

—PHILLIPS BROOKS

$\mathcal{E}$very person you meet knows something you don't know. Learn from them.

$\mathcal{D}$on't let the weeds grow around your dreams.

$\mathcal{B}$ecome someone's hero.

$\mathcal{I}$'ve learned that...

... children need loving the most when they are the hardest to love.

—AGE 79

... marriage is all about compromising and forgiving.

—AGE 35

I BELIEVE in the sacredness of
a promise, that a man's word
should be as good as his bond;
that character—not wealth
or power or position—
is of supreme worth.

I BELIEVE that love is the
greatest thing in the world;
that it alone can overcome hate;
that right can and
will triumph over might.

Things which matter
most must never be at
the mercy of things
which matter least.

—JOHANN WOLFGANG VON GOETHE

I hope I shall always
possess firmness and
virtue enough to maintain
what I consider to be the
most enviable of all titles:
the character of an
"Honest Man."

—GEORGE WASHINGTON

$\mathcal{L}$ive so that
when your children
think of fairness,
caring, and integrity,
they think of you.

Choose your
life's mate carefully.
From this one decision
will come 90 percent
of your happiness
or misery.

enthusiasms, the great devotions, who spends himself in a worthy cause, who best knows in the end the triumph of high achievement, and who at the worst, if he fails, at least fails while daring greatly, so that his place shall never be with those poor spirits who neither enjoy much nor suffer much because they live in the gray twilight that knows not victory nor defeat.

—THEODORE ROOSEVELT

It is not the critic who counts, not the man who points out how the strong man stumbles, or where the doer of deeds could have done them better. The credit belongs to the man who is actually in the arena, whose face is marred by dust and sweat and blood, who strives valiantly, who errs and comes short again and again, because there is no effort without error and shortcoming, but who does actually strive to do the deeds, who knows the great

Love is the only gold.

—ALFRED, LORD TENNYSON

Children will not
remember you for the
material things you provided,
but for the feeling that
you cherished them.

—GAIL SWEET

$\mathcal{I}$'ve learned that…

. . . children want discipline
and guidelines because
it shows you care.

—AGE 32

. . . if you're too busy to
do a friend a favor, you're
too busy.

—AGE 39

I don't know what
your destiny will be,
but one thing
I know: the only ones
among you who will be
really happy are those
who will have sought
and found how to serve.

—ALBERT SCHWEITZER

Give life
your best.
You'll never
regret it.

$\mathcal{G}$et your priorities
straight. No one ever
said on his deathbed,
"Gee, if I'd only
spent more time
at the office."

Fifty years from now, it will
not matter what kind of car you
drove, what kind of house you
lived in, how much you had in
your bank account, or what
your clothes looked like.
But the world may be a better
place because you were
important in the life of a child.

—ANONYMOUS

Try measuring your
wealth by what you are
rather than by what you
have. Put the tape
measure around your
heart rather than
your bank account.

—ANONYMOUS

$\mathcal{I}$'ve learned that...

... the person who is really kind will never be alone or unhappy.

—AGE 75

... I've never regretted the nice things I've said about people.

—AGE 38

Make a rule and pray to
God to help you keep it: never,
if possible, lie down at night
without being able to say,
"I have made one human
being a little wiser or a little
happier or at least a little
better this day."

—CHARLES KINGSLEY

$\mathcal{B}$e kinder
than necessary.

Treasure the love you
receive above all.
It will survive long
after your gold and good
health have vanished.

—OG MANDINO

which to reject? Using Immanuel Kant's proposition, which he called the categorical imperative, is one approach. In this method of determining the moral and ethical value of an act, one asks, "What would be the result to humankind if everyone did it?" For instance, what kind of world would we have if everyone were honest, self-disciplined, responsible, kind, generous, courageous, and virtuous? This is a question that deserves serious reflection and one you might use to examine and challenge the things which are important in your life.

Plato noted that the unexamined life is not worth living. With that in mind, I dedicate this book to all who seek a renewed sense of moral clarity and purpose.

We are all on the slippery stairs. But our steps can be sure and steady when we know our handrail is made of sturdy stuff.

Introduction

There is a fundamental question we all have to face. How are we to live our lives; by what principles and moral values will we be guided and inspired?

I once heard a minister compare life to a slippery staircase—an apt analogy. Slipping and sliding as we all do, we intuitively reach out for support, for anything to keep us from falling. There is a handrail. But its stability is determined by the values we have chosen to guide our lives. It is, therefore, no stronger, no more reliable, than the quality of the choices we have made.

Is there a clear and simple way to decide which principles to embrace and

Published in Nashville, Tennessee, by Rutledge Hill
Press, a Thomas Nelson Company, P.O. Box 141000,
Nashville, Tennessee 37214.

Book design and layout by Karen Phillips and Nikita
Pristouris

ISBN: 1-55853-803-8

Printed in the United States of America

1 2 3 4 5 6 7 8 9 — 04 03 02 01 00

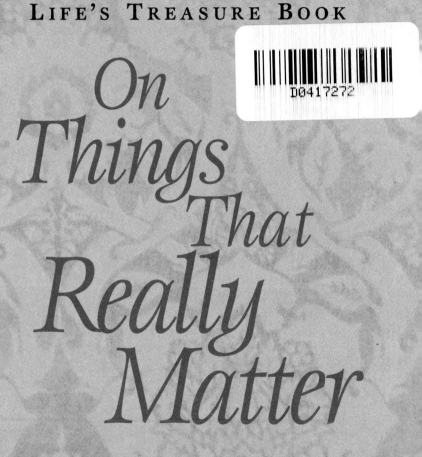

LIFE'S TREASURE BOOK

On
Things
That
Really
Matter

H. JACKSON BROWN, JR.